THE UNSEEN PROFESSORS

LEO AMINO
MINORU NIIZUMA
JOHN PAI

TINA KIM GALLERY   GREGORY R. MILLER & CO.

Table of Contents
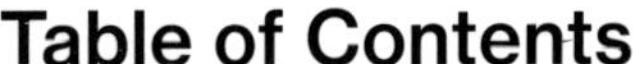

The Unseen Professors
John Yau

This publication and the related exhibition focus on the work of Leo Amino (1911–1989), Minoru Niizuma (1930–1998), and John Pai (b. 1937), three Asian sculptors who were born between 1911 and 1937 in Taiwan, Japan, and Korea, respectively, and immigrated to America. Eventually, all of them moved to New York City, where they worked and taught for many years in prestigious art programs. Despite being members of different generations, their teaching careers overlapped for more than a decade (1965–77), during which time a generation of artists associated with Minimalism and site-specific art gained much of the art world's attention. By reexamining this period through significant works by Amino, Niizuma, and Pai, the exhibition highlights the accomplishments of three independent Asian-American artists who were neither associated with a mainstream movement or style nor ever fully accepted by the art world, despite showing in prestigious New York venues, such as the Whitney Museum of American Art, the Metropolitan Museum of Art, and the Museum of Modern Art.

Equally important is that the work and material choices made by these Asian American artists have almost nothing in common with each other. Employing distinct processes, they rigorously pursued their own trajectories, never attempting to align themselves with the dominant currents of the art world. This refusal to adjust themselves to mainstream thinking may have been due partly to their realization that they would always be regarded as outsiders or outliers. This grasp of their problematic status in relationship to the dominant art world and its deeply embedded strain of inherent prejudices was first hinted at in 1997, when Amino, Niizuma, and Pai were shown together, along with other Asian American artists, in the exhibition: *Asian Traditions/Modern Expressions: Asian American Artists and Abstraction, 1945–1970*, organized by Jeffrey Wechsler for the Jane Voorhees Zimmerli Art Museum at Rutgers University (March 23–July 31, 1997). However, in contrast to that exhibition, which largely focused on Asian American painters and their relationship to abstraction, particularly gestural painting and the development of Abstract Expressionism, this exhibition centers on the relationship of three innovative sculptors and the alternative bodies of work they developed in the face of Minimalism and the dominant paradigm of avant-garde art that was developed by Donald Judd and Rosalind Krauss, starting in the mid-1960s.

In the early 1960s, when mainstream art critics of color were nonexistent in the American art world, much critical discussion revolved around the "death of painting," signaled by the rise of Andy Warhol and the use of silkscreen and other forms of mechanical reproduction. As the art world's attention continued to shift away from painting throughout the 1960s and ultimately focused on Conceptual art and other non-painting practices in the 1970s, a parallel "death of sculpture" began to take root around the mid-1960s, marked by David Smith's death in 1965. Influenced by painting's fallen status and the rejection of the handmade in favor of the machine-tooled object and modular forms, a generation of sculptors began to rely on industrial fabrication for the production of their work, while others incorporated store-bought objects into their sculptures. Working with fabricators or incorporating ready-mades into their work, artists such as Donald Judd, Dan Flavin, and Carl Andre began to receive critical acclaim for a cool and reductive hands-off approach that was soon designated by the term "Minimalism."

In his essay "Specific Objects" (1965), Donald Judd theorized, contextualized, and underscored why a change in approach and materials was historically unavoidable. Writing about sculpture, Judd states: "So far the most obvious difference within this diverse work is between that which is something of an object, a single thing, and that which is open and extended, more or less environmental."[1] In 1979, nearly fifteen years after Judd's essay was published, the artist historian Rosalind Krauss published "Sculpture in the Expanded Field" in *October*. In this essay, which Krauss later developed into a book, she elaborated upon Judd's idea of the "environmental" by applying a precise diagram to define the structural parameters of sculpture, architecture, and landscape art. Since their publication, Judd's and Krauss's essays have achieved canonical status, influencing the way sculpture is received,

        THE UNSEEN PROFESSORS

discussed, and evaluated. Although they were written fourteen years apart, what they have in common is a rejection of sculpture as a handmade object and as a "single thing" in favor of works of art that are fabricated and "environmental." While the authority of these texts has seldom been challenged, and their dominance has been evident, I want to offer another way of reading them.

By connecting themselves to a well documented, largely self-sustaining avant-garde tradition based on a belief in art's progress, both Judd and Krauss make aesthetic arguments rooted in the color-blind thinking associated with various Western philosophies, be it Plato, Immanuel Kant, or French post-structuralist theory. Although I don't presume any venomous design, neither "Specific Objects" nor "Sculpture in the Expanded Field" mentions a single artist of color, except as an afterthought, which is in keeping with the avant-garde tradition as it developed in America during the latter half of the twentieth century, in the aftermath of what Irving Sandler defined as "the triumph" of American art.[2] Further, to suppose that Judd's and Krauss's texts trace the only routes of advanced thinking for artists to take is to presume that everyone is born into the same culture and subscribes to the same avant-garde tradition. If, as Judd argues in his essay, "the disinterest in painting and sculpture is a disinterest in doing it again," then the identity of the person who decides the meaning of "doing it again" is the key here, isn't it?

Like Judd, Krauss emphasizes rupture. Judd and Krauss's shared belief in the importance of bursting away from the past, coupled with a focus on form, material, and process, ignores certain crucial issues, such as the historical and social circumstances the individual is born into, and the role that one's culture, race, upbringing, gender identity, and sexual orientation might play in the making of art. I am not arguing for an autobiographical or diary-like approach or even an "I" centered transparency. Rather, I am stating that the ideals proposed by Judd and Krauss efface the sociological aspects of the individual to such an extreme degree that it approaches Warhol's goal of being machine-like, which is a way of denying racial and/or suppressing cultural and gender difference and the role they might play in the making of art. By doing so, Judd and Krauss fail to recognize their resistance to recognizing race and culture as an important feature in the production of art, as well as deny their complicity with an aesthetics that shares something with colonialist-imperialist thinking and the so-called "triumph" of American art.

If we further examine Judd's "disinterest in doing it again," we are compelled to ask why he never acknowledged Leo Amino, who began using polyester resin (plastic) around the end of World War II, and had work in all but two Whitney Annuals for sculpture (the precursor to the Whitney Biennial), between 1947 and 1962. It is unlikely that Judd was unaware of Amino's work, as they both had work in the 1965 group show *Plastics*, which the conceptual artist Dan Graham organized at the now legendary John Daniels Gallery (1964–65) that he opened and ran. It was in *Plastics* that Amino debuted his cast resin pieces collectively titled *Refractionals*. Five years later, in 1970, Amino's work was included in the large touring group show *A Plastic Presence*, which was organized by Tracy Atkinson, director of the Milwaukee Art Center. *A Plastic Presence* opened at the Jewish Museum (November 19, 1969–January 4, 1970) in New York and after traveling to the Milwaukee Art Center (January 30, 1970–March 8, 1970) concluded its tour at the San Francisco Museum of Art (April 24, 1970–May 24, 1970). Along with Amino, the exhibition of nearly fifty artists included work by Richard Artschwager, Eva Hesse, Craig Kauffman, Helen Pashgian, and Richard Van Buren.

In her discussion of the intersection of sculpture, architecture, and landscape art, Krauss never mentions Isamu Noguchi, who was commissioned by Marcel Breuer to design a Japanese garden adjacent to UNESCO's headquarters in Paris in 1957. One likely reason for Krauss's rejection is that Noguchi's site-specific installation did not sufficiently conform to her aesthetics to rank consideration. By her standards, a Japanese garden was neither American nor avant-garde enough. By insisting that their views are the only viable measures that can be used to assess a work of art, Judd and Krauss appoint themselves gatekeepers to

    THE UNSEEN PROFESSORS

a community of individuals who deny the existence of those who do not subscribe to their ideologies. It is against this backdrop that Amino, Niizuma, and Pai made their work. In their invisibility in the art world, and erasure from history, they share something with other artists of Asian descent, such as Wifredo Lam, Isamu Noguchi, and Ruth Asawa, who exhibited their work in America but did not go on to become celebrities (like Yayoi Kusama and Yoko Ono).

In Volume II of *"Primitivism" in 20th Century Art: Affinity of the Tribal and the Modern* (1984, edited by William S. Rubin), Evan Maurer, in his essay, "Dada and Surrealism," makes the following observation:

> This was [Wifredo] Lam's greatest synthesis as a Surrealist: He combined a close contact with tribal rituals with the cultural and artistic sophistication of a Western intellectual.

Maurer's observation is based on an earlier statement made by William S. Rubin, the director of the department of painting and sculpture at MoMA from 1973 to 1988, in *Dada, Surrealism, and Their Heritage* (1968, 2nd edition 1977):

> Wifredo Lam was the first Surrealist to make primitive and ethnic sources central to his art.

Neither Rubin nor Maurer mentions Lam's race; he was the son of a Chinese father and Afro-Spanish-Cuban mother. However, when it comes to writing about Picasso, much attention has been paid to biographical details, down to the day a particular work was completed. Maurer's "close contact" suggests that there is no autobiographical connection between the artist and "tribal rituals"; it certainly does not convey that he participated in these religious practices as a child. The fact that Lam's godmother, Mantønica Wilson, was a Yoruba priestess, and that he formed a lasting relationship with the Black Martinican poet Aimé Césaire, one of the founders of the Négritude movement, are considered irrelevant by Rubin and Maurer. Rather, Lam possessed the "cultural and artistic sophistication of a Western intellectual," which is code for white. Nothing about Lam's racial and cultural background is considered worthy of consideration. It is within this situation of invisibility and suppression based on hierarchical thinking that Amino, Niizuma, and Pai lived and made their work.

Leo Amino was born in Taiwan in 1911 and grew up in Tokyo, Japan. In 1929, he immigrated to the United States, where he lived south of San Francisco, studying for two years at San Mateo Junior College. He then moved to New York, where he studied briefly at NYU. After leaving the university before finishing his degree, he remained in New York and began working for a Japanese wood importing firm and taking home ebony samples to carve. Although Amino had no formal art training, he grew increasingly interested in sculpture. In 1937, he studied briefly at the American Artists School with Chaim Gross, a leading proponent of direct carving. In 1938, Amino traveled to England, where he saw the work of Henry Moore and Moore's use of pierced volumes. In 1939, Amino and Isamu Noguchi were paired in an exhibition at the World's Fair in New York. In 1940 he had his first solo exhibition at the cooperative Artists Gallery, where Josef Albers and Ad Reinhardt also showed. It is where Albers first learned of Amino's work, and later Albers invited him to teach at Black Mountain College.

On December 12, 1941, Amino and six other artists of Japanese descent who were living in New York penned and signed a letter expressing their shock at the bombing of Pearl Harbor on December 7, declaring they were ready to "bear arms if necessary to insure the final victory for the democratic forces of the World." During World War II, while being made to translate for the United States Navy, he became interested in the sculptural possibilities of polyester resin (or plastic) after it was declassified by the military, and he began casting it in 1945, long before artists such as DeWain Valentine and Rockne Krebs began (and became known for) using resin in their work.

 THE UNSEEN PROFESSORS

Looking back at Amino's career from when he first carved wood in the early 1930s and in the late '40s began casting, it seems to me that he was engaged with issues of form, from totems and vertical structures to transparency, color, and light (which might have been inspired by his contact with Albers and Bauhaus thinking). Working with two radically different materials (wood and plastic), which he at times combined, and employing two different processes (carving and casting), while focusing on form, light, color, and transparency without making any overt reference to being Asian, did not gain Amino a larger circle of attention. As with other artists of color working in America in the twentieth century, there was a barrier he could not break through.

In addition to inviting Amino to teach at Black Mountain (summer 1946 and 1950), Albers helped secure him a position at Cooper Union, where he taught from 1952 until 1977, despite having no formal education or college degree, and where he introduced his student Jack Whitten to direct carving. Albers, who left Germany with his wife, Anni, in 1933, when the Nazis closed the Bauhaus, was an instrumental figure in Amino's life, more so than any other American artist. In addition to inviting Amino to teach, Albers invited Jacob Lawrence and Gwendolyn Knight Lawrence to teach at Black Mountain College in 1946, a few years after the school began to incorporate African American culture and history into its programming. In order to protect the Lawrences from the world of Jim Crow and institutionally sanctioned racism, especially below the Mason-Dixon line, Albers got the school to provide private transportation to bring them to the campus, which they did not leave during their residency. The rest of America did not mirror Albers's open embrace of artists of color.

In addition to being included in many Whitney Annuals, Amino had work in other important group shows, including *Carvers-Modelers-Welders* at the Museum of Modern Art, New York (1950), and *American Sculpture* at the Metropolitan Museum of Art, New York (1951), and he was one of six sculptors who had work in *The New Decade: 35 American Painters and Sculptors* (1955) at the Whitney Museum of American Art.

As I cited earlier, in 1965, Dan Graham put on the exhibition *Plastics* (1965) at John Daniels Gallery. In 1969, Vito Acconci wrote this about Amino's resin works in *ARTNews*:

> The over-all form looks solid, holding the viewer away from it, while the inside is elusive and tempts the viewer in. Seen from one direction, there is an agglomeration of color, while, seen from another, the color almost disappears; the viewer enters it unconsciously.[3]

It is clear from Acconci's description that the views of Amino's resin works change, and this is caused by the side you are looking at. This is just one of the many experiential conditions that Amino attained in his work, particularly the *Refractionals*.

I have cited these events in Amino's career because they convey something of the gap between having your work seen and having it recognized, in his case, for its innovative use of materials. Both Graham and Acconci called attention to Amino's resin works, but these instances did not lead to a larger recognition. This means that Amino's work is seen, but remains under the radar, and he remains a largely invisible or peripheral presence. After his death in 1989, his work was not exhibited in a New York gallery for thirty years. It is this condition of near invisibility that Niizuma and Pai, who were born two decades or more after Amino, enter into when they begin teaching in New York.

Minoru Niizuma was born in Tokyo in 1930, and graduated from Tokyo National University of Fine Arts and Music in 1955. In order to make modern art in a society that provided little institutional support and had few galleries, Niizuma became a member of an artist-run group in Tokyo, the Modern Art Association (1954–58). He was elected a permanent jury member in 1957. During this time, he taught sculpture and drawing at Seijo School, Tokyo (1955–58), and his work began to gain attention. In 1956, he was awarded

                    THE UNSEEN PROFESSORS

a commission for a public monument by the city of Tokyo and in 1958 by the Tokyo Asia Center. Shortly after, realizing that there were no real opportunities to exhibit, other than being included in the group shows organized by the Modern Art Association and other artist-run groups, Niizuma immigrated to New York in 1959.

He worked as an instructor at the Brooklyn Museum Art School (1964–70). In addition to teaching and making sculpture, he photographed Yoko Ono's performances, such as the legendary *Cut Piece* (1964), performed at the Carnegie Recital Hall on March 21, 1965. The photographs that Niizuma took of Ono's performances from the 1960s to the early '70s – often the only record – are considered iconic and have been reproduced many times.

In 1966, Niizuma had his first solo show in New York at Howard Wise Gallery. His work was included in two Whitney Annuals (1966 and 1968). In 1966, he was one of forty-six artists whose work was included in *The New Japanese Painting and Sculpture* at the Museum of Modern Art, organized by Dorothy Miller and William S. Lieberman, and in the early 1970s he showed with Gimpel and Weitzenhoffer. Despite exhibiting in New York, and being included in museum shows, Niizuma attained greater recognition outside of America. In 1976, he had a retrospective at the Seibu Museum of Art in Tokyo and a decade later, in 1986, at the Gulbenkian Museum in Lisbon, Portugal.

In his review in *The New York Times* (April 15, 1972), the conservative critic John Canaday stated: "Mr. Niizuma has two loves, marble and the abstract patterns of traditional Japanese art. He makes the most of both by cutting and polishing his stones to reveal grains and colors in shapes that echo the patterns of folk art, fabrics and ritual vessels." While Canaday sees a connection between Niizuma's Japanese heritage and his sculptures, he also isolates him from Western art, implicitly suggesting that the work is solely Japanese. This reductive review does not recognize what Niizuma got from Western art, particularly Minimalism and its reliance on geometric forms and the use of repetition. This is not particularly surprising, but it does reveal some of the inherent prejudices that Niizuma faced in America, which was still celebrating the "triumph" of American art.

That Niizuma carved in stone further isolated him from the commercial New York art world, which, under the influence of Pop Art and Minimalism, had pivoted away from the handmade and begun focusing almost exclusively on works that involved fabrication, modular repetition, and the use of commercially available objects. If the work could not be made by others or assembled from obtainable things, it was considered traditional because it did not break with a Western notion of the past. And yet, Niizuma's work and the philosophy informing it can be seen as both a break with Japanese traditional art and an implicit critique of Western materialism and the belief in timelessness and art's permanent status.

In works such as *Unknown* (Italian marble, c. 1986), *Water Fall* (c. 1986), and *Unknown* (Italian Paonazzo marble, c. 1986), Niizuma explores his longstanding interest in states of constant change, as signified by waterfalls and rivers. This was not an abstract concept to Niizuma, who had worked as a fisherman in Hokkaido, Japan's northernmost prefecture, when he was a young man. No doubt, he was also familiar with the archetypal motif in East Asian art of a scholar contemplating a waterfall, which was regarded as an emblematic sign of change and dissipation. By working in stone, Niizuma effectively dislodges a motif common to ink painting and the pictorial world, and introduces it into the domain of sculpture and the three-dimensional. Whereas the painter can use a brush to depict the scholar contemplating the waterfall, Niizuma had to find a way to address this phenomenon in stone without becoming pictorial. This is what is new about Niizuma's sculptures, and why it is wrong to regard him as a traditional artist because he carved directly in stone.

In Niizuma's sculptures, the elements and forces of water (liquid), descending forms (gravity), and destruction (water crashing against stone) become stone and stillness, polished finish and rough surface. Viewers might even find themselves asking, what forces made this work? Was it water that polished these stones just as it has smoothed the glass found at the beach? Or did crashing water break this piece, leaving different surfaces jagged? Niizuma's recognition of nature's power is fundamentally different from the attitudes common to the Minimalists, who believe they can impose a permanent form on nature but seldom recognize its power in their work.

This is how Sakai Tadayasu described the tension between smooth and rough in Niizuma's work:

> It is not so much that the work has been abandoned in an unfinished state but that an uncanny contrast has been created between the sharply chiseled areas which are seemingly caressed to a polish and areas that remain in their rough, untouched state.[4]

This is one of the contrasts found in Niizuma's work. Others can been seen in works such as *Water Fall* and *Unknown* (Italian Paonazzo marble) (both c. 1986), in which the artist establishes an interplay between the stone's blue veining and the shape and interaction of the cut pieces. This is another one of Niizuma's innovations, which I think was not recognized in America. Canaday got a trace of it, but I don't think he fully grasped what the sculptor was up to.

In the beginning of the 1980s, Niizuma started working in Portugal. During this decade, he helped form a link between Portugal and Japan. This included bringing Japanese art to Portugal and introducing Portuguese artists to Japan. One reason he was attracted to working in Portugal was because of the marble and other stones that he discovered were available.

In *Castle of the Eye III* (c. 1985), which Niizuma carved from pure white Portuguese marble, the four facing surfaces are identically marked by physically receding, incrementally smaller nesting rectangles whose parameters are established by the previous rectangle. The shallow, physically receding space pulls the viewer in, but does not permit entry to the interior. The first *Castle of the Eye* (1964), which employs repetition without relying on fabrication, is in the collection of the Museum of Modern Art, and should be paired with one of Judd's boxes in an exhibition.

Do we want to contemplate the material surface of Niizuma's marble or the way Judd reproduced the industrial world of color and material in art? I am not of the mind that there is only one way. Do we want a work marked by the artist's repetitive but changing labor or a smooth, shiny, timeless presence? What is the dialogue works by Niizuma and Judd would have with each other if placed in the same room?

Widely appreciated in Portugal, thirty pieces were installed in the Minoru Niizuma Sculpture Garden, which the collector and patron José Berardo established next to his Bacalhoa Winery-Museum. I believe that the attention and accolades that Niizuma received during his life, mostly in Portugal and Japan, and the current invisibility of his work in America, where he lived and worked for nearly forty years, suggest that we give his work another look.

In his sculptures, Niizuma often juxtaposes a polished surface with a rough, pitted area. In contrast to the Western tradition, as epitomized by Constantin Brancusi's complete control over a stone, resulting in an embodiment of perfected essence and "timelessness," Niizuma acknowledged time's inescapable effects. By having the outer edges of *Unknown* (black marble, 1982) rough, he anticipates the ultimate effects of time. Is *Unknown* — with a hole piercing each of the kitty-corner sides — complete or broken off from something larger that we cannot see, even in our mind's eye? This recognition of fragmentation and erosion stands in contrast to the impeccable Minimalist works by Judd, the stainless steel geometries of David Smith, and the Cor-Ten steel totems of Beverly Pepper. It is in his synthesis of geometric forms such as a cube or a pyramid that one sees the influence of Minimalism. However, by presenting the split or broken halves of a highly polished form, Niizuma recognizes that nothing is impervious to time, not even a work of art, and that it is an illusion to think otherwise. In this regard, he believed that art was part of life, rather than separate from it.

In other works, Niizuma's carving transforms a solid column of stone into fluid surfaces, suggesting that change is also inescapable, and that marble — that sign of empire and permanence — is not a bulwark against time. This is the opposite

          THE UNSEEN PROFESSORS

of Western thinking, and one of Niizuma's great accomplishments; he transforms stone into something both unblemished and broken, impervious and vulnerable. He underscores that the cycle of time we live in is far vaster and more powerful than we can imagine.

John Pai was born in Seoul, Korea, in 1937, the youngest of three children. His father, an activist Korean Presbyterian minister committed to Korean liberation, was often away, and Pai did not meet him until the end of World War II, when he was 8. His mother, who spent her childhood in Russia, where she received her education, and which she and her family were forced to leave during the Russian Civil War (1917–1922), raised him and his older siblings. During World War II, and the Japanese occupation, the mother brought the children to Ilsan, a rural area northwest of Seoul. Because of his parents' political leanings, Pai and his family were isolated from other Korean families, and he spent much of his time alone, as he was much younger than his brother and sister. Pai began to draw at an early age and his mother taught him to play the piano. When he was 8, his mother arranged for him to study art with a man who had received French academic training.

In 1949, shortly after North and South Korea became formally separate countries, Pai's father wrote to some of his friends about bringing his family to the United States. Reverend Arthur Pritchard, who was one of his classmates from McCormick Seminary in Chicago, proposed that he bring his family to Wheeling, West Virginia, where Pritchard was the pastor of a small church in nearby Warwood. After landing in San Francisco, the Pai family took a Pullman train to Saint Paul, Minnesota, where John's older brother was a student at Macalester College. After that they stopped in Chicago, Toledo, and New York before going on to Wheeling. In Toledo, they stayed with the Reverend Kenneth Cutler, who told John's father that his two younger children should have American names. John's father decided on the spot that their names should be John and Mary. After staying with Pritchard for a few weeks, the Pai family found an apartment. When John was 15, his parents returned to Korea, and he began living with an American family in Wheeling. By this time, his brother and sister were on their own, trying to start their lives.

In an oral history that Pai did with Leyla Vural during the summer of 2021 (June 3, June 10, June 24, July 22, and August 5, 2021), he said that while in Wheeling, he soon became involved with sports, particularly football, as he saw it as a way to belong to a group as well as demonstrate his athleticism in a contact sport. It was also at this time that Pai, who had been going to Saturday art classes, had his first solo exhibition at the Oglebay Institute in Wheeling. Six years later, at the age of 21, he received a full scholarship to attend Pratt Institute, and moved to New York, where he lived with his sister and studied industrial design. Two years later, in 1960, inspired by the steel sculptures of Theodore Roszak, which he had seen in the exhibition *New Images of Man* at the Museum of Modern Art, he called Roszak up and eventually began working as his studio assistant as well as helped him install a show at the Pierre Matisse Gallery. Deeply affected by the war, and the Holocaust, the Polish-born Roszak began working with welded metals after the end of World War II. In an email he sent to me in 2019, Pai described Roszak as "patient and caring," and he believes his time working for him accelerated his education, especially with materials.

In 1962, Pai graduated from Pratt with a BFA in industrial design and two years later, he got an MFA in sculpture there. In 1965, he became the youngest professor to start teaching at Pratt and was appointed head of the sculpture department. This means that within a period of three years, Pai went from being an undergraduate to a professor assigned to direct a department.

During the mid-1960s, as he was starting his teaching career at Pratt, Pai got married, bought a carriage house in the Clinton Hill area of Brooklyn, and had two children. He and his wife, Eunsook, also began having parties for diasporic Korean artists, musicians, and writers living in New York. This is when he met Nam June Paik, who moved to New York from Germany in 1964, along

     THE UNSEEN PROFESSORS

with Kim Whanki, a pioneer of abstract painting in Korea, and Kim Tschang-yeul, who became known for his waterdrop paintings after he moved to Paris in 1969. Pai recounted to me that although he and Paik never talked about their art, he enjoyed singing Korean folk songs while Paik played the piano, joined by others at the party. Although Pai was younger than Whanki, who lived in New York from 1963 until 1974, and Kim Tschang-yeul, who lived in New York from 1966 to 1969, they were supportive of him and his work. Later, Whanki's widow helped Pai get a gallery in Korea.

Although Pai was younger than these three artists, his steady teaching job and financial stability meant that he was able to host, as he told me, "parties for Korean artists, musicians, and writers, along with some Korean students" in the house that he shared with his wife and family. This group of diasporic Koreans was Pai's community, which existed apart from the mainstream, white art world. It seems to me that this coterie of artists, who knew each other at a crucial point in their careers, has never been acknowledged as an important force in New York. Their encounter with New York art had a different effect on each of them, even as it also inspired them to be more resolute in their pursuit of art that had little to do with Western popular culture or mechanical reproduction.

Recognizing their roots in Korean culture and a history of striving for liberation — a struggle in which Pai's activist parents played significant roles — Whanki and Tschang-yeul did not try and assimilate and become Western artists. This attitude is crucial to understanding Pai's sculpture, which does not resemble anything else being made in New York during the 1970s and '80s. In the review "Sculptor John Pai weaves life into wires" by Kwon Mee-yoo that appeared in the *Korea Times*, Pai said this about his use of steel wire in his sculptures: "Steel wires are affordable and durable, but can disappear after becoming rusty. I like such a nature of wire, because it is similar to that of a living thing."

In the unpublished oral history conducted by Vural, Pai makes a further distinction about his use of steel.

> [...] [David Smith] loved working with heavy pieces of
> metal. [...] So there was a branch of people who liked the
> idea of working with heavy chunks of metal, geometric,
> and I think the basic strength of steel. So they wanted
> steel to look like steel. Whereas I think I was beginning
> to see the other side of steel, which with a welding
> torch, you're taking something very strong and solid and
> you're melting it until it's liquid. So, that's the side that
> fascinated me, because it seemed to offer an incredible
> range of flexibility. So from there, I began to experiment
> with what the torch can do.

In these two statements about steel, one sees that Pai is working
out of an aesthetic that is rooted in a different worldview than
the ones espoused by Western sculptors, including David Smith,
Donald Judd, and Richard Serra. Pai's recognition of impermanence
and liquidity shares little with Smith's placement of stainless steel
sculpture in the fields around his house in Bolton Landing, New
York, Judd's placement of concrete sculptures in Marfa, Texas,
or Serra's *Afangar* ("Standing Stones") on Viðey Island, a national
preserve across the harbor from Reykjavík, Iceland. While these
artists impose their work on the landscape, Pai is informed by
his interest in various branches of science, including physics and
biology, and states of change. Given his early intention to study
architecture, it seems to me that he has expanded his interest in
visible structures to include invisible and theoretical ones. Both
Smith and Judd believe in permanence, while Pai and Niizuma
have a different understanding of nature, materials, and time.

In 1963, in response to assisting Roszak, he developed
a way of making art that has characterized his work ever since.
This is how he put it to me in an email after I asked him when he
decided to work solely with thin steel rods, which may or may not
be copper coated:

> I wanted to reduce the amount of tooling & machining
> and simplify the process so that it would be more like

   THE UNSEEN PROFESSORS

drawing in space. Reducing the size of the basic unit gave me a lot of freedom.

Working within a strong and visible material constraint of steel wire, Pai's process is slow and incremental, literally attaching one section to another until a form emerges. Many of Pai's pieces consist of open, swirling, and climbing forms made of thin steel rods welded together. The grids seem capable of attaining any contortion, torque, or change in size. He does not do a drawing for the works, and the final outcome is the result of an open-ended process, which he likens to that of a jazz musician. I think it is telling that the composer he most often listens to while working is Bach.

A number of open, self-contained, freestanding works are composed of a form inside a form inside a form. In the masterful *Involution* (1974), one sees the circular perimeter of an open linear grid rising off the floor until it becomes a plump, vase-like form that is open to investigation. As it rises from the floor, the grid swells out and then curls in until it forms a circular opening at the top. As the opening descends, like a tunnel, into the interior of the outer shell, it becomes a visual, three-dimensional echo of the outer form. Inside this interior form we see a teardrop form rising – a form sits inside a form, which sits inside a larger form, all of which are connected by a flexible grid of lines. *Involution*'s pot-like form evokes a state of continuous change. Instead of imposing the work on the landscape while claiming perfection and permanence, Pai addresses change as a constant in his dynamic structures made of twisting and bending lines and curving and collapsing planes.

Pai's sculptures are not static. Works such as *Involution* seem to be in a state of change; in some cases, it is like a three-dimensional record of a transformation that has been stilled, so that we might scrutinize it. We see his forms as well as see through them. They feel solid and vulnerable, sturdy and delicate. Largely eschewing solid forms, Pai's sculptures are precise three-dimensional drawings in space. Working with the simplest, most pared-down means – cut, bent, and welded steel rods – Pai has attained a remarkable fluidity in his work. They are meticulous drawings in space, but they are also far more than that. They are meditations on inescapable change and disruption, topographical models of unseen forces.

In different ways, Amino, Niizuma, and Pai have explored a lifelong concern with change, rather than the desire to make a permanent and timeless monument. It is a distinction worth pondering in light of our continued arrogance toward and degradation of our environment, and just one of many reasons why their work deserves a longer, sustained look.

Endnotes

1   Donald Judd, "Specific Objects," *Arts Yearbook* 8 (1965).
2   In *The Triumph of American Painting: A History of Abstract Expressionism* (New York: Harper & Row, 1970), Irving devotes a chapter to the eleven artists he feels are central to Abstract Expressionism. None of them are women or artists of color. In his follow-up book about the second generation, *The New York School: The Painters & Sculptors of the Fifties* (1978), Sandler writes about thirty-nine artists, six of whom are women. There are no artists of color.
3   Vito Acconci, "Leo Amino," *ARTnews*, May 1970, 20.
4   Sakai Tadayasu, "Listening to Stone: Niizuma Minoru," in *Niizuma* (Paris: Galerie Nichido, 1989), n.p.

  THE UNSEEN PROFESSORS

CHRONOLOGY

1895
The Empire of Japan defeats the Qing Dynasty of China
in the first Sino-Japanese War. China recognizes the total
independence of Korea and officially cedes Taiwan, but
not without five months of conflict after local resistance to
Japanese occupation.

1910
Korea is annexed by the Empire of Japan, beginning decades
of violent colonial rule.

1931
Japan annexes Manchuria, kickstarting more than a decade
of Japanese conquest in China and the broader Asia-Pacific
region.

1937
The Second Sino-Japanese War begins with the fall of Beijing
to Japanese forces.

1939
World War II begins.

1911
Leo Amino is born in Japanese-occupied Taiwan.

1910s or early 1920s
Leo Amino relocates to Tokyo.

1929
Leo Amino immigrates to the United States. He enrolls at San
Mateo Junior College.

1930
Minoru Niizuma is born in Tokyo, Japan.

1937
Leo Amino begins studying direct carving under Chaim Gross
at the American Artists School.

John Pai is born in Seoul, Korea.

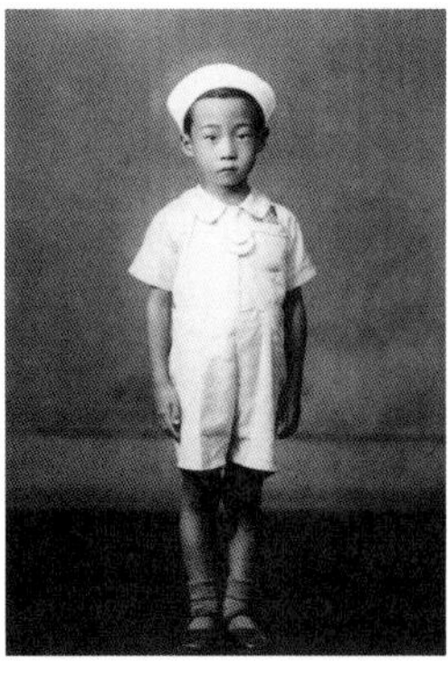

1939
Leo Amino exhibits at the World's Fair in New York alongside
Isamu Noguchi.

1940
Leo Amino debuts his first solo exhibition at Artists Gallery
in New York.

CHRONOLOGY

1941

Japan bombs Pearl Harbor, triggering the United States' entry into World War II.

1942

American President Franklin D. Roosevelt authorizes Executive Order 9066, forcibly interning 120,000 people of Japanese ancestry in concentration camps. Leo Amino is not interned.

1945

After the bombings of Hiroshima and Nagasaki by the United States, Japan surrenders, ending World War II in Asia.

Early 1940s

Leo Amino is made to translate for the Navy following Pearl Harbor, beginning his first forays into plastics shortly after the military declassified polyester resin. Amino was one of the first American artists to incorporate plastics into his artistic practice.

1945

John Pai's father, Rev. Minsoo Pai, a Presbyterian minister who advocated for independence during the Japanese occupation of Korea, returns to Korea after exile.

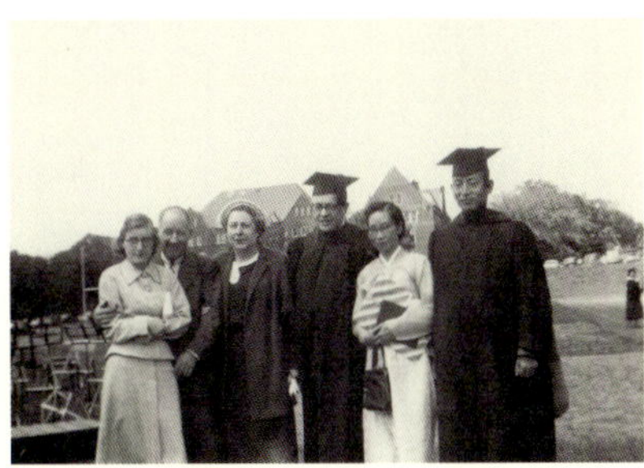

1946

Leo Amino begins teaching summer classes at Black Mountain College under the directorship of Josef Albers, influencing students such as Kenneth Noland and Ruth Asawa.

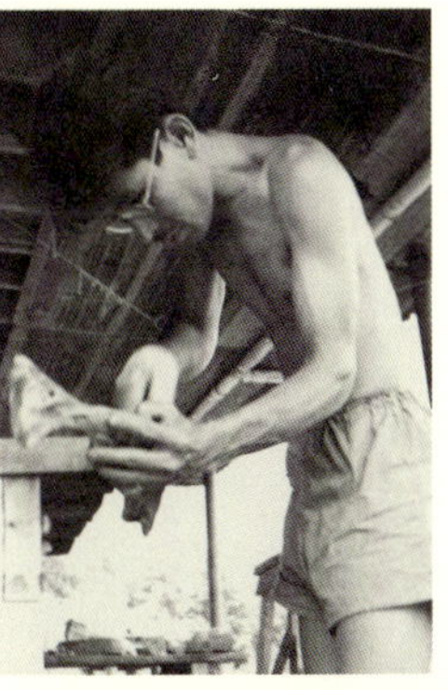

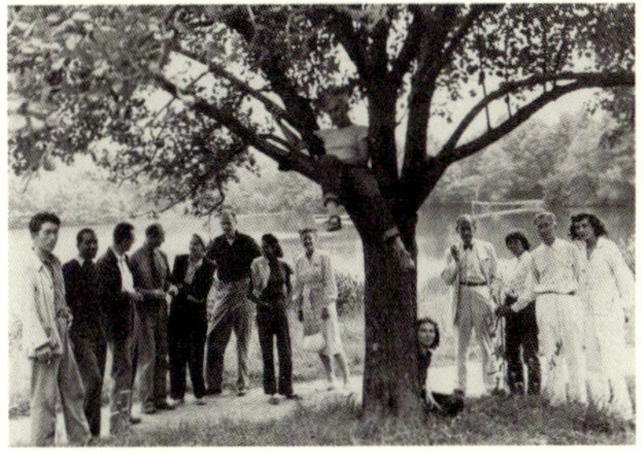

1947

Leo Amino is invited to participate in his first of twelve Whitney Annual Exhibitions.

1949

John Pai and his family immigrate to the United States, arriving in San Francisco in January 1949.

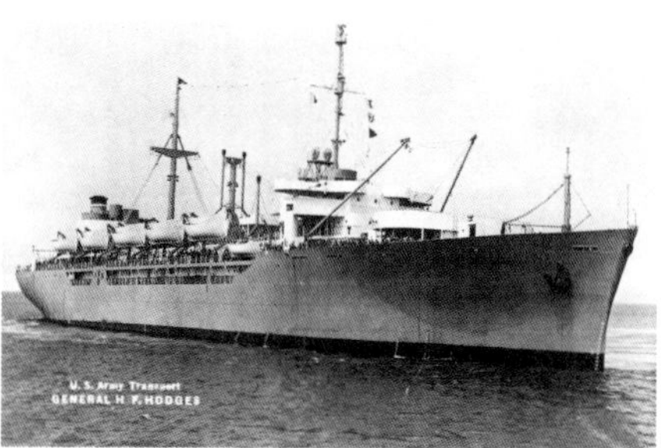

1950

North Korea's army crosses the 38th parallel, triggering the Korean War.

1950

Leo Amino shows in MoMA's *Carvers-Modelers-Welders* exhibition.

1951

Leo Amino shows in the Metropolitan Museum of Art's *American Sculpture.*

1952

The Walter-McCarran Act nullifies the United States' federal anti-Asian exclusion laws, allowing all Asians to become naturalized U.S. citizens.

1952

Leo Amino begins teaching at Cooper Union, where he mentors Jack Whitten.

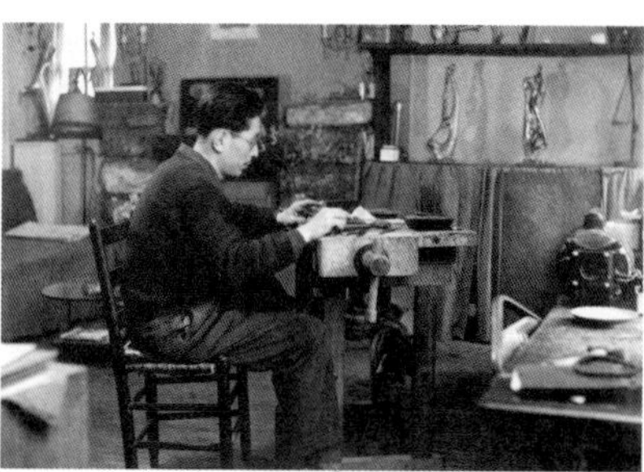

15-year old John Pai holds his first one-person show at the Oglebay Institute in Wheeling, West Virginia.

John Pia to Display Paintings in First 'One-Child' Art Show

For the first time in the history of Oglebay Institute's Art Department, a child will be featured in a "One-Child" show, planned for the early spring. Youthful John Pai, a Korean, will exhibit his paintings.

"John's ability as an artist is demonstrated by the quality and number of pictures that he has painted," said Harry Holbert, in charge of art. "This 'One-Child' show will be unique in that it marks the first time that a member of the Children's Art Classes has been able to provide enough pictures for a complete show," Harry concluded.

1953

The Korean Armistice Agreement is signed, dividing Korea in two and effectively ending the Korean War. North and South Korea are officially divided by the DMZ.

1954

Minoru Niizuma begins exhibiting with the Modern Art Association, Tokyo.

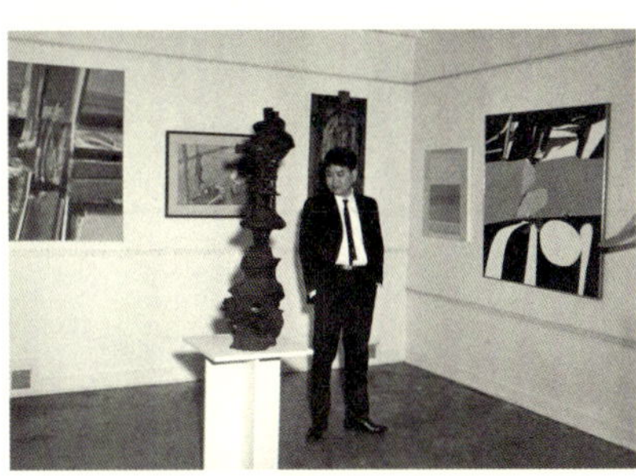

1955

Minoru Niizuma graduates from Tokyo National University of Fine Arts and Music.

1958

John Pai receives a full scholarship to the Pratt Institute and moves to New York.

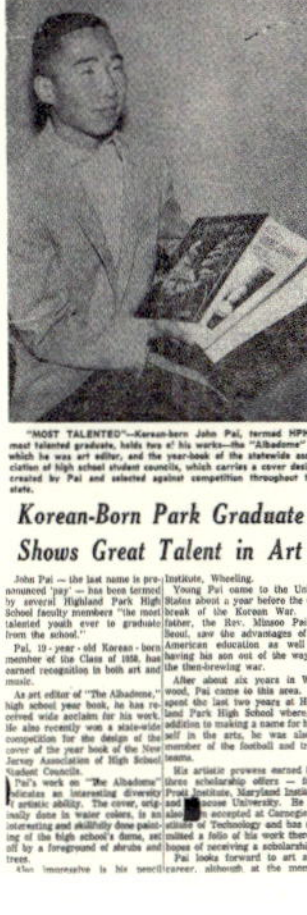

"MOST TALENTED"—Korean-born John Pai, termed HPHS' most talented graduate, holds two of his works—the "Albadome" of which he was art editor, and the year-book of the statewide association of high school student councils, which carries a cover design created by Pai and selected against competition throughout the state.

Korean-Born Park Graduate Shows Great Talent in Art

John Pai — the last name is pronounced 'pay' — has been termed by several Highland Park High School faculty members "the most talented youth ever to graduate from the school."

Pai, 19-year-old Korean-born member of the Class of 1958, has earned recognition in both art and music.

As art editor of "The Albadome," high school year book, he has received wide acclaim for his work. He also recently won a state-wide competition for the design of the cover of the year book of the New Jersey Association of High School Student Councils.

Pai's work on "The Albadome" indicates an interesting diversity of artistic ability. The cover, originally done in water colors, is an interesting and skillfully done painting of the high school's dome, set off by a foreground of shrubs and trees.

Also impressive is his pencil

Institute, Wheeling.

Young Pai came to the United States about a year before the outbreak of the Korean War. His father, the Rev. Minsoo Pai of Seoul, saw the advantages of an American education as well as having his son out of the way of the then-brewing war.

After about six years in Warwood, Pai came to this area. He spent the last two years at Highland Park High School where, in addition to making a name for himself in the arts, he was also a member of the football and track teams.

His artistic prowess earned him three scholarship offers — from Pratt Institute, Maryland Institute, and Syracuse University. He has also been accepted at Carnegie Institute of Technology and has submitted a folio of his work there in hopes of receiving a scholarship.

Pai looks forward to art as a career, although at the moment

1959

Minoru Niizuma immigrates to the United States, moving to New York.

1960

John Pai begins working for sculptor Theodore Roszak.

1962

John Pai graduates from Pratt with a BFA in industrial design.

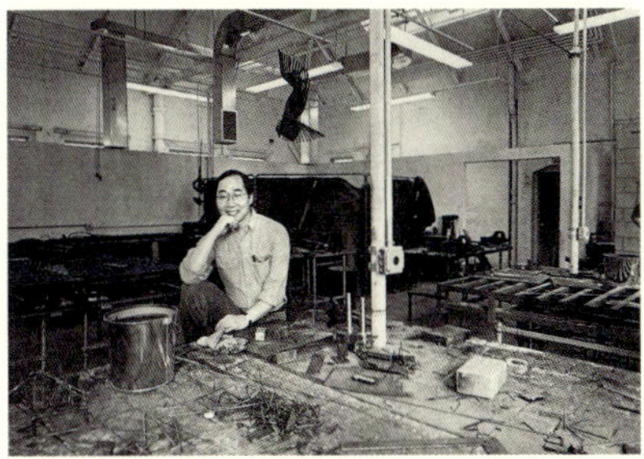

John Pai graduates from Pratt with an MFA in sculpture.

Minoru Niizuma begins teaching at the Brooklyn Museum Art School.

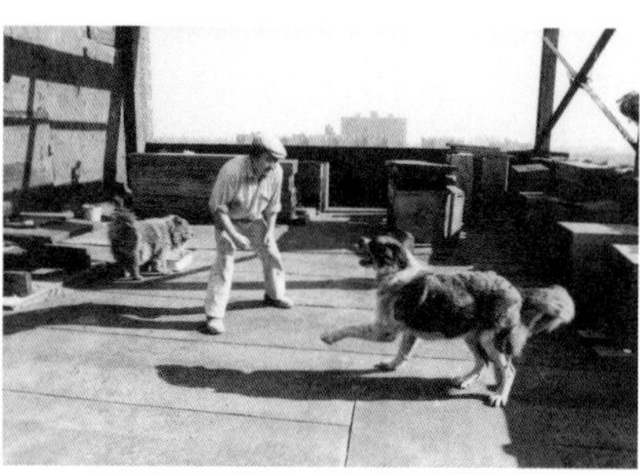

1965

John Pai starts teaching at Pratt as the youngest ever hired professor at the age of 27.

Minoru Niizuma participates in the MoMA's exhibition *The New Japanese Painting and Sculpture*.

Leo Amino debuts his *Refractionals* at the John Daniels Gallery show *Plastics*.

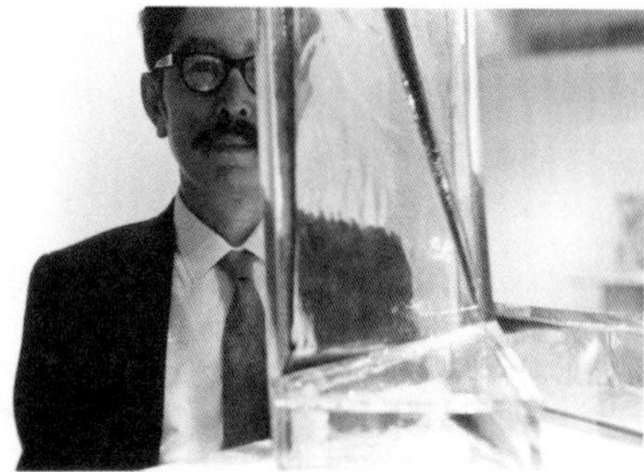

John Pai becomes the head of the undergraduate sculpture department at Pratt.

Mid-1960s

As a young professor, John Pai begins hosting community parties for Korean diasporic artists, including Kim Whanki, Kim Tschang-yeul, Nam June Paik, Hwang Byungi, and Kun-woo Paik.

1968

Emma Gee and Yuji Ochioka coin the term "Asian American," in the midst of a surge in hate crimes and growing solidarity amongst multiracial coalitions of activists.

1971

John Pai becomes director of the Division of Fine Arts at Pratt.

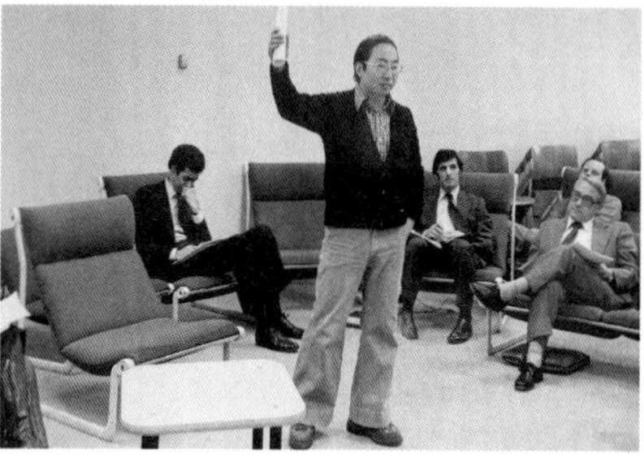

CHRONOLOGY

Minoru Niizuma begins teaching at Columbia University.

1980
John Pai participates in FIAC in Paris, France with the support of the Whanki Foundation, breaking through onto the international stage.

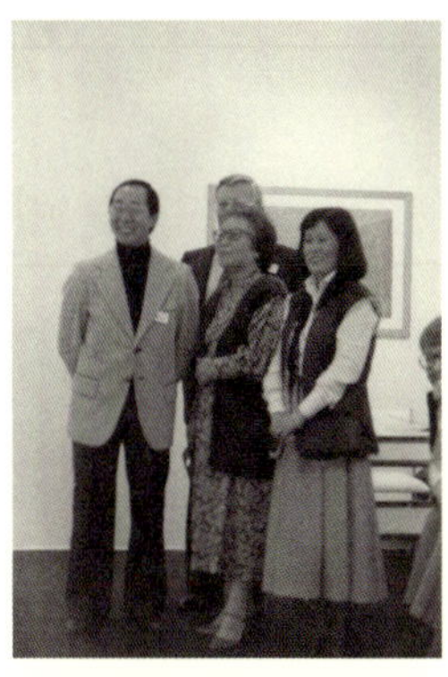

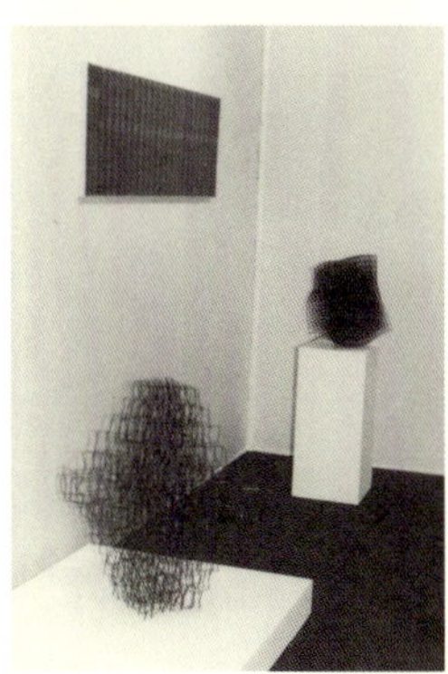

1981
Minoru Niizuma travels to Portugal to participate in the Evora Symposium. There he discovers the abundance of marble and other stones available in Portugal, which becomes a hub for his practice.

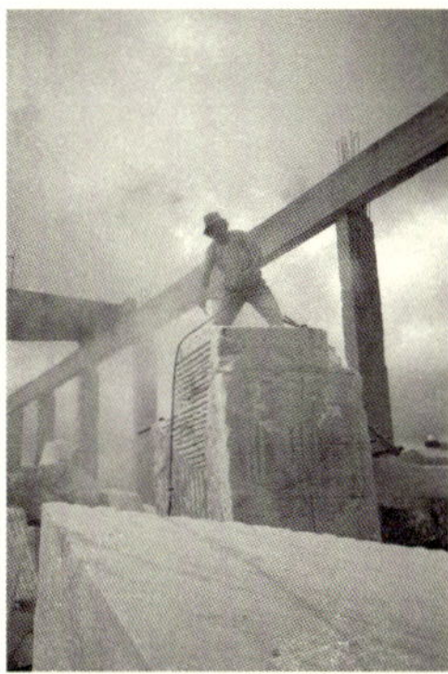

John Pai participates in group exhibitions at the Brooklyn Museum in New York and the National Museum of Modern and Contemporary Art, Korea.

Minoru Niizuma begins working with Portuguese president
Mario Soares to promote artistic exchange between Portugal
and Japan.

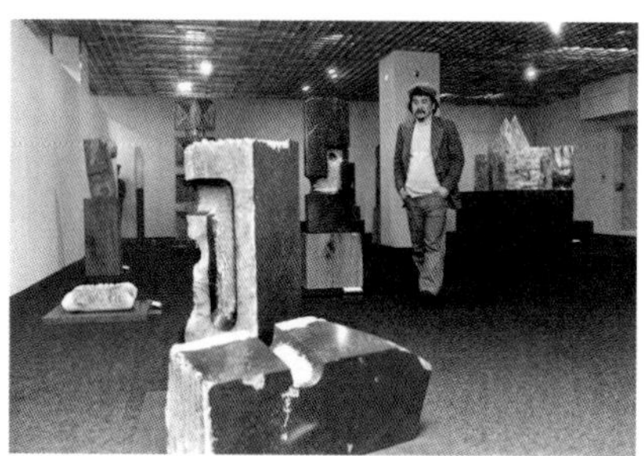

1986
The Immigration Reform and Control Act imposes civil
and criminal penalties on employers who knowingly hire
undocumented aliens, widely affecting Asian American
communities.

1987
The White House commemorates Asian Pacific American
Heritage Week for the first time. This celebration would later
become Asian Pacific American Heritage Month.

1988
President Ronald Reagan signs the Civil Liberties Act of
1988, apologizing for Japanese Internment and paying
$20,000 in reparations to each victim.

1989
Leo Amino, aged 78, dies in New York, NY.

1997
Leo Amino, Minoru Niizuma, and John Pai all show works in
Asian Traditions/Modern Expressions at the Zimmerli Art
Museum in New Brunswick, NJ. This is the only show in which
all three artists have exhibited together.

1998
Minoru Niizuma, aged 67, dies on Long Island, NY.

2000
John Pai resigns from teaching at Pratt to commit full-time to
his artistic practice.

2003
John Pai participates in a group show, *Dreams and Reality:
Korean-American Contemporary Art*, held at the Smithsonian
International Gallery in Washington, D.C.

2008–2011
John Pai participates in exhibitions *Poetry in Motion*, at
Galerie Beyeler, Basel, and *Floating Hours: Moon Is the Oldest
Clock*, at the National Museum of Modern and Contemporary
Art, Deoksugung, Seoul, South Korea.

Leo Amino's work is included in *Leap Before You Look: Black Mountain College 1933–1957,* at the ICA Boston, the Hammer Museum, Los Angeles, and the Wexner Center for the Arts, Columbus, OH.

Present
Leo Amino is posthumously given a solo exhibition, *The Visible and the Invisible,* at David Zwirner Gallery, curated by Genji Amino.

John Pai is preparing for his upcoming retrospective (2022) at the Korean Cultural Center New York for the center's inaugural exhibition. Pai currently works and lives in Stamford, Connecticut.

THE UNSEEN PROFESSORS

Curated by John Yau
Tina Kim Gallery, New York
November 18, 2021–February 26, 2022

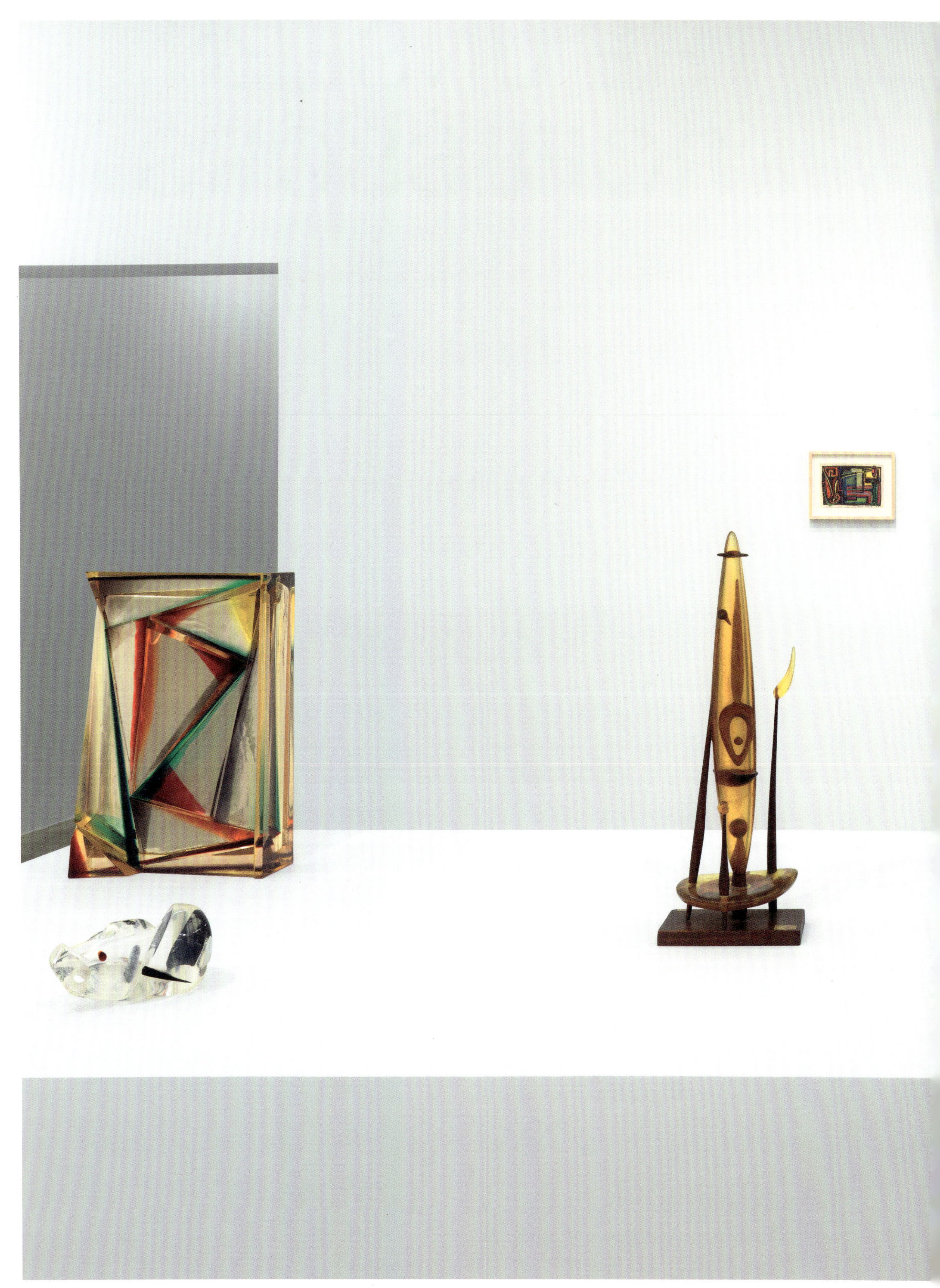

THE UNSEEN PROFESSORS

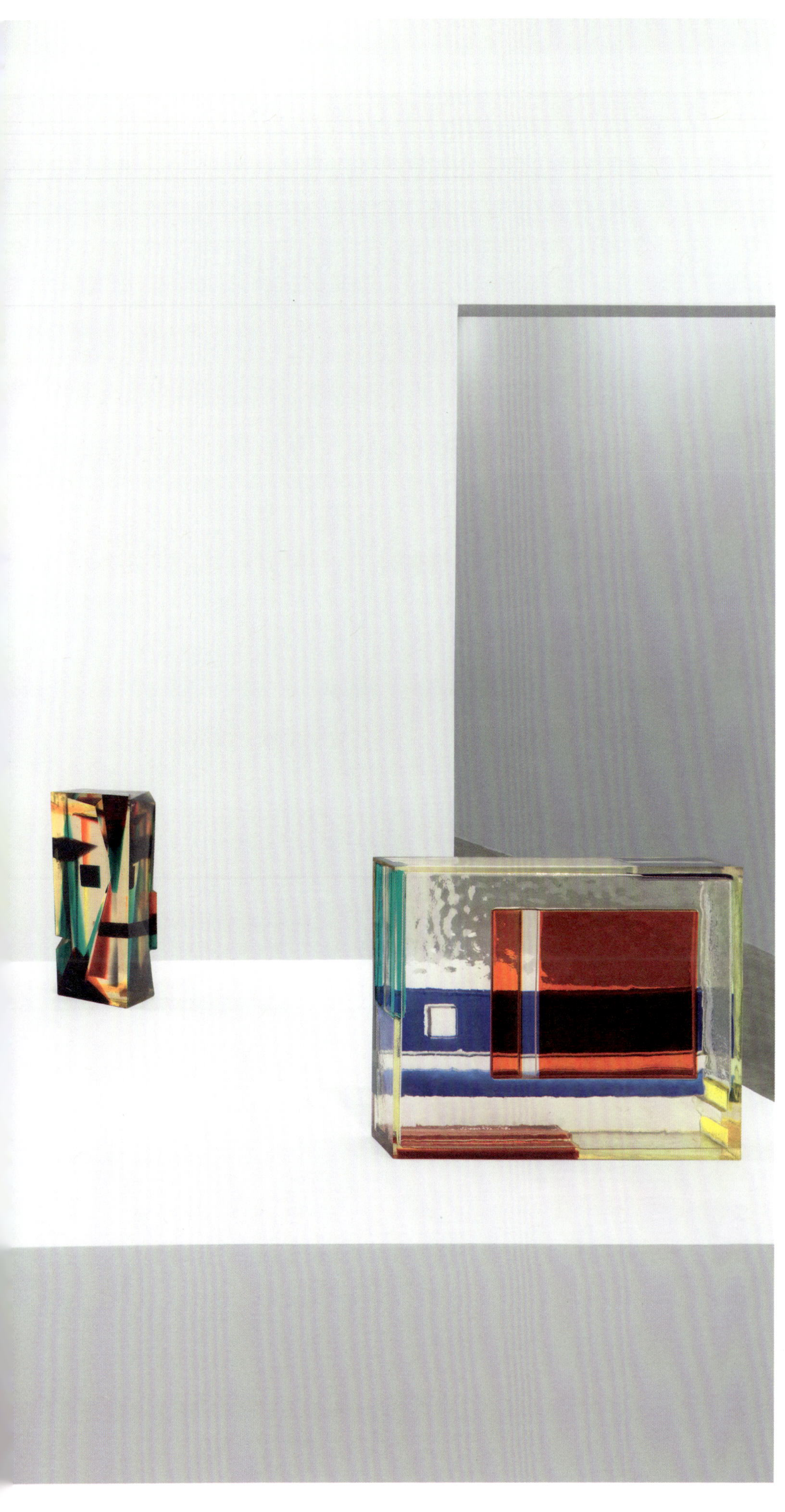

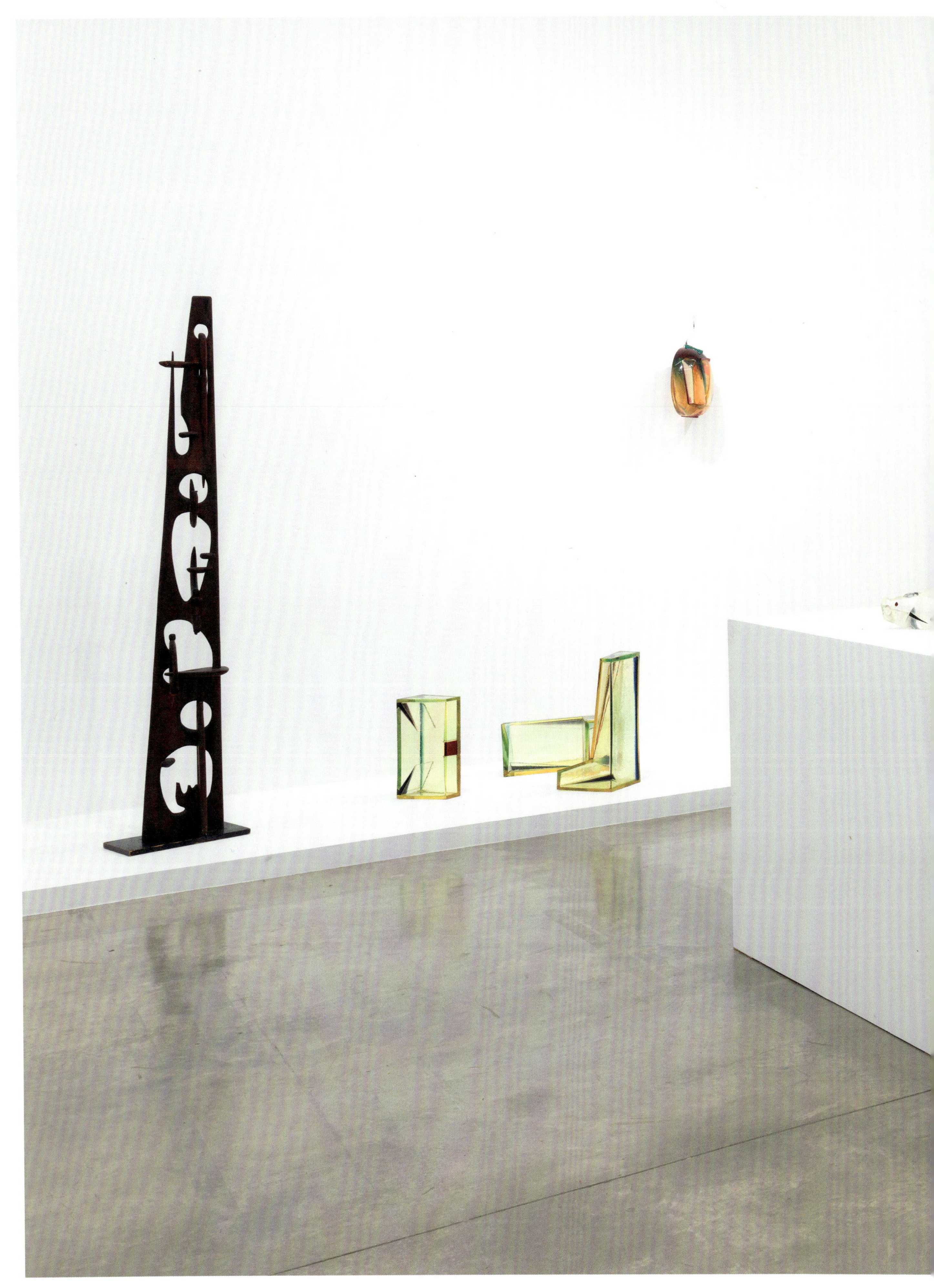

THE UNSEEN PROFESSORS

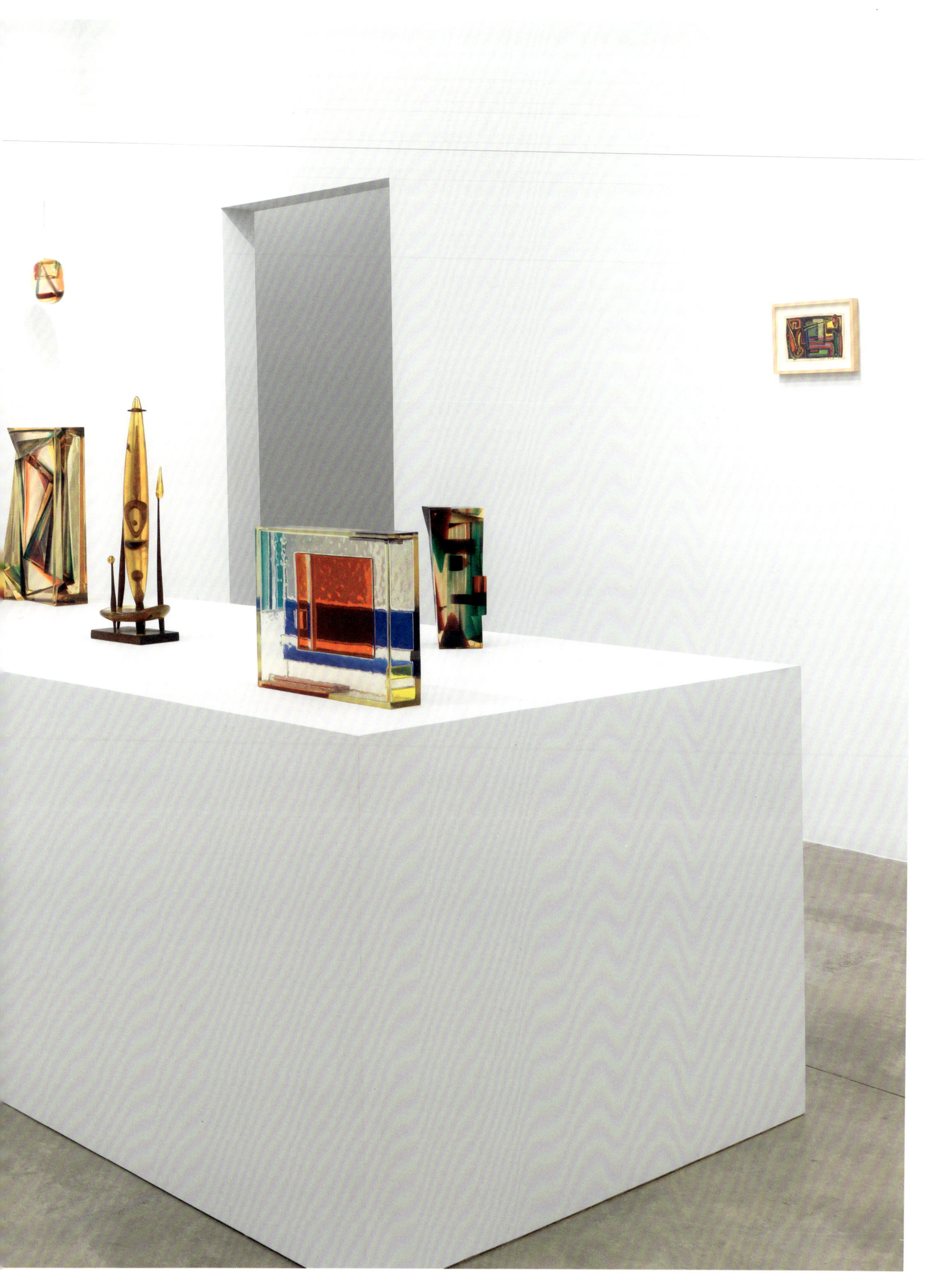

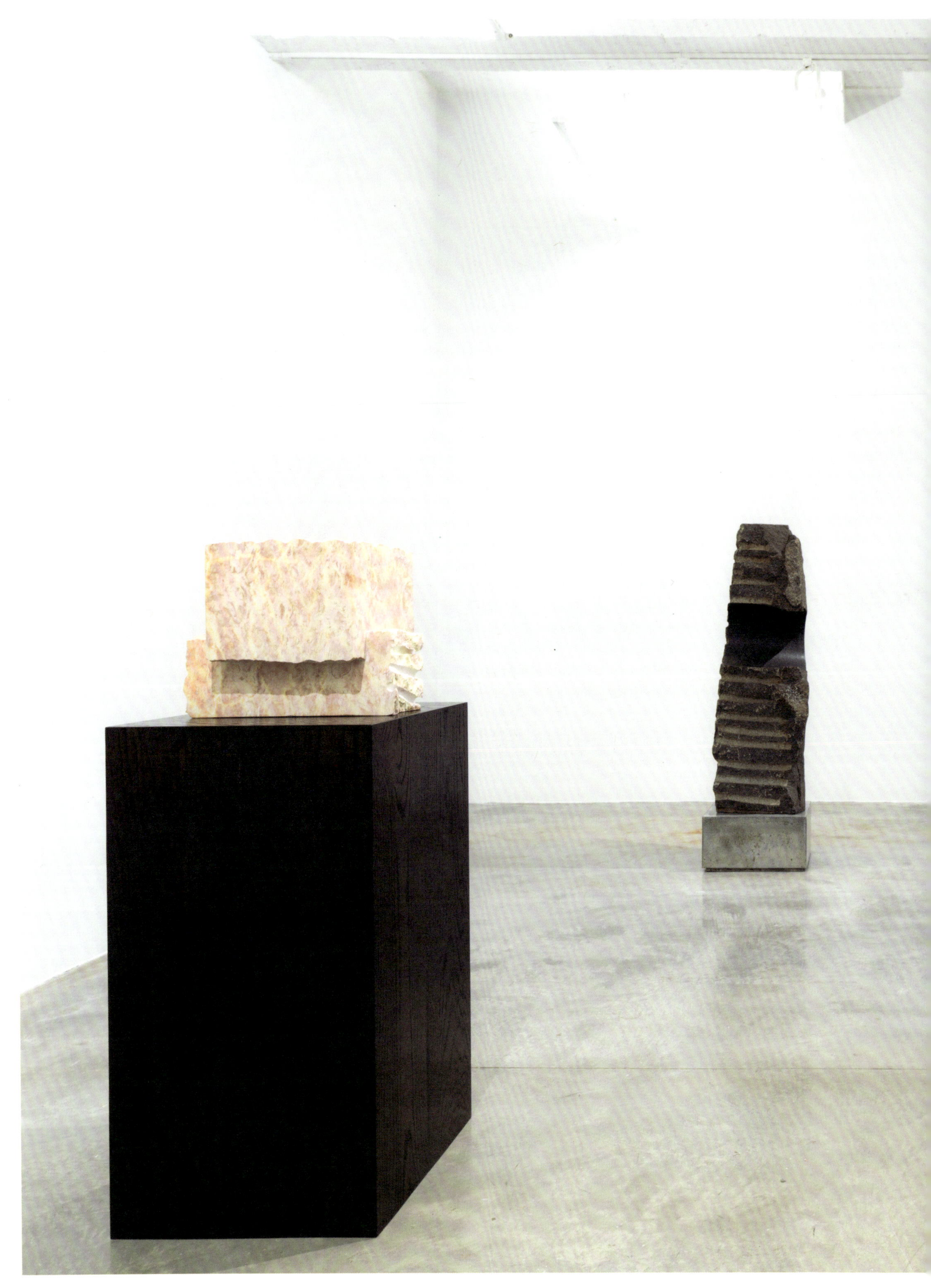

   THE UNSEEN PROFESSORS

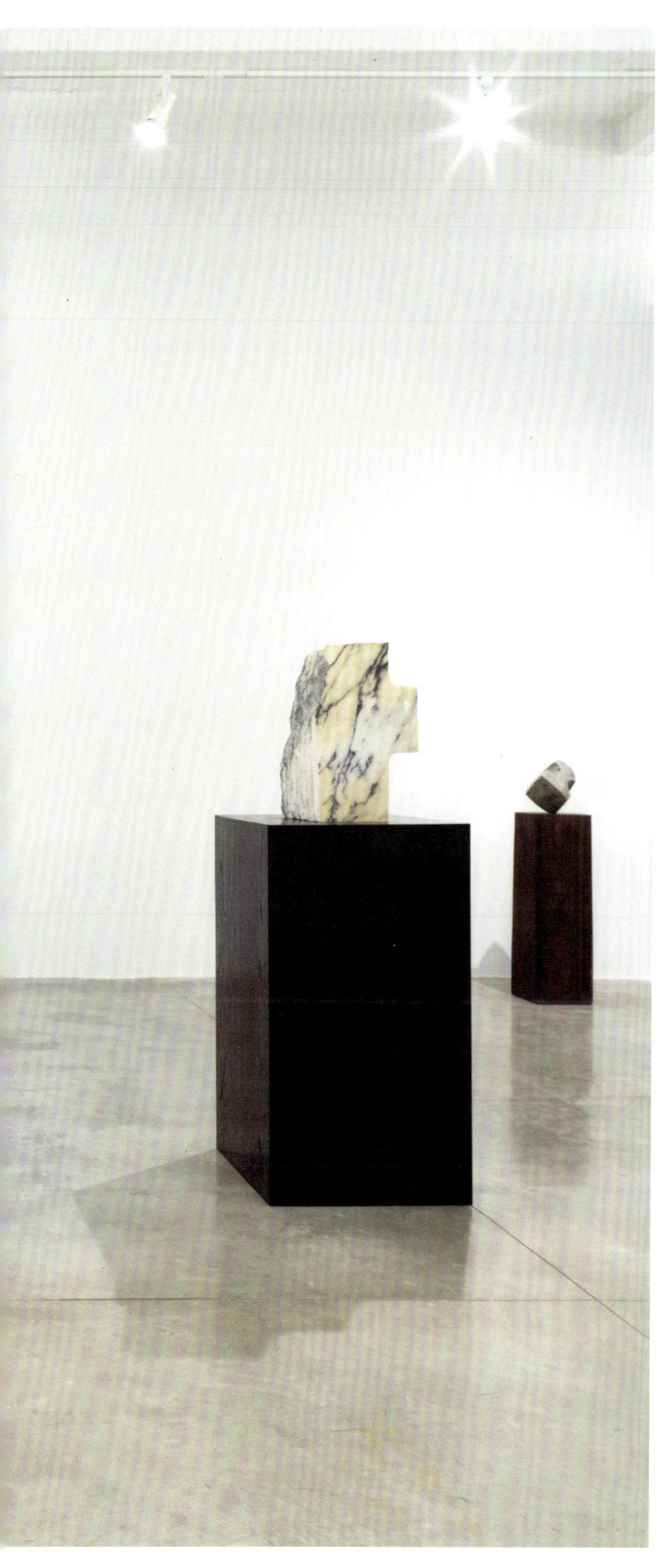

INSTALLATION VIEWS

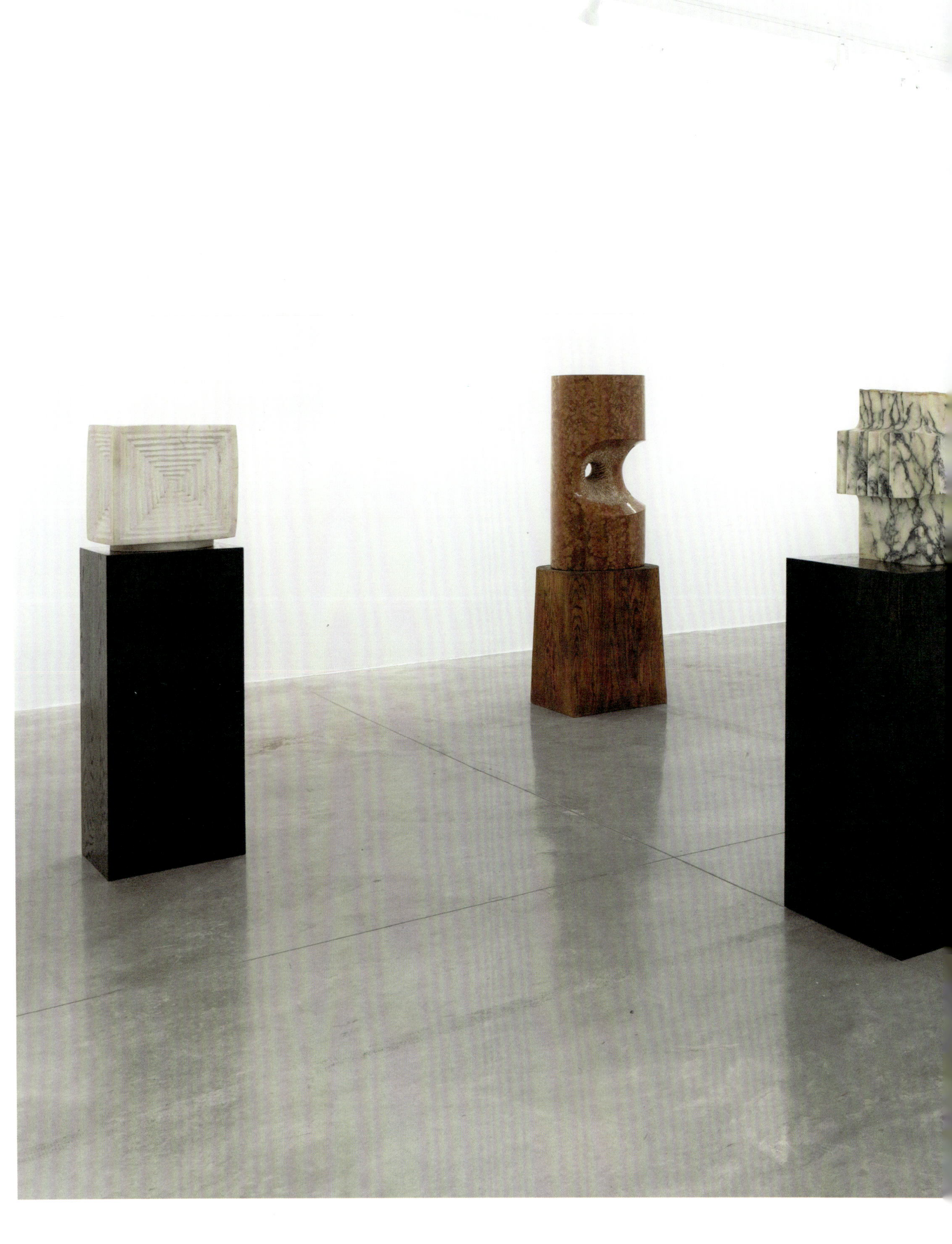

THE UNSEEN PROFESSORS

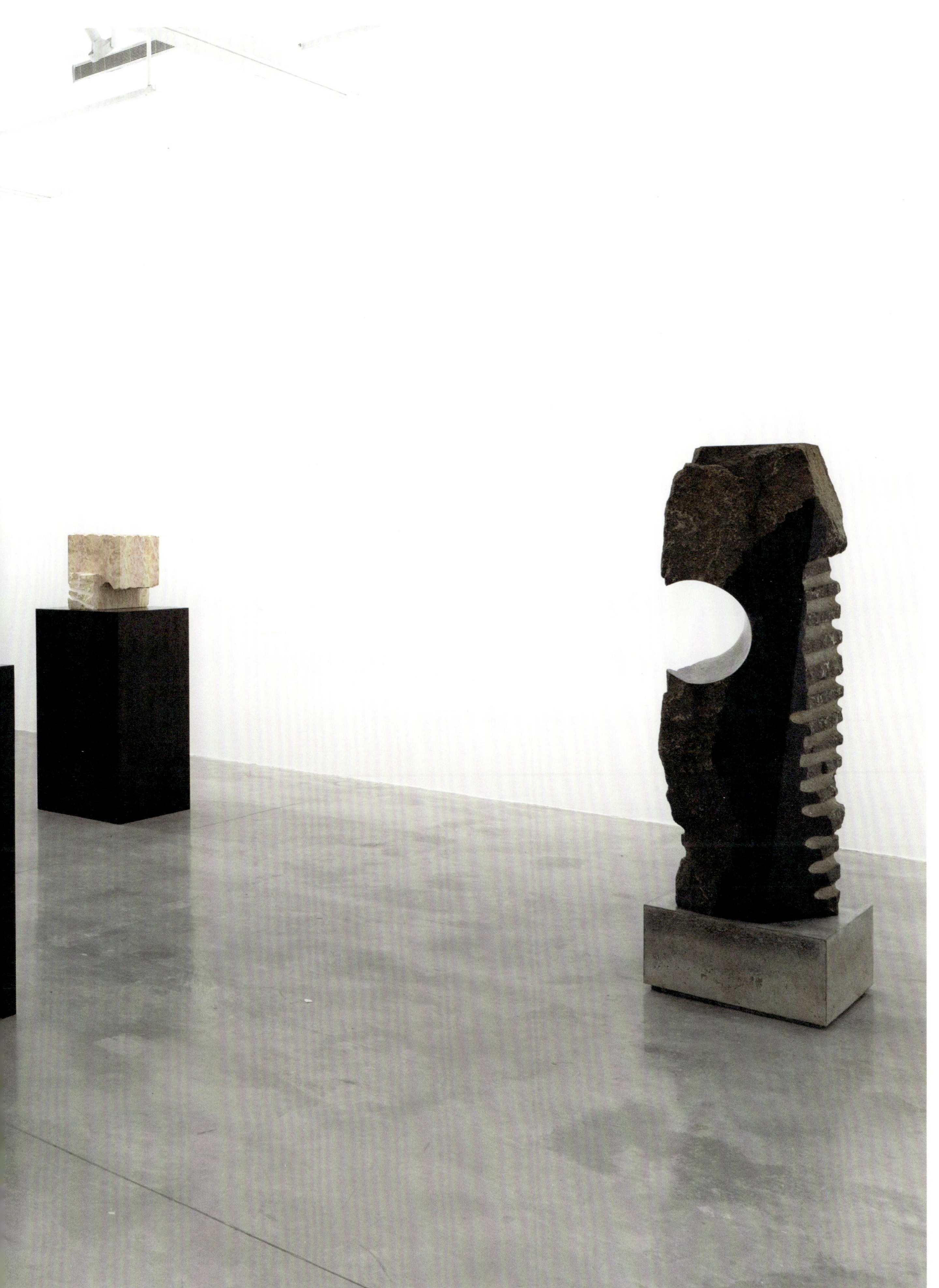

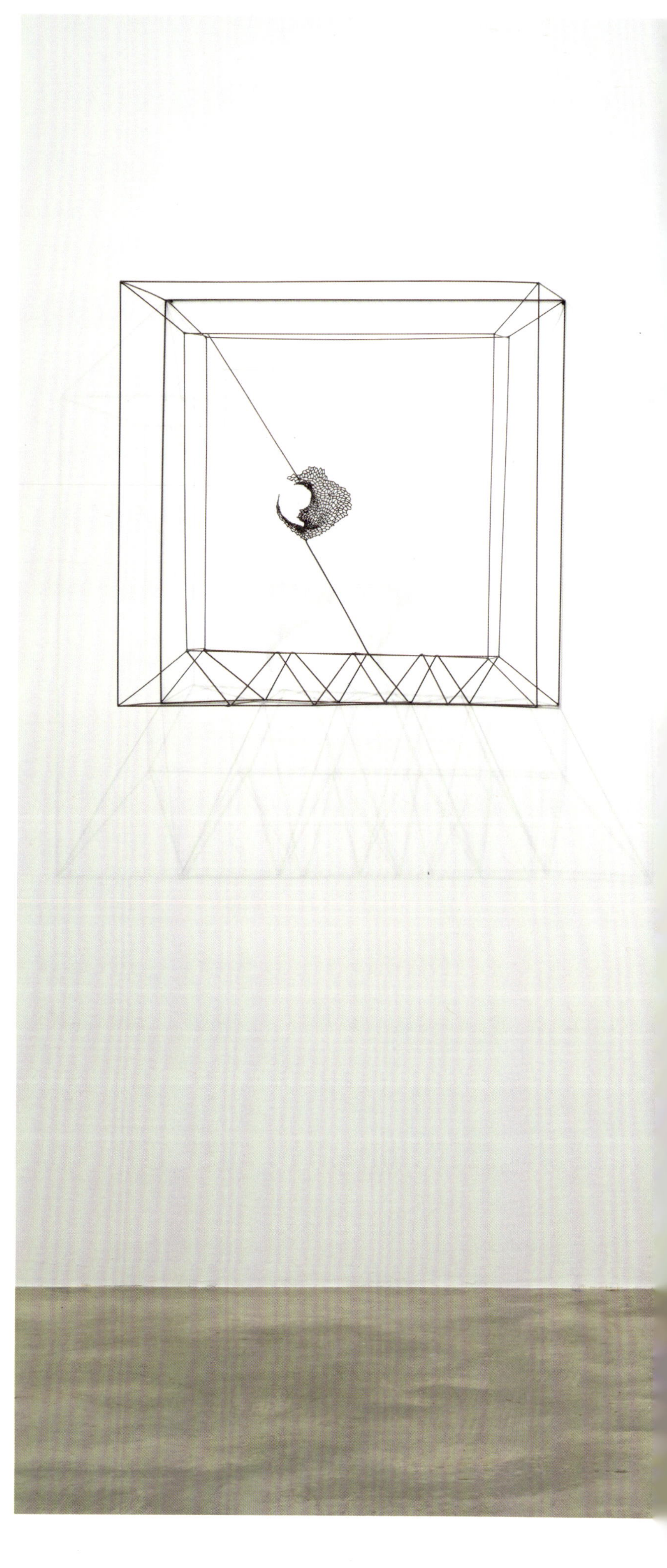

THE UNSEEN PROFESSORS

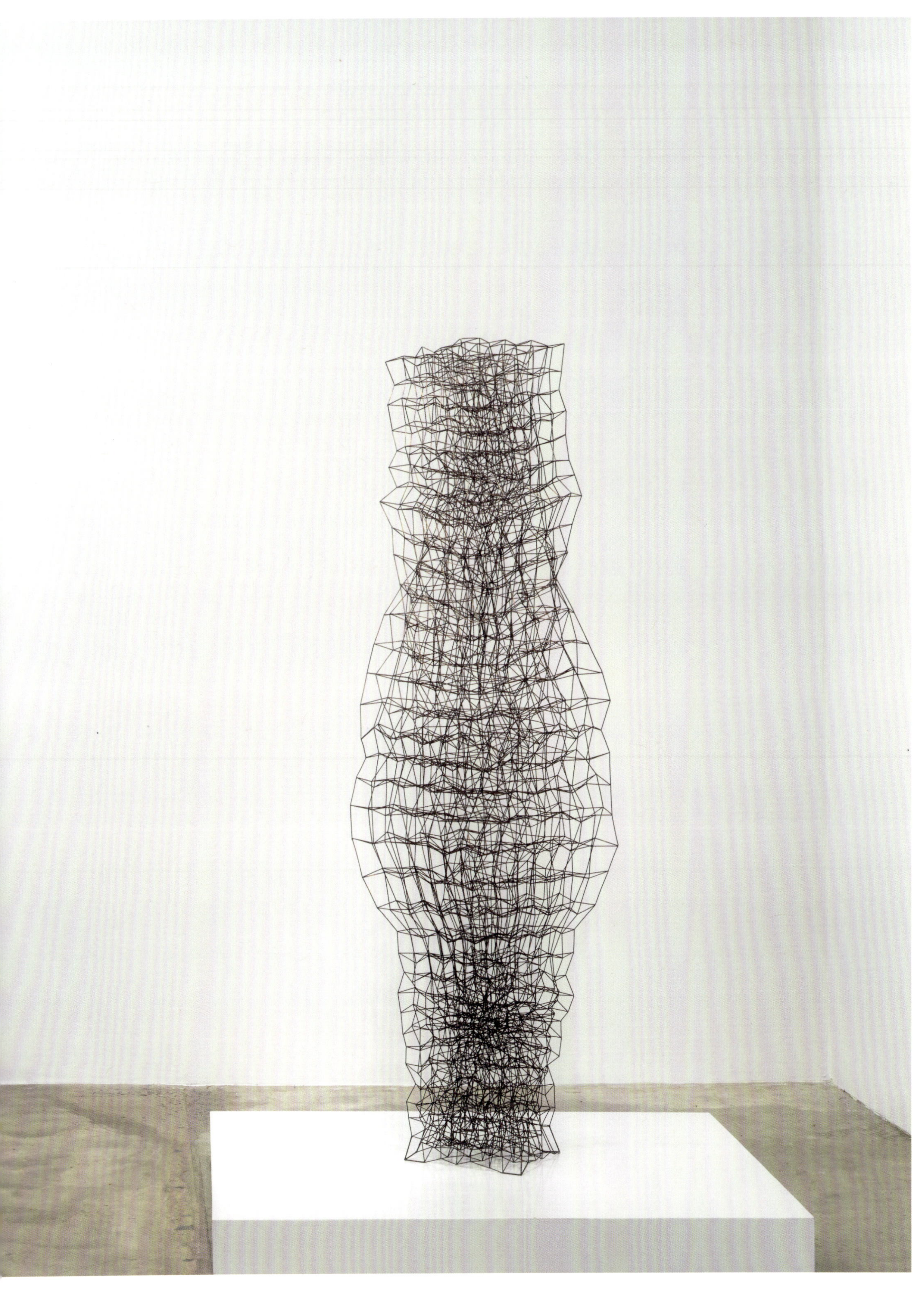

INSTALLATION VIEWS 43

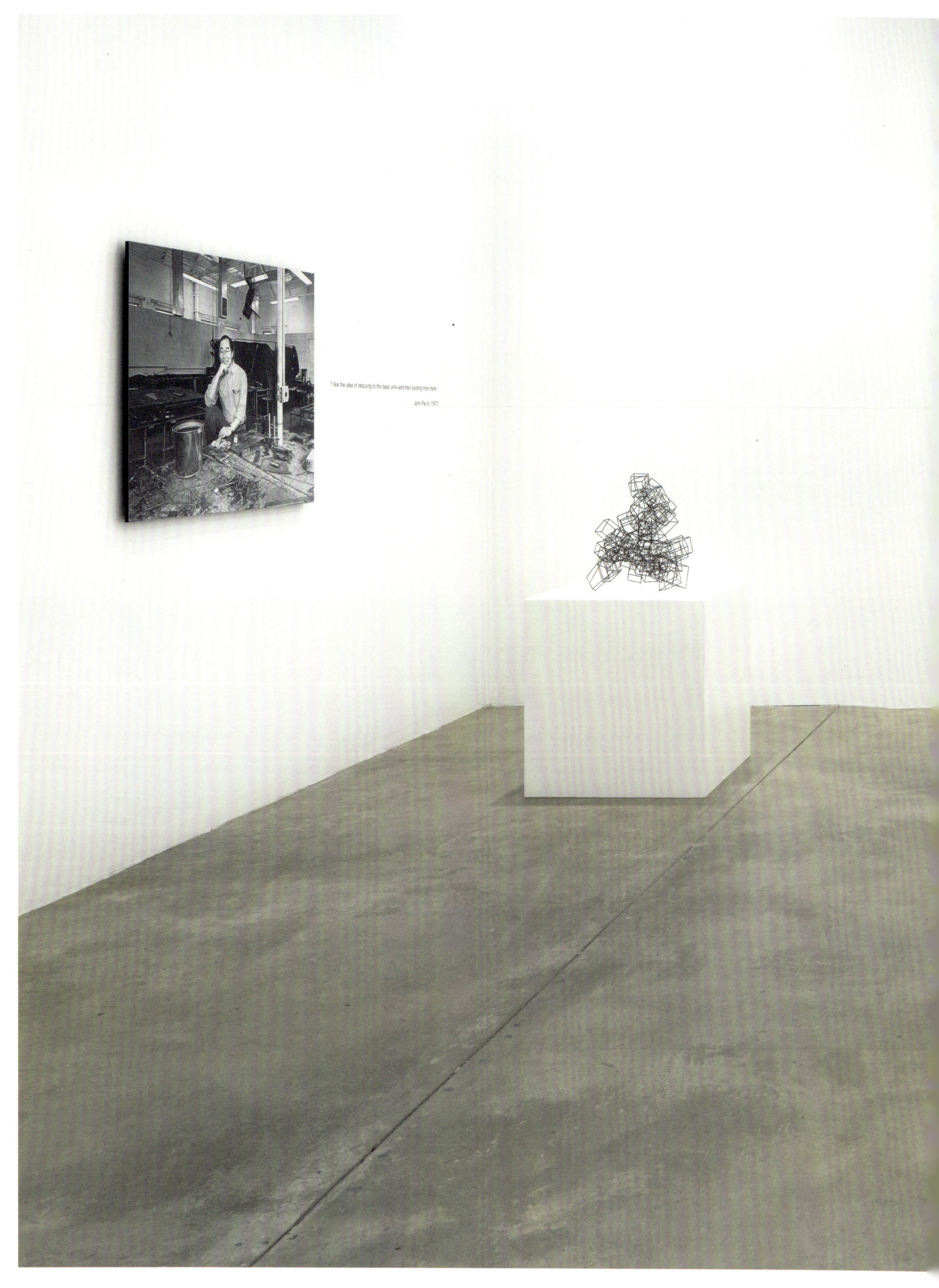

THE UNSEEN PROFESSORS

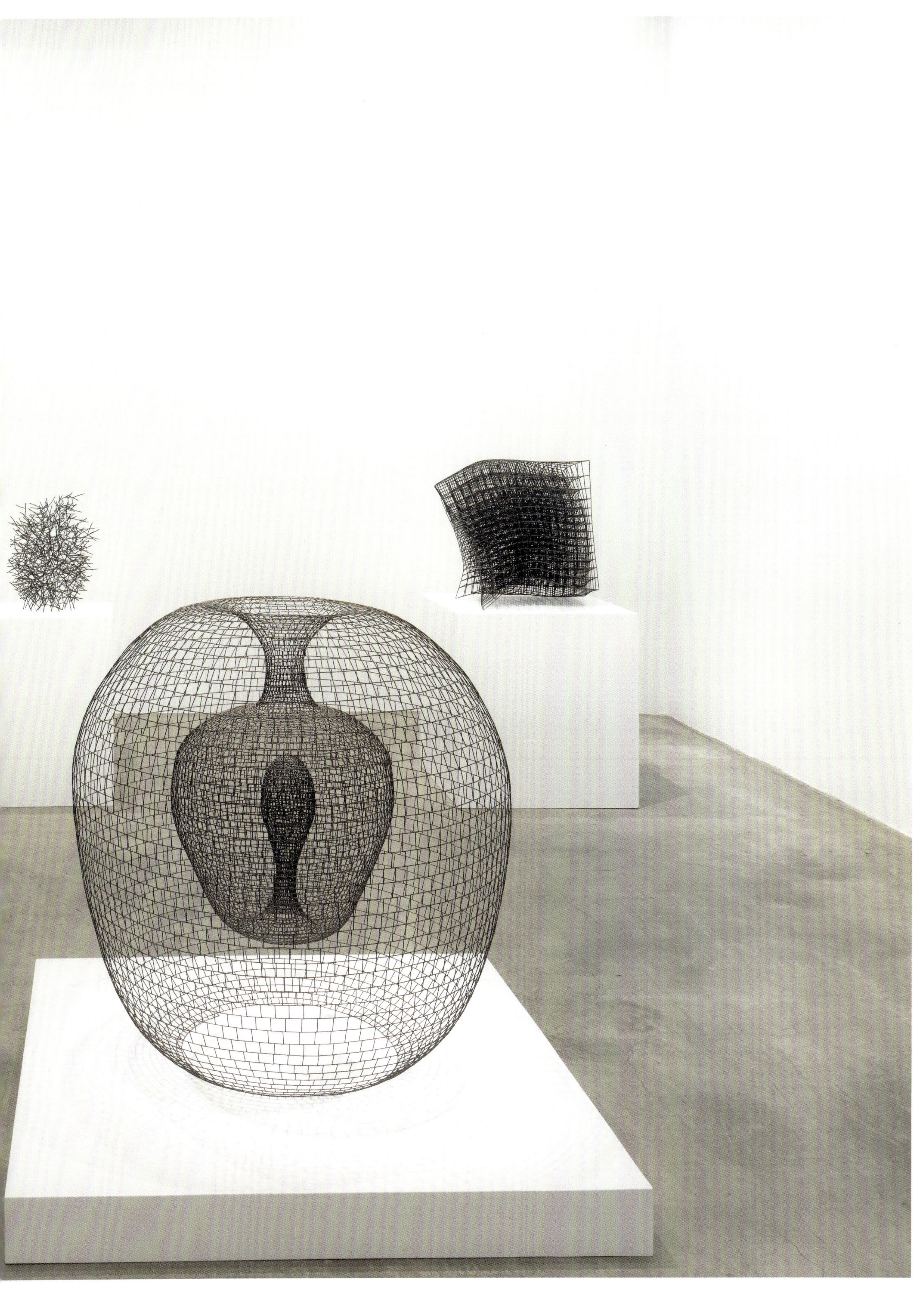

LEO AMINO
MINORU NIIZUMA
JOHN PAI

LEO AMINO

(1911–1989)

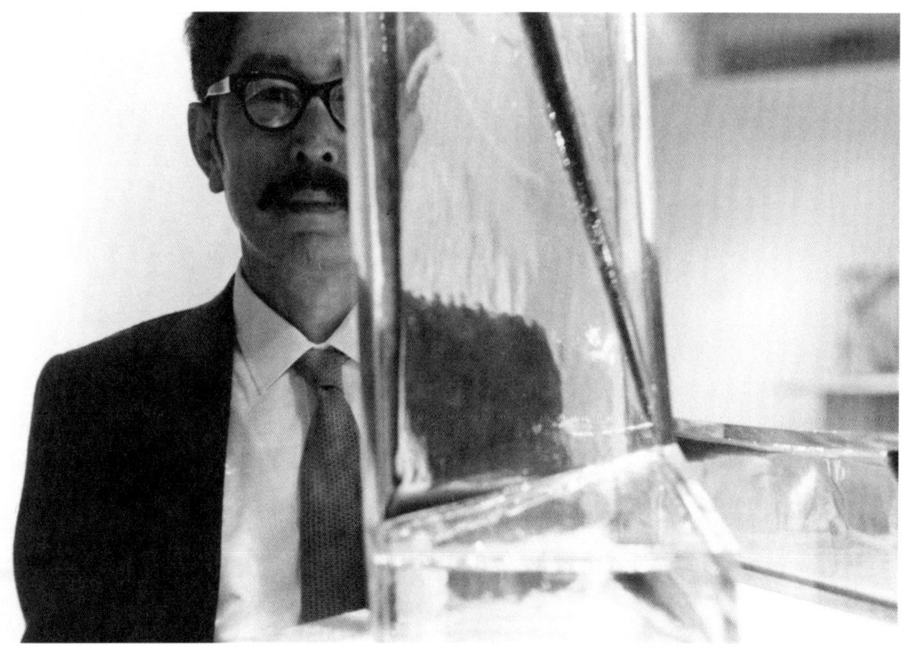

Leo Amino at the opening for his 1971 exhibition *Leo Amino: "Refractional" Plastic Sculpture 1945–1970*, Sculpture Center, New York (detail). Courtesy The Estate of Leo Amino and David Zwirner Gallery

Work selection for *The Unseen Professors* presentation of Leo Amino made by Genji Amino on behalf of The Estate of Leo Amino. Exhibition design for Amino's presentation developed in collaboration with Genji Amino on behalf of The Estate of Leo Amino.

 LEO AMINO

Leo Amino was born in 1911 in the then-Japanese colony of Taiwan, to a mother who practiced ikebana and father who practiced calligraphy. He moved to Tokyo at a young age, before immigrating to the United States in 1929 as an 18-year-old. He lived for six years in California, where he attended San Mateo Junior College, before crossing the country to New York, where he attended classes at New York University. Amino briefly studied direct carving with Chaim Gross at the American Artists School in 1937, where he received coverage in the *New York Times* alongside the artist. Amino stepped out onto a national artistic stage through his inclusion alongside Isamu Noguchi at the 1939 World's Fair in New York. 1939 also marked the first hostilities of World War II, during which Amino was made to translate for the U.S. Navy following Pearl Harbor. He became interested in the sculptural possibilities of polyester after the military's declassification of the medium. Its transparent, malleable qualities inspired his forays into resin sculpture, making him one of the earliest artists in the United States to work with plastics, a practice he continued through the rest of his life.

Invited to teach at Black Mountain College by Josef Albers for two summers in 1946 and 1950, Amino flourished as an educator and artist. Amino was one of only three faculty of color to teach at the Black Mountain Summer Arts Sessions, alongside Jacob Lawrence and Gwendolyn Knight Lawrence. He touched the educational paths of Ruth Asawa and Kenneth Noland before returning to New York, his preferred home base. In the midst of his teaching, Amino was included thirteen times over fifteen years in the Whitney Museum of American Art's annual exhibitions for sculpture from 1947 to 1962, the most of any artist of color besides Isamu Noguchi. He was also featured in the decade-defining 1950 *Carvers-Modelers-Welders* at the Museum of Modern Art, as well as the 1951 *American Sculpture* at the Metropolitan Museum of Art. In 1965, Amino debuted his "refractional" series in the fabled group show *Plastics* at John Daniels Gallery, New York, carrying this series through the late 1980s.

Amid wide success on the New York exhibition circuit, Amino joined the faculty of Cooper Union through the recommendation of Josef Albers. He taught there from 1952 to 1977, mentoring generations of artists, including Jack Whitten, who he trained in direct carving. He passed away in 1989.

LEO AMINO

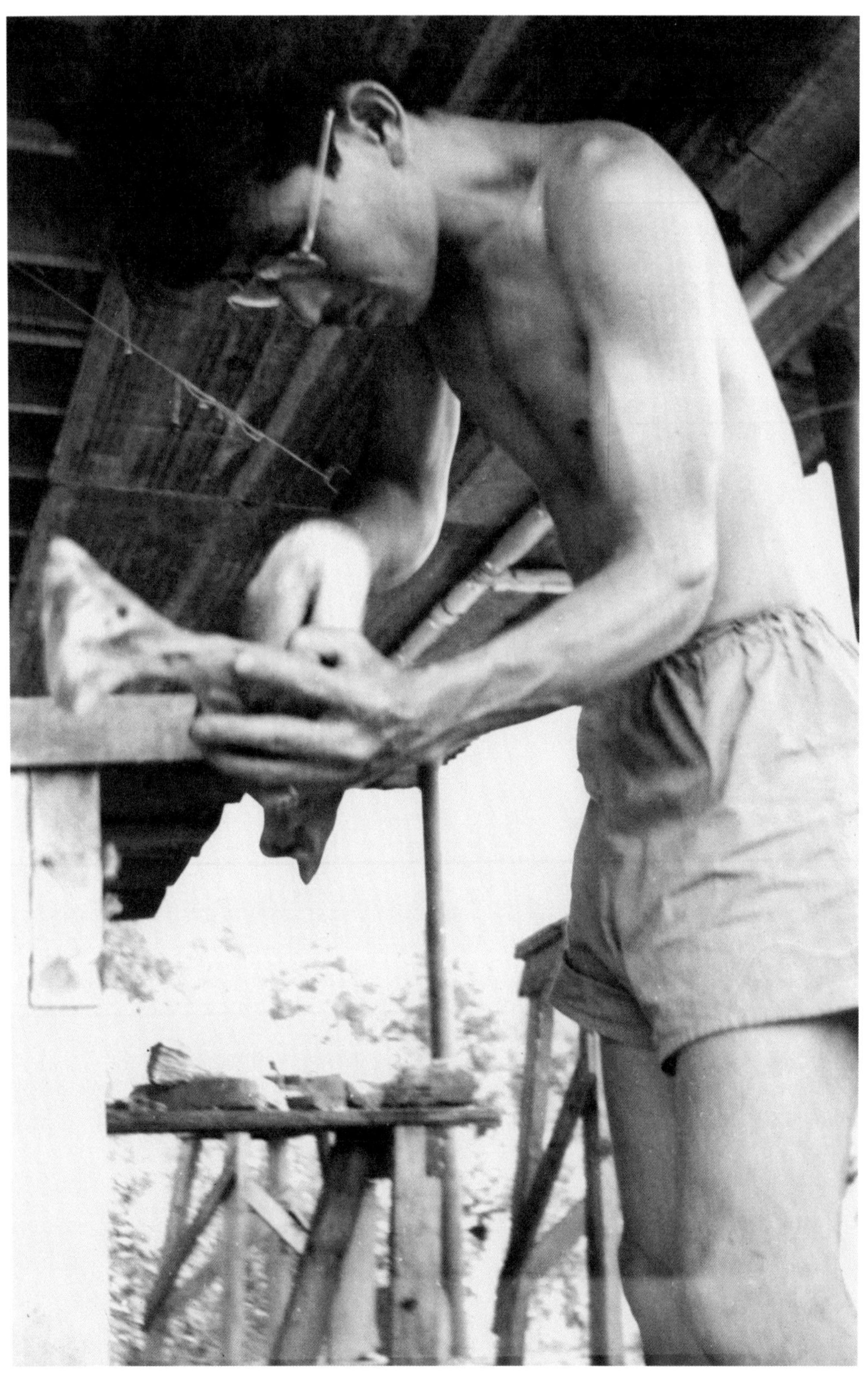

Leo Amino's course in sculpture at Black Mountain College, summer 1946.

(1911–1989)

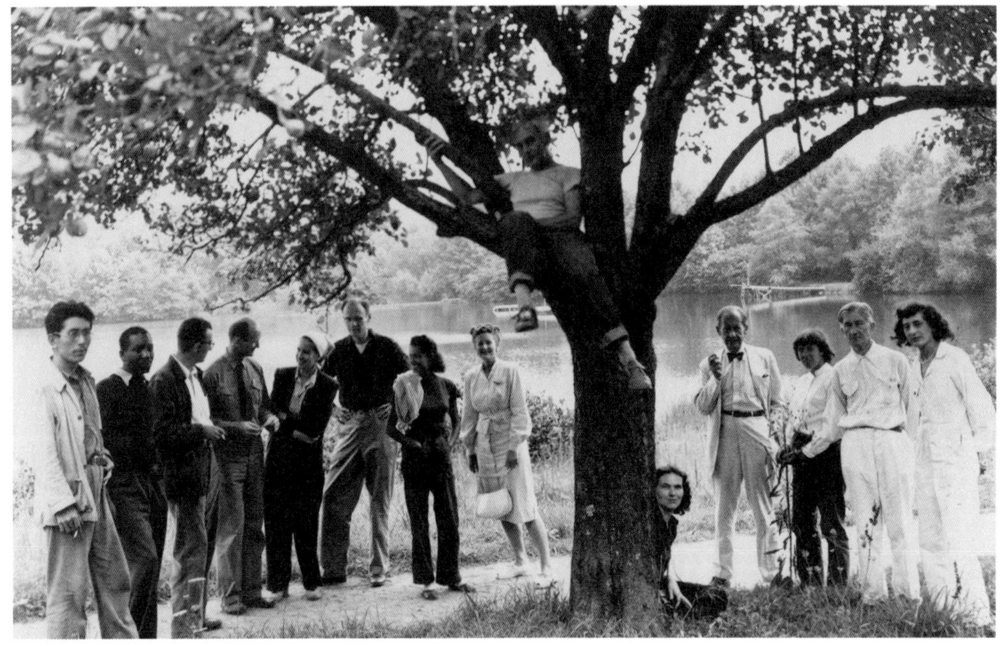

Leo Amino and Jacob Lawrence (far left), Josef and Anni Albers (far right) and Black Mountain College Faculty, Summer Art Session 1946.

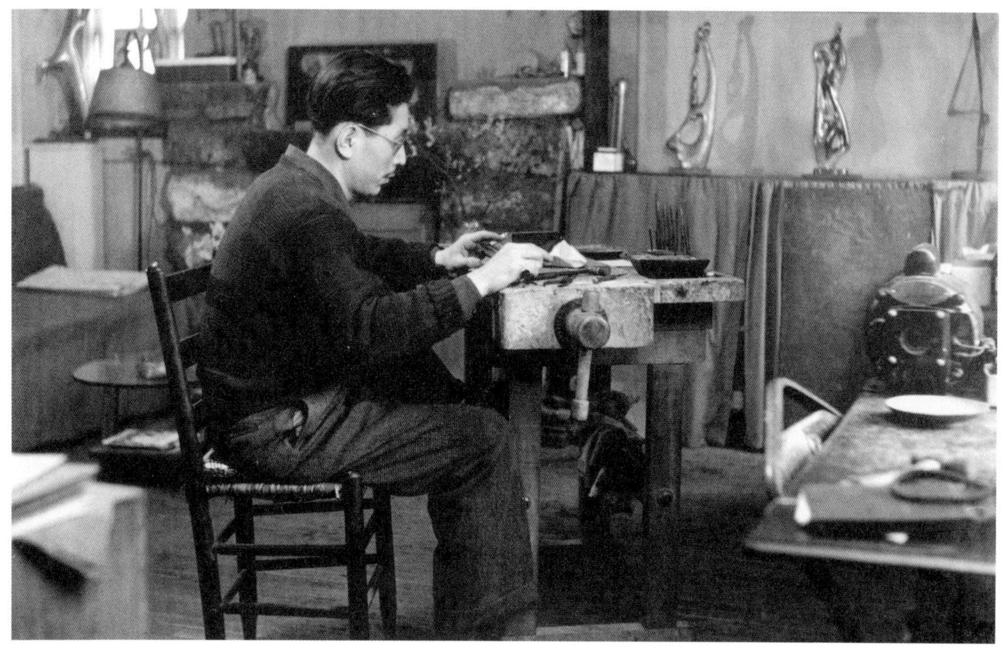

Leo Amino at work in his Perry Street apartment studio, Greenwich Village, c. 1946.

LEO AMINO

I feel that my grandfather's investigations into the mutual implication of mind, eye, and body proceeded from questions about what other worlds could be revealed to exist already in this one. I believe he found something to think with in his readings in phenomenology, insofar as they provided him with a companion for his intuition that what appears to be most near to perception might actually be what is most far, and vice versa. That some limber attunement of critical and sensuous attention is called for to disaggregate and reconstruct appearances toward a revision of the prevailing terms of relation: subject and object, figure and ground, interior and environment. I believe my grandfather remained convinced of and committed to an incontrovertible intimacy between these terms, understanding that what we know of ourselves remains rooted in what we know of our every encounter with something else, understanding that the question of interiority is not an accomplishment of human exception but a matter of perceptual entanglement by which our senses prove to be theoreticians in their own right. He would often repeat a favorite, somewhat refracted phrase of Heidegger's — "Thrown in the world!" — and I think that more than the heroic existential drama, what interested him in this predicament was the problem of encounter, of the possible apprehension and description of existence. I think that for him this went beyond the question of relativity, meaning beyond the question of relation in the way it is usually conceived. To me the proposal in

(1911–1989)

his work—as much ethical as aesthetic—has less to do with figure-
ground relation than with the intuition of a radical indebtedness
of the figure to its ground. Of that which is seen to that which
is unseen. A conviction that our seeing is always ambivalently
invested, reformed, even fundamentally disarticulated by the
anticipation and return of a transformative potential inherent in
the most basic unit of experience.

> *unredoubted to expose*
> *in this way necessitated*
> *visited*
> *by proximity*
> *having the excuse of*
> *containment*
> *relation*
> *of composure*
> *lapidary*
> *filled out*
> *by belatedness*
> *anticipation*

My mother tells stories about how during the summers the family
spent in a cabin in Glen Gardner, New Jersey, Leo would often
call her attention to the way that the eye could allow itself to be
led astray, brought around, irrevocably moved by the contour of a
branch, leaf, or stone. In his manner of expression, "It will tell you."
I believe it is this openness to absorption, surrender, the structural
as much as aleatory imposition of time and space, that renders
even his most minimal and rigorously geometrical resin works so
rich in sensuous investigation and display. The intervention of a
novel industrial material into this bucolic setting and vocabulary
may seem incongruous to some, but to Leo it was not. He had in

LEO AMINO

fact little interest in the oppositions between man and nature, craft
and industry, art and life, which were so defining for many American
artists at midcentury. At a time when the American avant-garde
was preoccupied with the notion of authentic gesture or automatic
revelation, Leo could not help but defer this notion of immediacy
in favor of the radically mediated, a penchant for conceiving
expression at perception's formal and philosophical juncture, an
impingement of the exterior so complete as to render the distinction
between inside and outside a matter of attention. In a period during
which American sculpture moved between statements of mass
and contour and their reversal into the negativity of open work in
structure or gesture, Leo's engagement with translucency invited
a second look. Not the self or the world, the subject or the object,
but an interim between which holds our seeing.

brightly lit
shiftless and latent
state
description
evoked
cauterized
recuses to be into
frequency
tandem
anthem

From one point of view, the history of Leo's engagement with the
shifting ground beneath sensuous and philosophical investigation
casts a queer shadow against the backdrop of several decades
of American sculpture across which one of the most robust
imaginaries is reserved for the idea of the monument. I don't believe
Leo made his work to stand in or against history, at least not a history

(1911–1989)

that had yet been imagined. I'm not sure how he would have liked
the idea of the uprightness of his own posthumous standing, at
least within this history, for much the same reason. Apart from
which he would have been the first to see the limits of revising or
repopulating a canon, which artists of color have a way of falling
into only to fall out. It is after all not built to conserve the possibility
of their appearance, which in any case these artists will continue
to exceed. I believe Leo would have wanted his memory to remain
a blessing for those stories, those practices, those resistances and
reservations that remain submerged. This is the way I remember
him today.

LEO AMINO

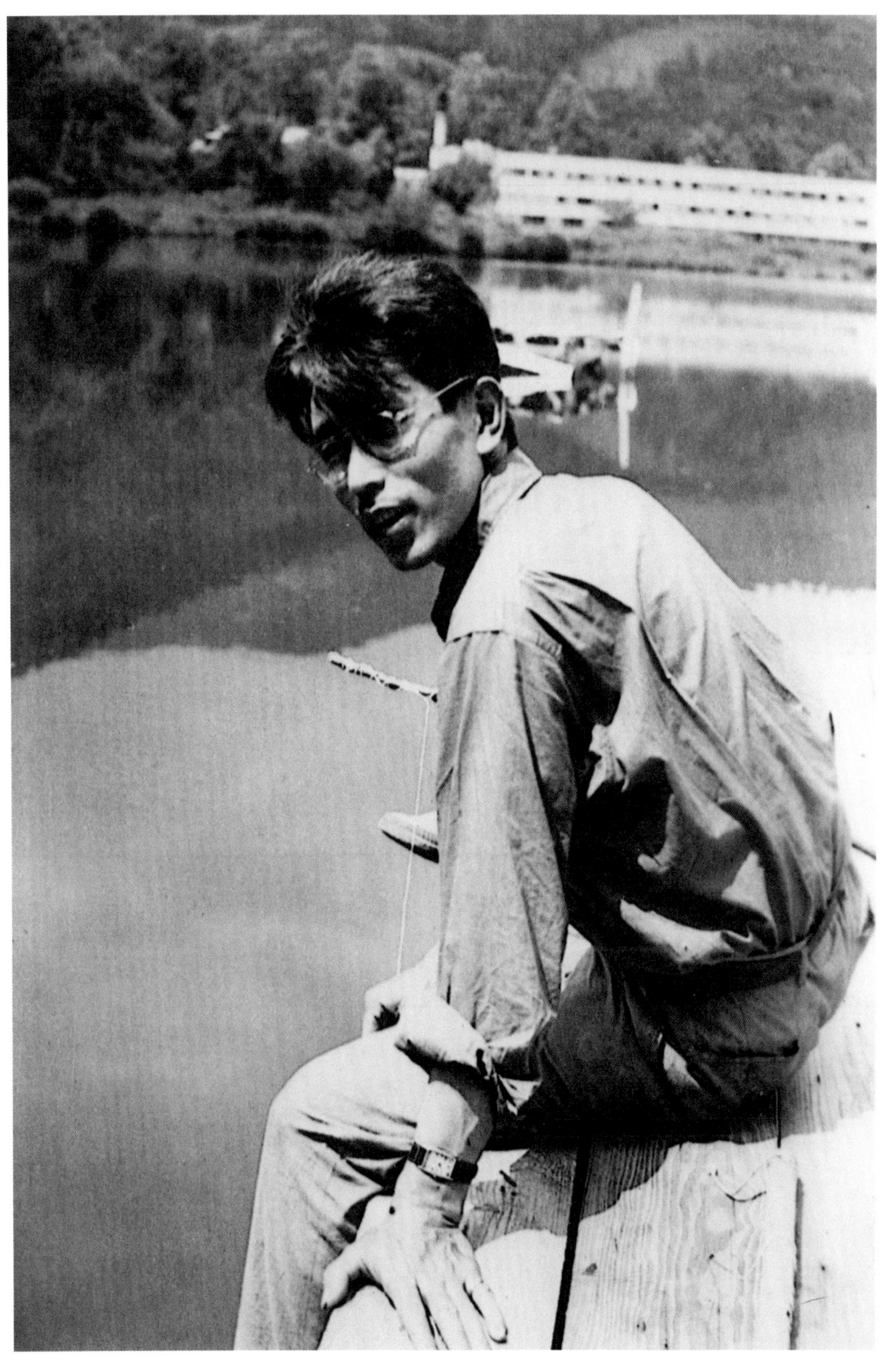

Leo Amino at Black Mountain College, 1946.

(1911–1989)

Born 1911, Taiwan
Died 1989, New York, NY

Education

1929   San Mateo Junior College
1935   New York University
1937   American Artists School

Selected Solo Exhibitions

2020   *Leo Amino: The Visible and the Invisible*, David Zwirner Gallery, New York, NY
1973   *Leo Amino, Recent Plastic Sculpture*, SculptureCenter, New York, NY
1971   *Leo Amino: Plastic Sculpture 1945-1970*, SculptureCenter, New York, NY
1970   *Leo Amino: Refractional Plastics*, East Hampton Gallery, New York, NY
1969   *Leo Amino: Refractional Plastics*, East Hampton Gallery, New York, NY
1957   *Leo Amino*, SculptureCenter, New York, NY
1954   *Leo Amino: Twelfth One-man Exhibition*, SculptureCenter, New York, NY
1953   *Leo Amino*, Behn-Moore Gallery, Boston, MA
1952   *Selected Works by Leo Amino,* SculptureCenter, New York, NY
1951   *Leo Amino: Tenth One-Man Exhibition*, SculptureCenter, New York, NY
1949   *Leo Amino*, Sculptors Gallery, New York, NY
1948   *Leo Amino: Sculpture in Plastics*, Sculptors Gallery, New York, NY
1947   *Leo Amino: Sculpture in Plastics*, Sculptors Gallery, New York, NY
1946   *Leo Amino*, Sculptors Gallery, New York, NY
1945   *Leo Amino*, Bonestell Gallery, New York, NY
1943   *Recent Sculptures by Leo Amino*, Artists Gallery, New York, NY
1941   *Leo Amino*, Clay Club, New York, NY
1940   *Sculpture Exhibition by Leo Amino*, Montross Gallery, New York, NY
1940   *Leo Amino*, Artist's Gallery, New York, NY

Selected Group Exhibitions

2021–22   *American Modernisms*, Rollins Museum of Art, Winter Park, FL
2021   *I AM A CITIZEN OF THE WORLD*, Black Mountain College Museum + Arts Center, Asheville, NC
2019   *Color, Form and Light*, Georgia Museum of Art, Athens, GA
2015–17   *Leap Before You Look: Black Mountain College 1933–1957*
            Institute of Contemporary Art, Boston, MA
            Hammer Museum, Los Angeles, CA
            Wexner Center for the Arts, Columbus, OH
2003   *Black Mountain College: Una aventura americana*, Museo Nacional Centro de Arte Reina
            Sofía, Madrid, Spain
2001   *Vital Forms: American Art and Design in the Atomic Age*
            Brooklyn Museum, New York, NY
            Walker Art Center, Minneapolis, MN
            Frist Center for the Visual Arts, Nashville, TN
            San Diego Museum of Art, CA
            Phoenix Art Museum, AZ
1997   *Asian Traditions/ Modern Expressions*, Zimmerli Art Museum, New Brunswick, NJ
1991   *Abstract Sculpture In America 1930-1990*, American Federation of Arts
            Lowe Art Museum, Coral Gables, FL
            Museum of Arts and Sciences, Macon, GA
            Akron Art Museum, OH
            Fort Wayne Museum of Art, IN
            Musée National des Beaux-Arts du Québec, Canada
            Terra Museum of American Art, Chicago, IL
1987   *Recent Acquisitions,* National Museum of American Art, Washington, DC
1987   *The Arts at Black Mountain College 1933–1937*
            Edith C. Blum Art Institute, Annandale-on-Hudson, NY
            Grey Art Gallery, New York, NY
1969   *A Plastic Presence*
            The Jewish Museum, New York, NY
            Milwaukee Art Center, Milwaukee, WI
            San Francisco Museum of Art, San Francisco, CA

                LEO AMINO

1965	*Plastics*, John Daniels Gallery, New York, NY
1962	*Annual Exhibition of Contemporary American Sculpture, Watercolors and Drawings,* Whitney Museum of American Art, New York, NY
1960	*Annual Exhibition of Contemporary American Sculpture, Watercolors and Drawings,* Whitney Museum of American Art, New York, NY
1959	*Annual Exhibition of Contemporary American Sculpture, Watercolors and Drawings,* Whitney Museum of American Art, New York, NY
1958	*Annual Exhibition of Contemporary American Sculpture, Watercolors and Drawings,* Whitney Museum of American Art, New York, NY
1956	*Annual Exhibition of Contemporary American Sculpture, Watercolors and Drawings,* Whitney Museum of American Art, New York, NY
1955	*The New Decade: 35 American Painters and Sculptors,* Whitney Museum of American Art, New York, NY
1954	*Annual Exhibition of Contemporary American Sculpture, Watercolors and Drawings,* Whitney Museum of American Art, New York, NY
1953	*Annual Exhibition of Contemporary American Sculpture, Watercolors and Drawings,* Whitney Museum of American Art, New York, NY
1952	*Annual Exhibition of Contemporary American Sculpture, Watercolors and Drawings,* Whitney Museum of American Art, New York, NY
1951	*American Sculpture,* Metropolitan Museum of Art, New York, NY
	Annual Exhibition of Contemporary American Sculpture, Watercolors and Drawings, Whitney Museum of American Art, New York, NY
1950	*Carvers-Modelers-Welders,* Museum of Modern Art, New York, NY
	Annual Exhibition of Contemporary American Sculpture, Watercolors and Drawings, Whitney Museum of American Art, New York, NY
1949	*Annual Exhibition of Contemporary American Sculpture, Watercolors and Drawings,* Whitney Museum of American Art, New York, NY
1948	*Annual Exhibition of Contemporary American Sculpture, Watercolors and Drawings,* Whitney Museum of American Art, New York, NY
1947	*Annual Exhibition of Contemporary American Sculpture, Watercolors and Drawings,* Whitney Museum of American Art, New York, NY
1939	*1939 World's Fair,* New York, NY

Collections

Addison Gallery of American Art, Andover, MA
Asheville Art Museum, NC
Carnegie Museum of Art, Pittsburgh, PA
Los Angeles County Museum of Art, CA
Montclair Art Museum, NJ
Museum of Modern Art, New York, NY
Newark Museum, NJ
Smithsonian American Art Museum, Washington, DC
Whitney Museum of American Art, New York, NY
Zimmerli Art Museum, New Brunswick, NJ

(1911–1989)

SELECTED WORKS

(1911–1989)

Composition #8
1947
Polyester resin
10.43 × 9.65 × 3.62 inches
26.5 × 24.5 × 9.2 cm

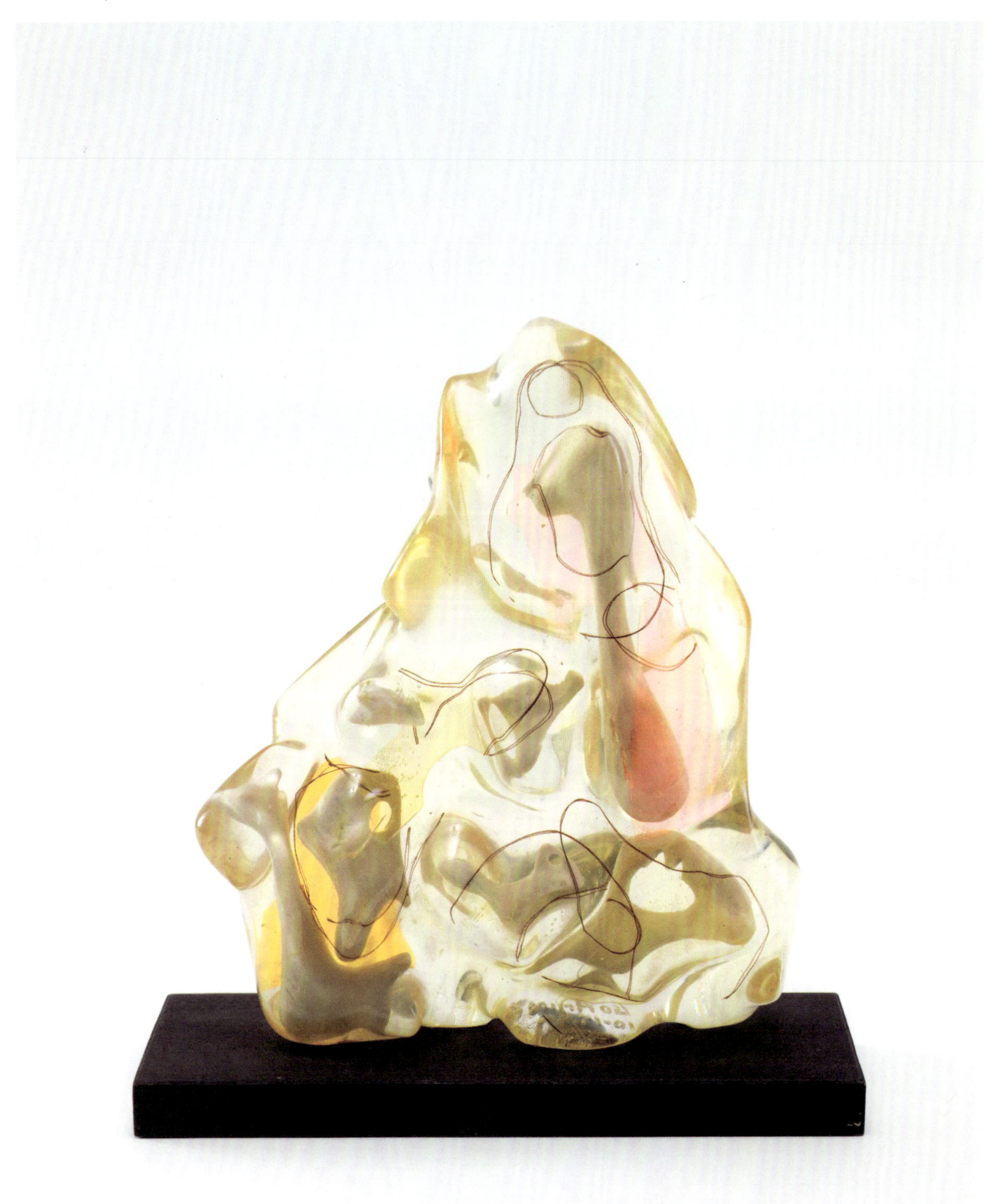

LEO AMINO

Composition #10
1948
Acrylic and pigment
4.5 × 6.5 × 4.75 inches
11.4 × 16.5 × 12.1 cm

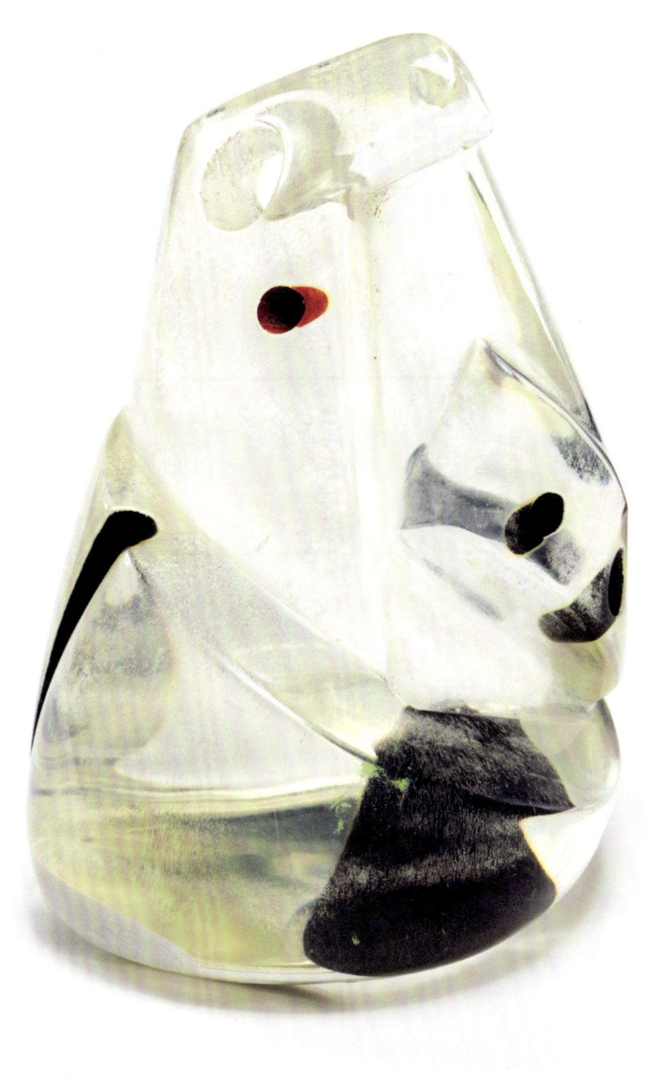

No. 42
1949
Crayon and ink on paper
6 × 9 inches
15.2 × 22.9 cm
Framed Dimensions:
9.25 × 12.25 inches
23.5 × 31.1 cm

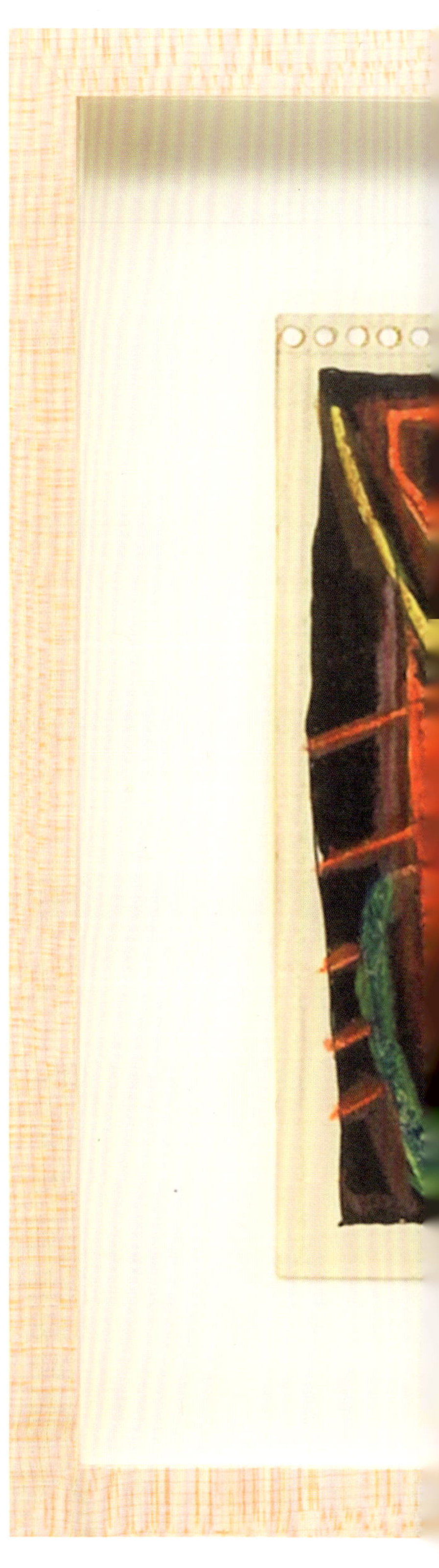

LEO AMINO

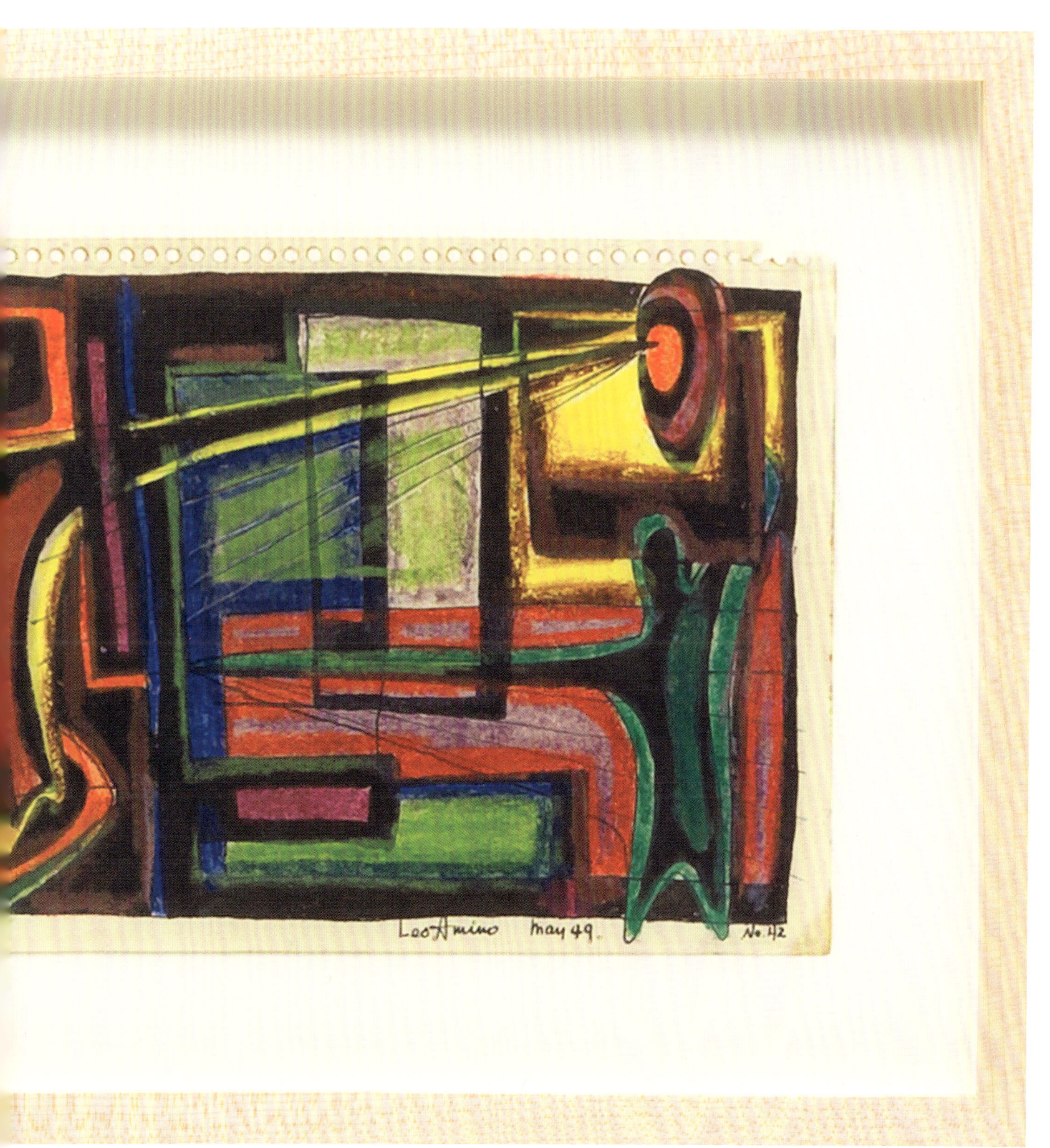

(1911–1989)

Family Totem
1951
Wood and granite
75 × 13 × 10 inches
190.5 × 33 × 25.4 cm

LEO AMINO

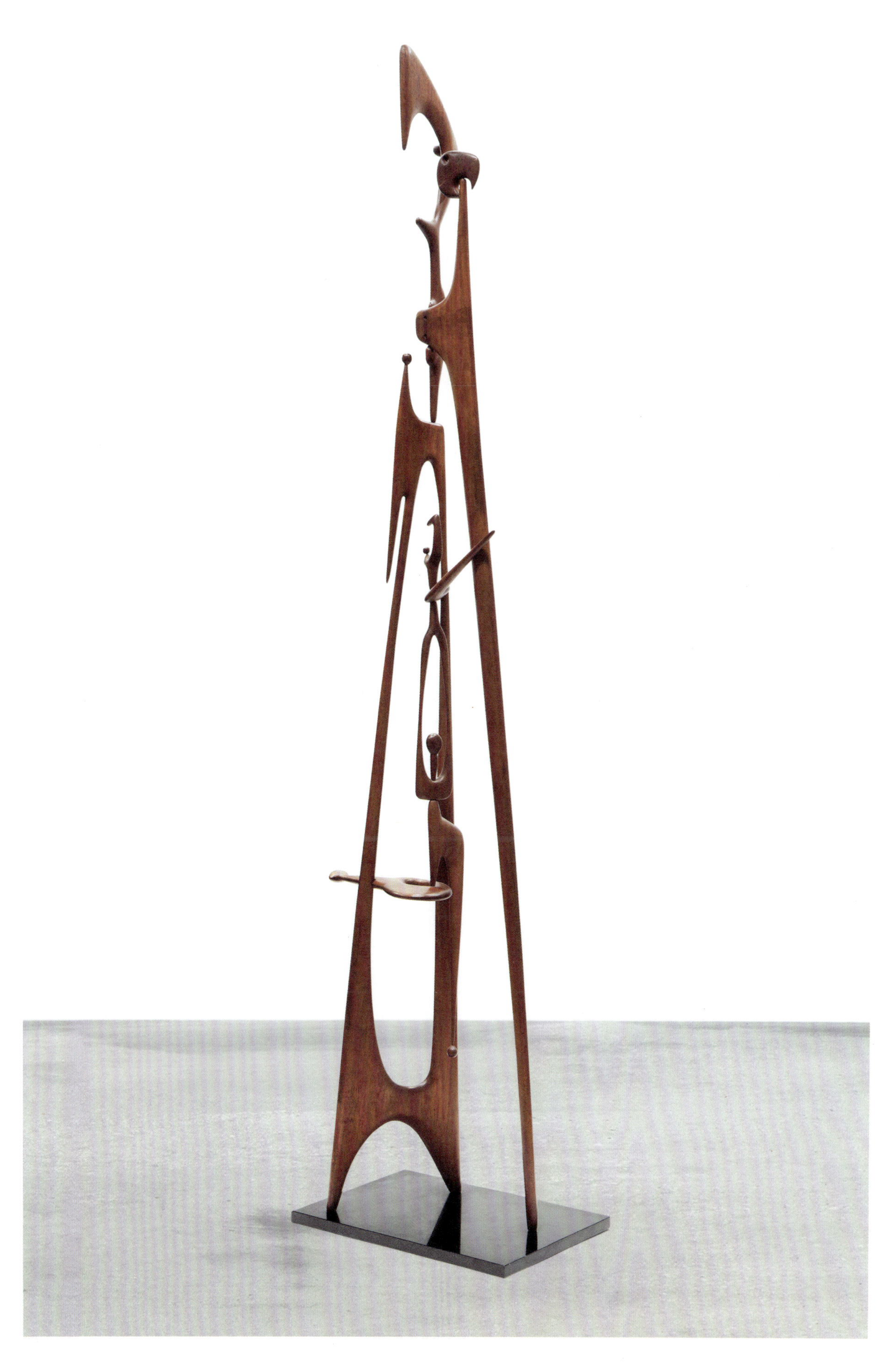

(1911–1989)

Stamen
1952
Polyester resin and wood
22.52 × 8.11 × 6.14 inches
57.2 × 20.6 × 15.6 cm

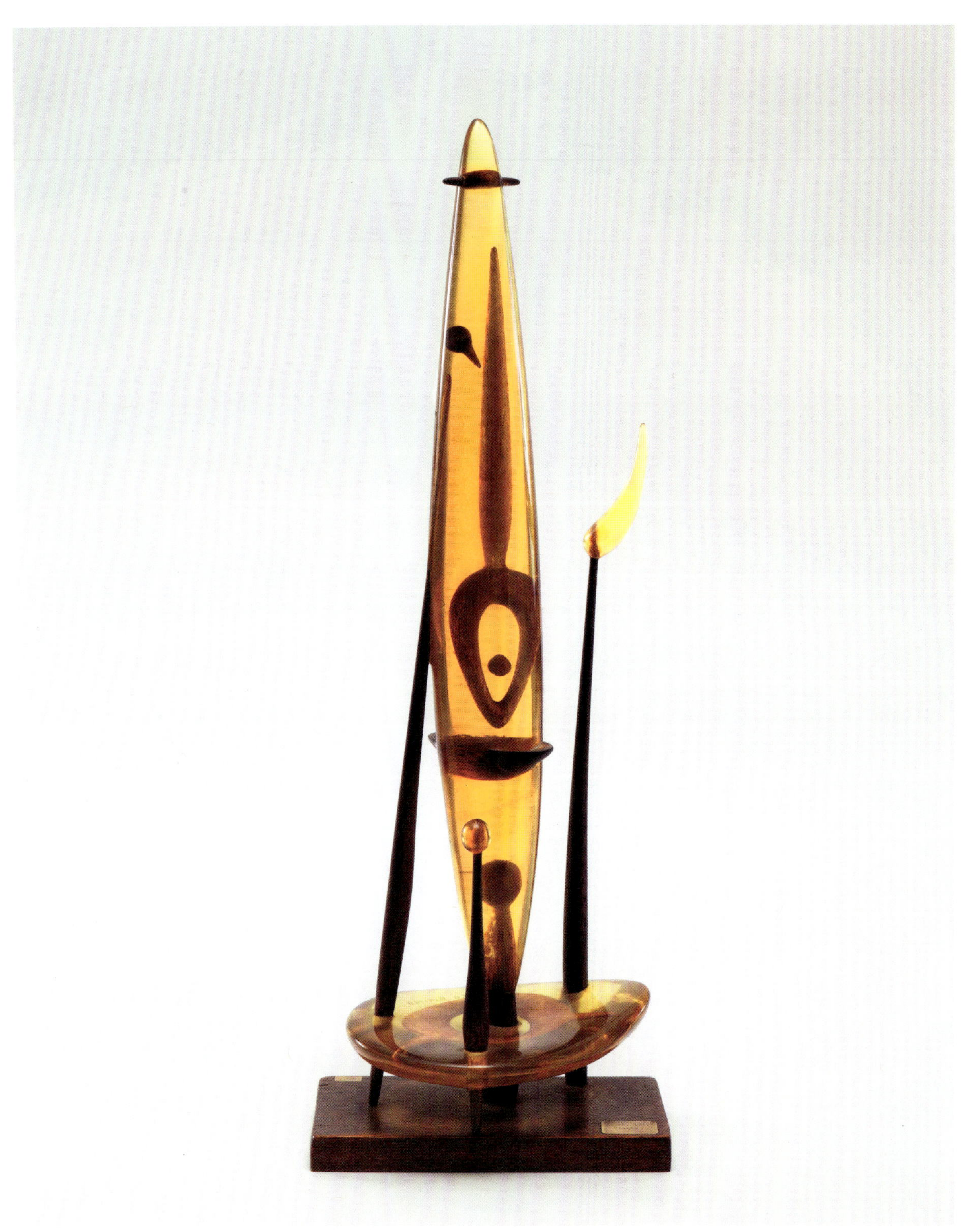

   LEO AMINO

Untitled
1956
Wood
72.52 × 15 × 9.02 inches
184.2 × 38.1 × 22.9 cm

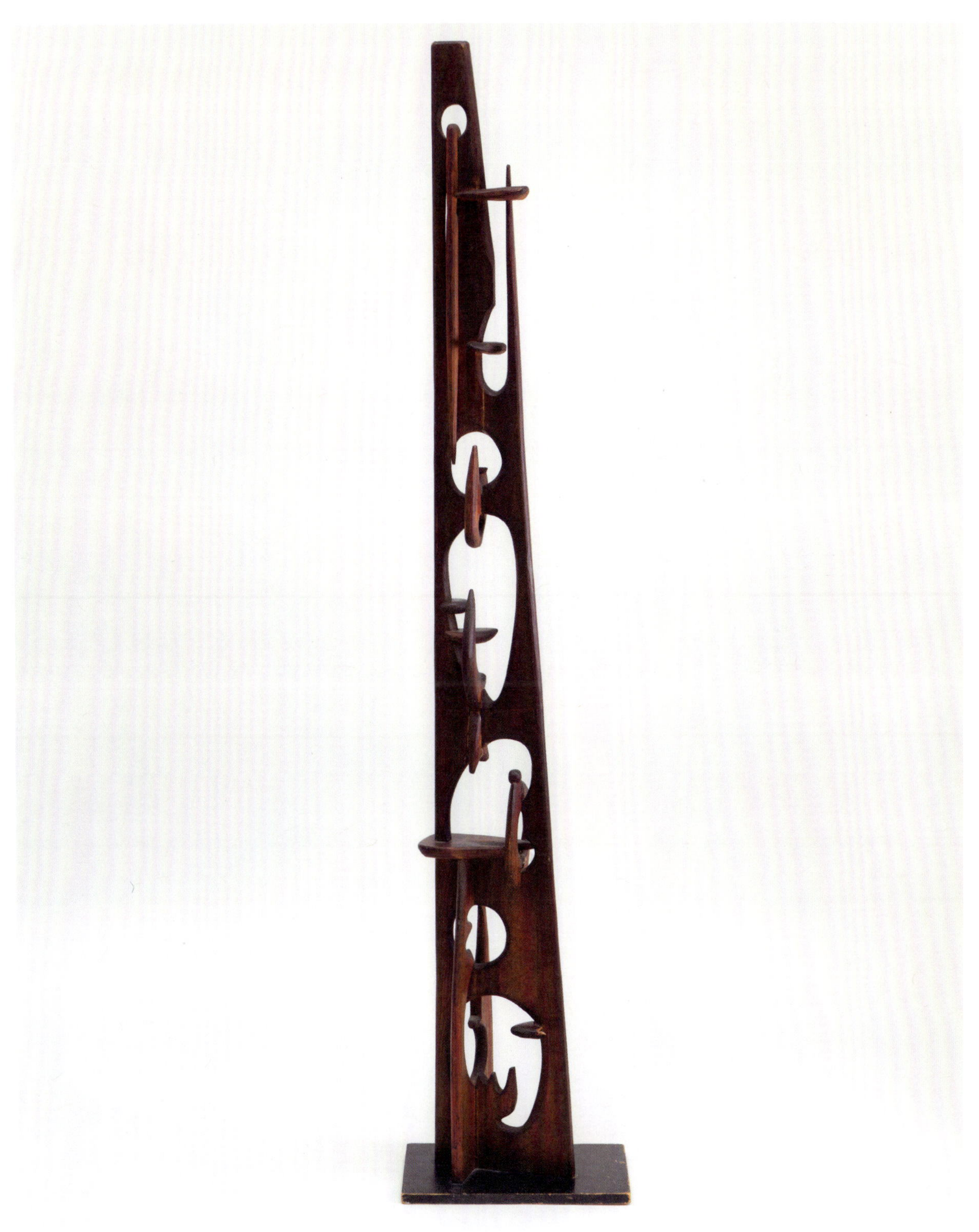

Landscape II
c. 1956
Wood
11 × 39 × 4.5 inches
27.9 × 99.1 × 11.4 cm

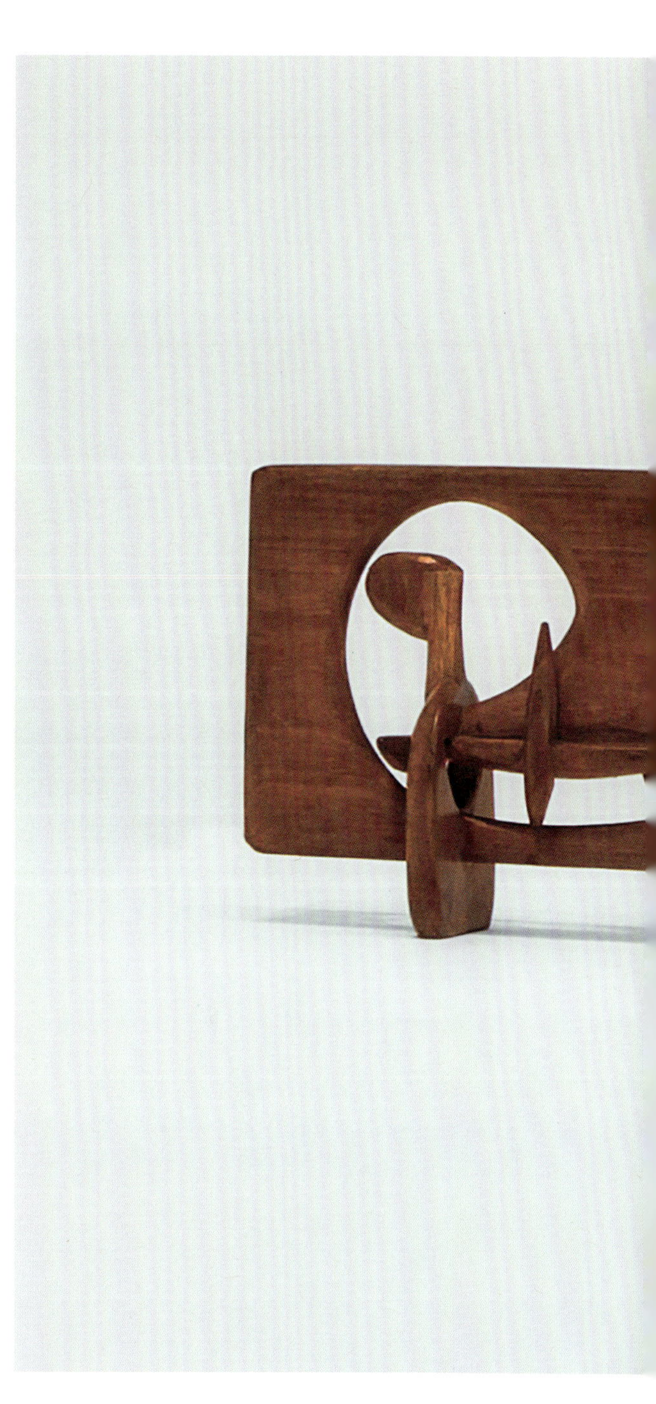

LEO AMINO

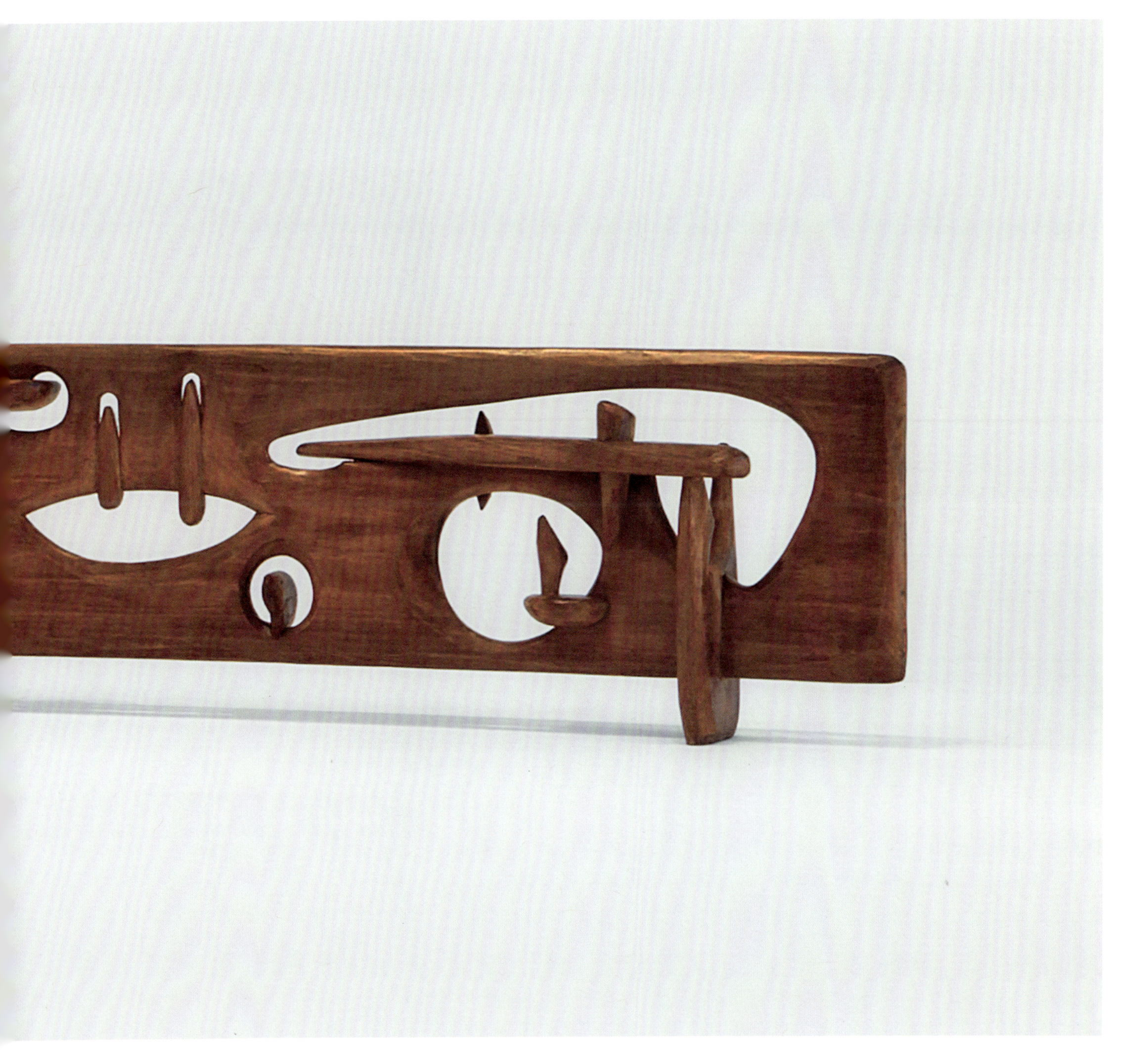

(1911–1989)

Hovering
1963
Polyester resin and wood
4 × 34 × 1.5 inches
10.2 × 86.4 × 3.8 cm

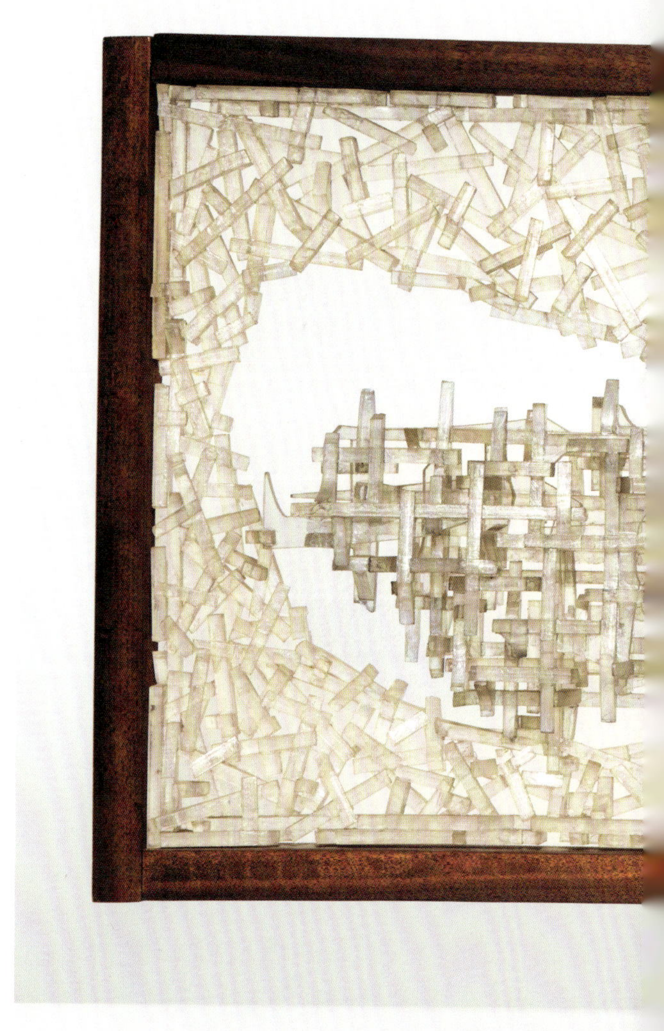

LEO AMINO

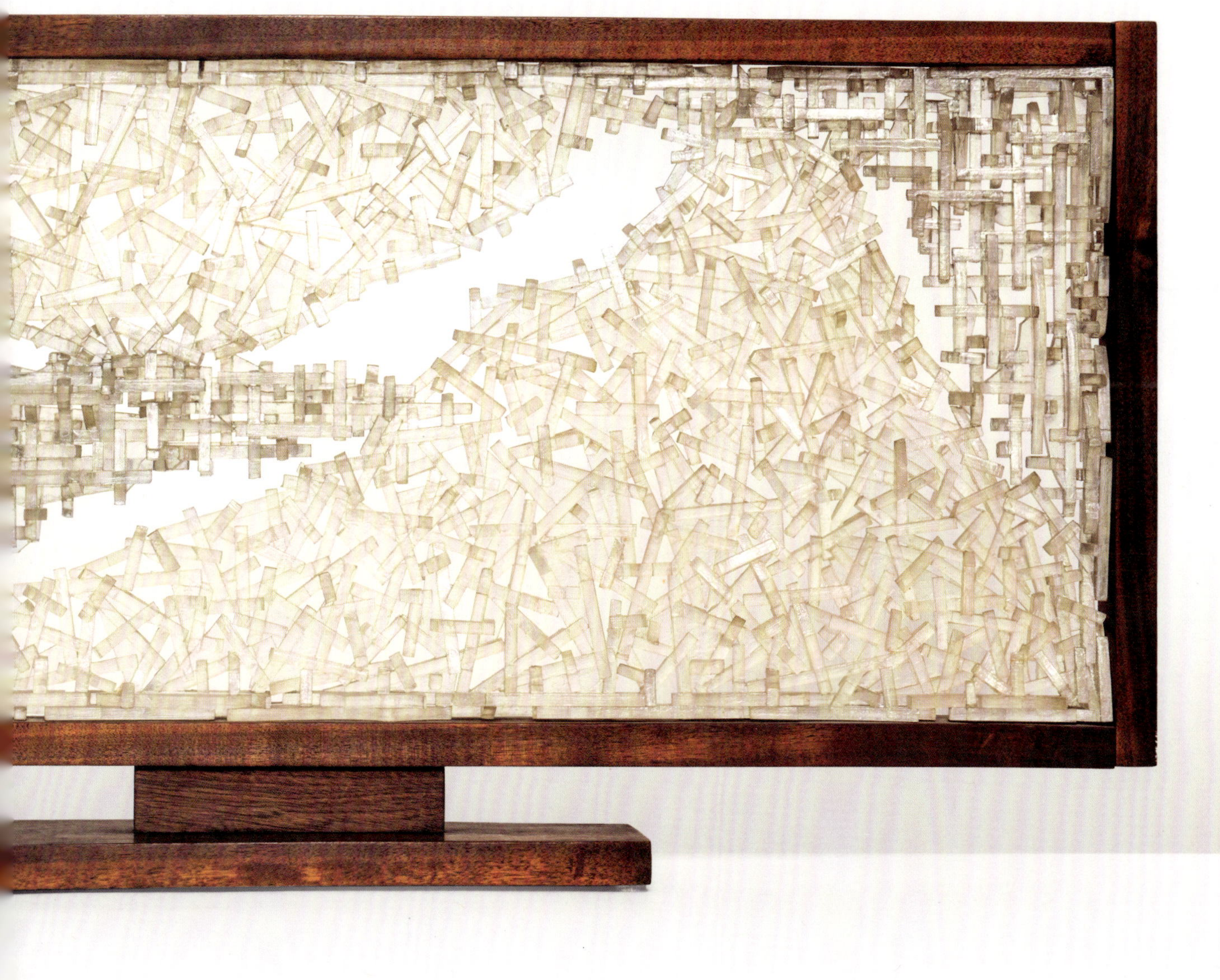

(1911–1989)   77

Refractional #27A
1966
Polyester resin
12.25 × 5.5 × 4.75 inches
31.1 × 14 × 12.1 cm

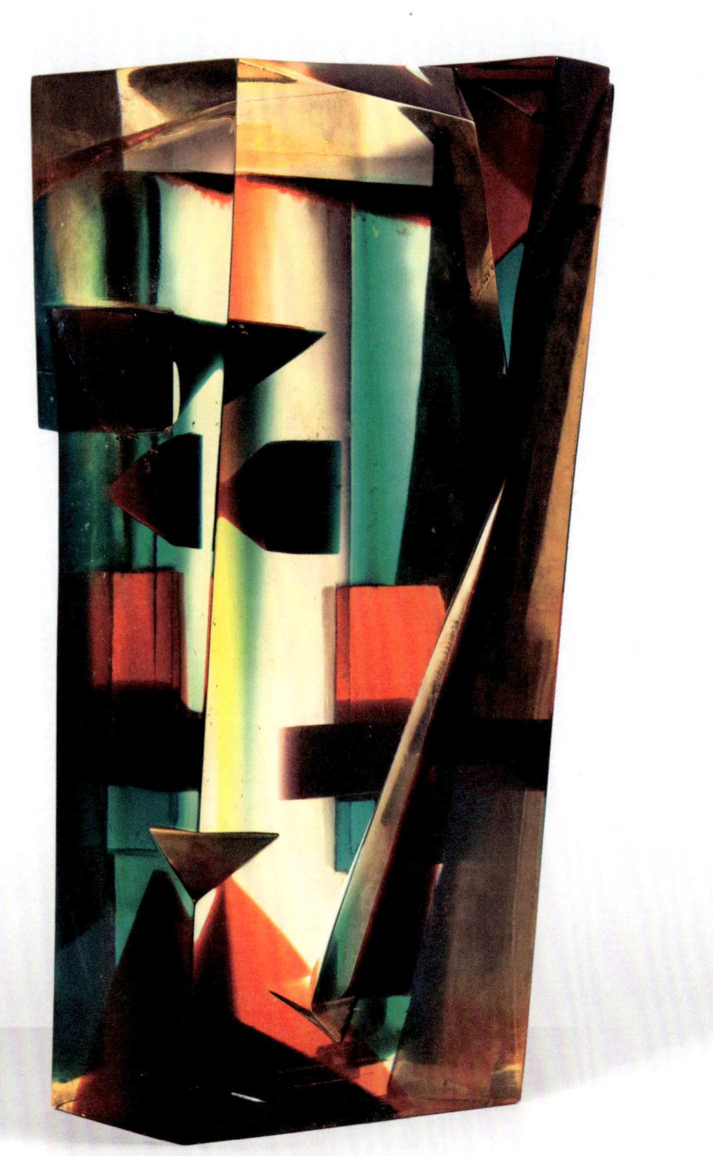

　　　LEO AMINO

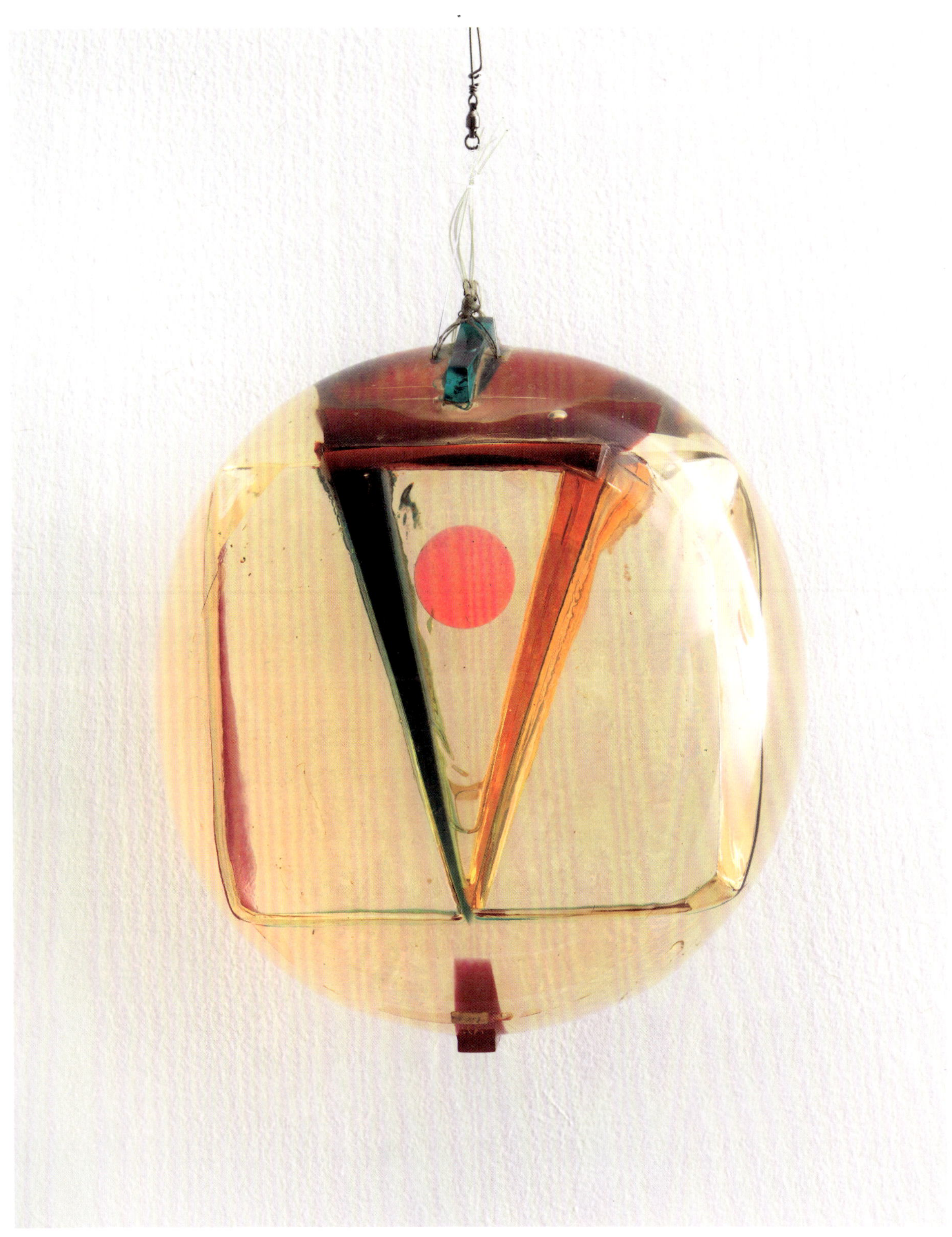

Refractional #21
1967
Polyester resin
20 × 13.62 × 4.37 inches
50.8 × 34.6 × 11.1 cm

LEO AMINO

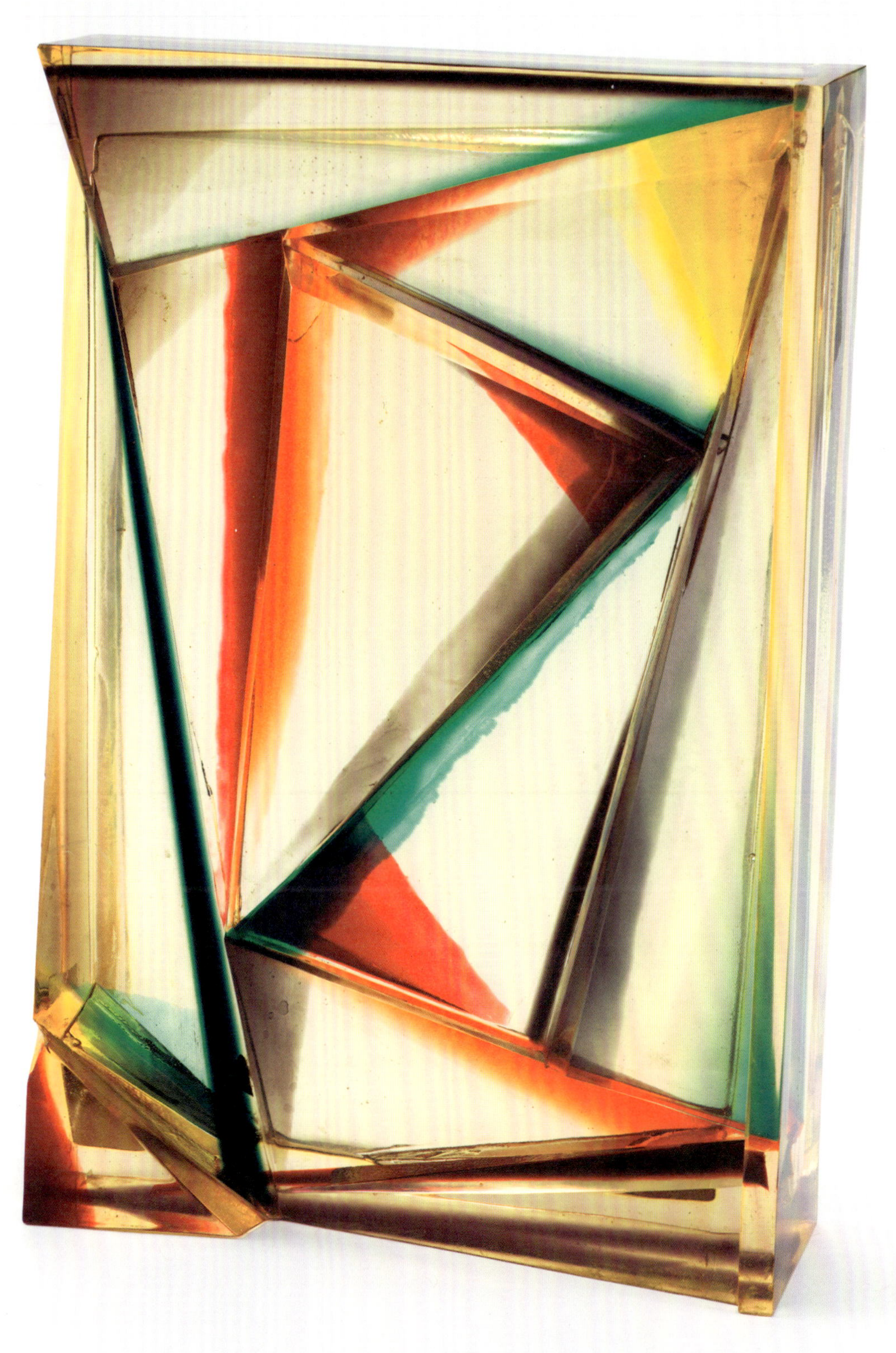

(1911–1989)

Refractional #44
1969
Polyester resin
14 × 28 × 7 inches
35.5 × 71 × 17.75 cm

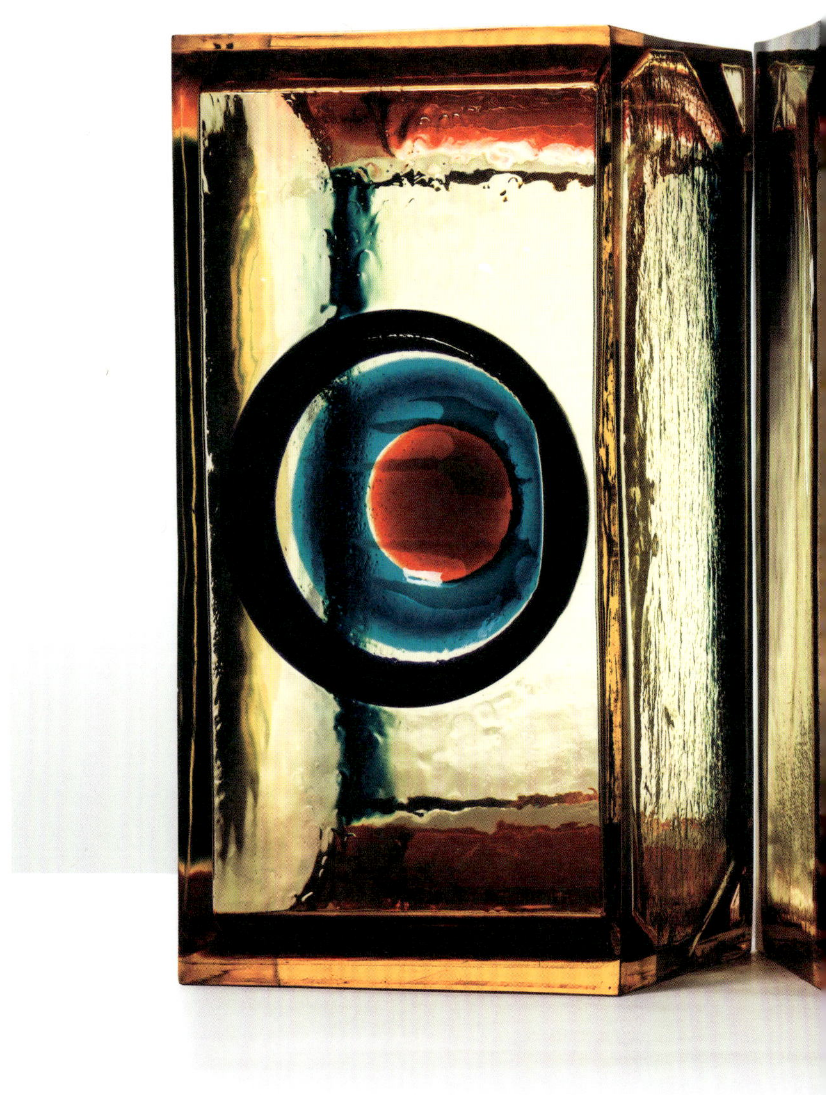

LEO AMINO

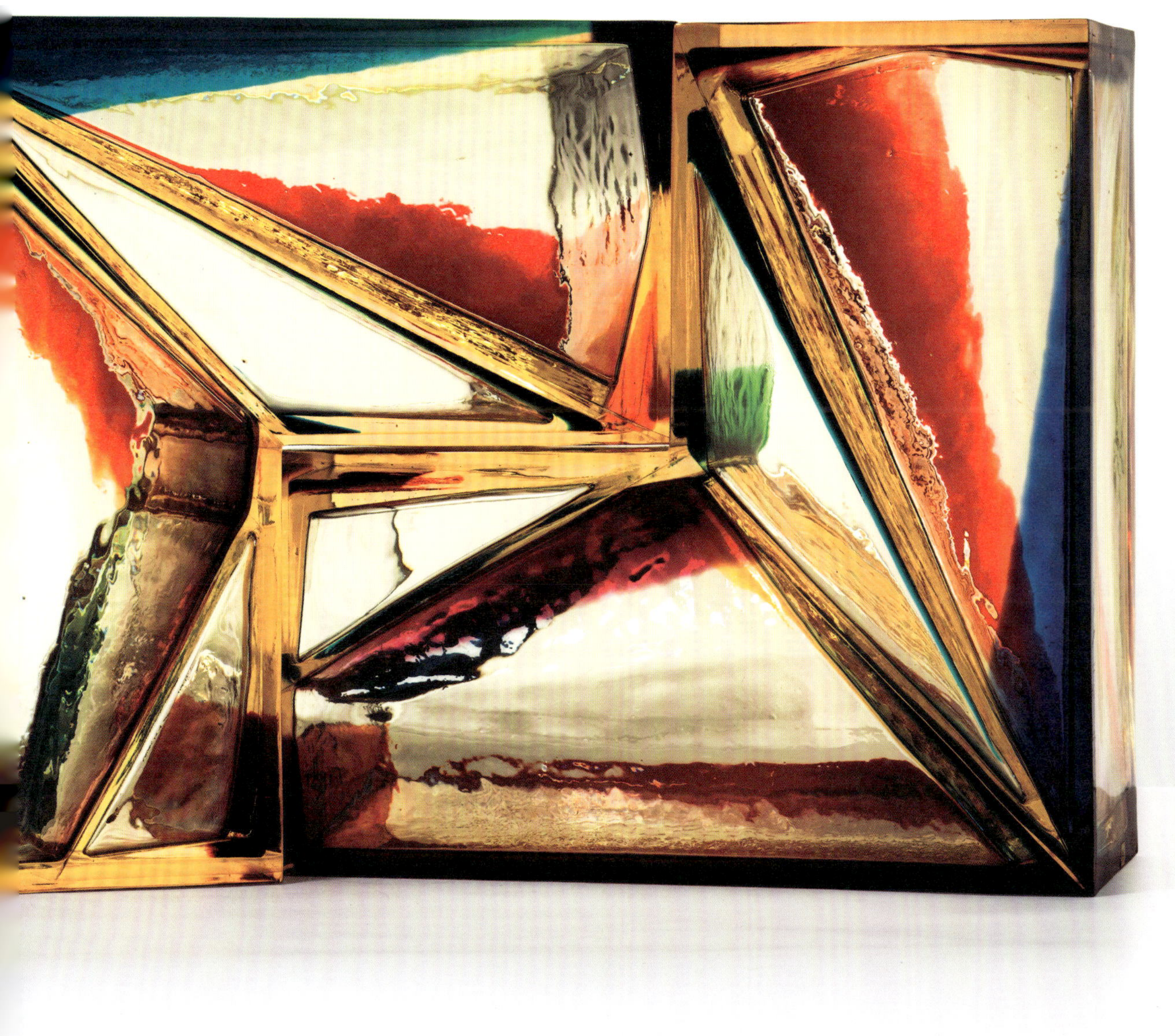

(1911–1989)

Refractional #56
1970
Polyester resin
Assembled Dimensions:
19.5 × 5 × 5 inches
49.5 × 12.7 × 12.7 cm

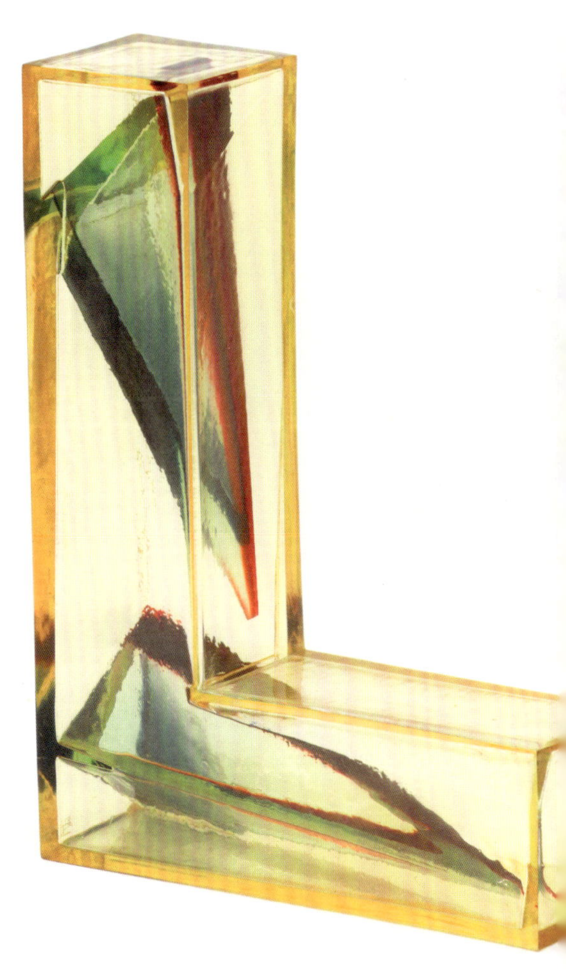

LEO AMINO

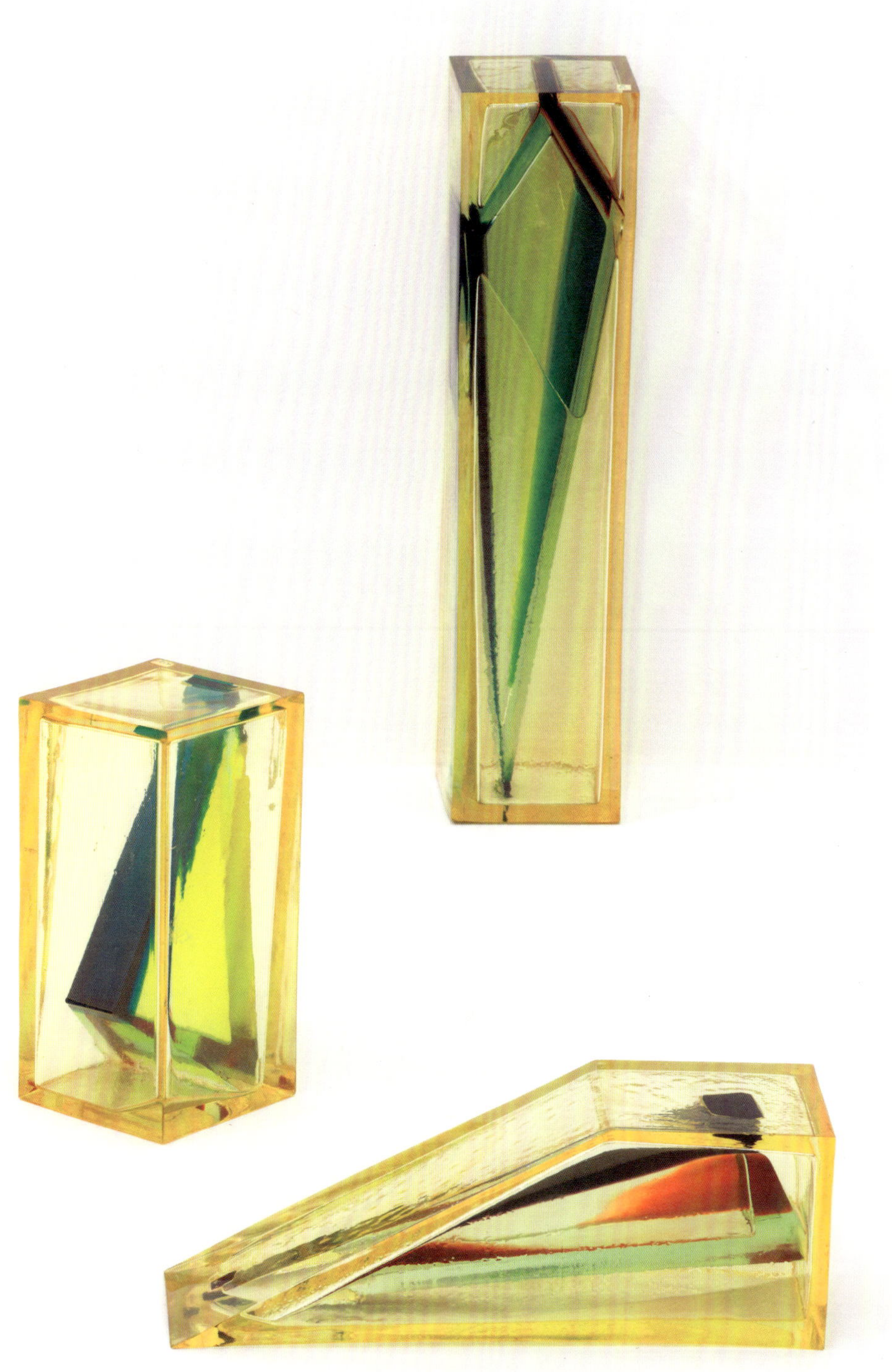

(1911–1989)

Refractional #73
1971
Polyester resin
11.9 × 14.75 × 3.9 inches
30.3 × 37.5 × 9.7 cm

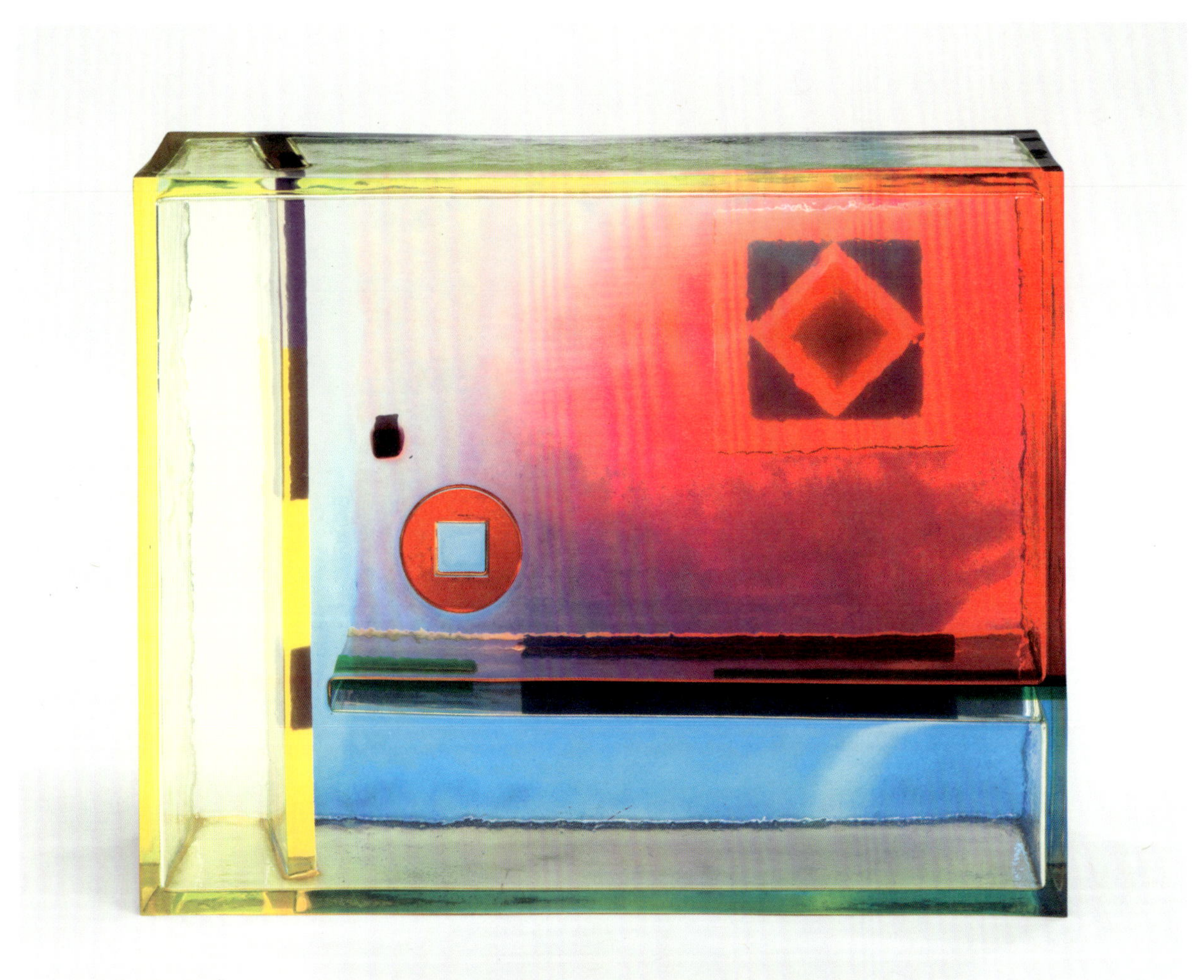

LEO AMINO

Refractional #75
1972
Polyester resin
11.9 × 14.9 × 3 inches
30.2 × 37.8 × 7.6 cm

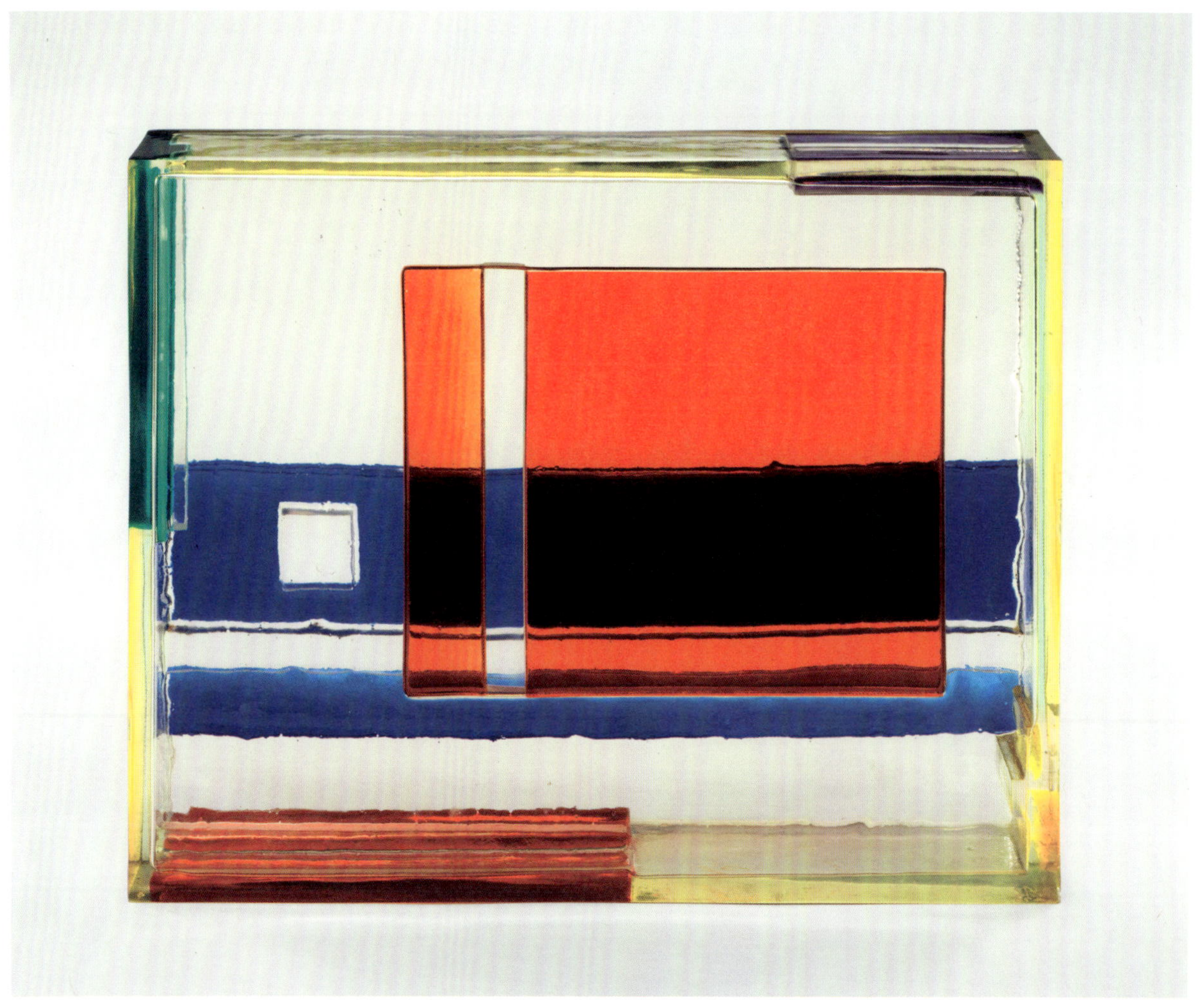

Refractional #106 (Rectangular Female)
1975
Polyester resin
14.9 × 10 × 2.9 inches
37.8 × 25.4 × 7.3 cm

LEO AMINO

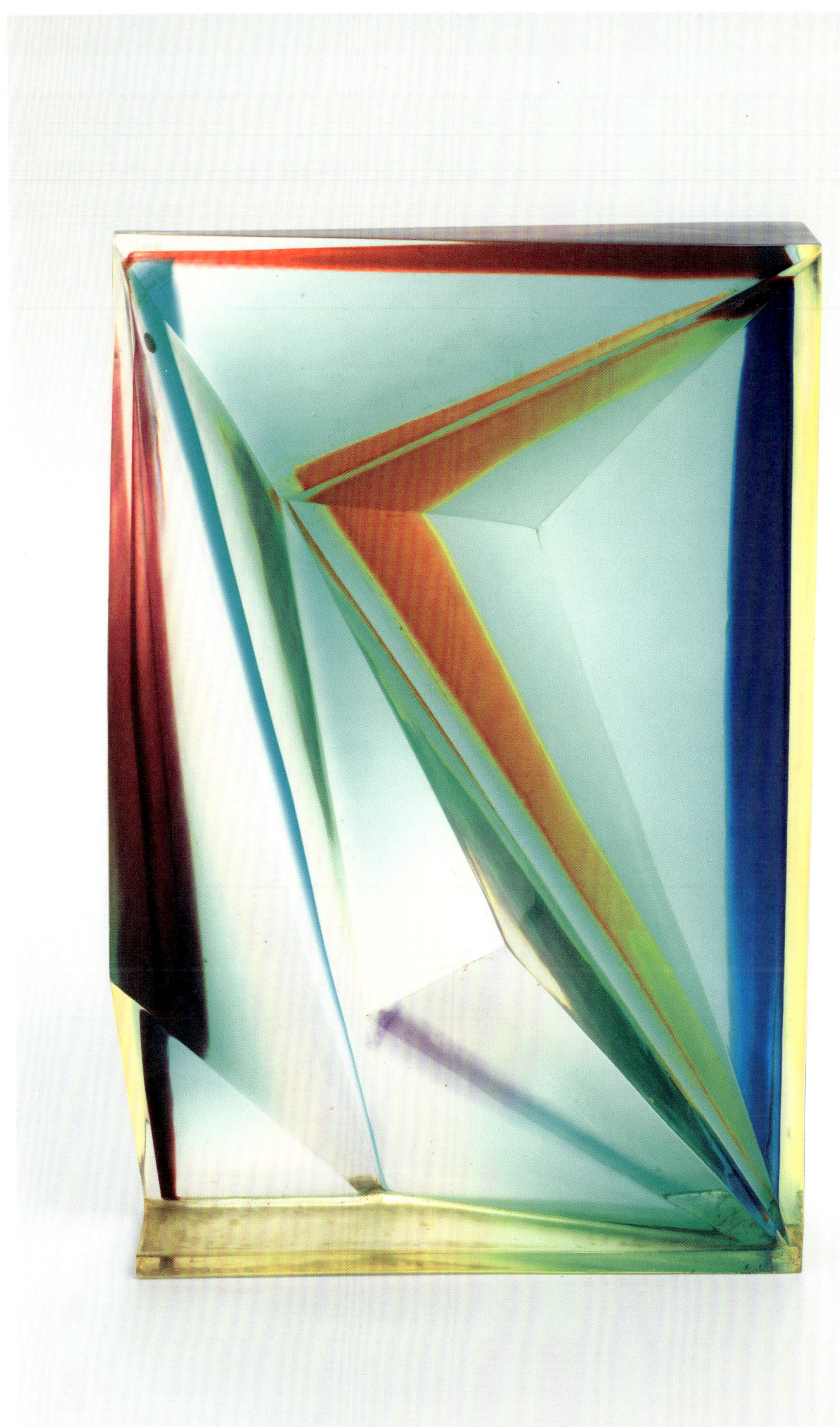

(1911–1989)

Refractional #117
1978
Polyester resin
5.5 × 5.5 × 5.5 inches
14 × 14 × 14 cm

LEO AMINO

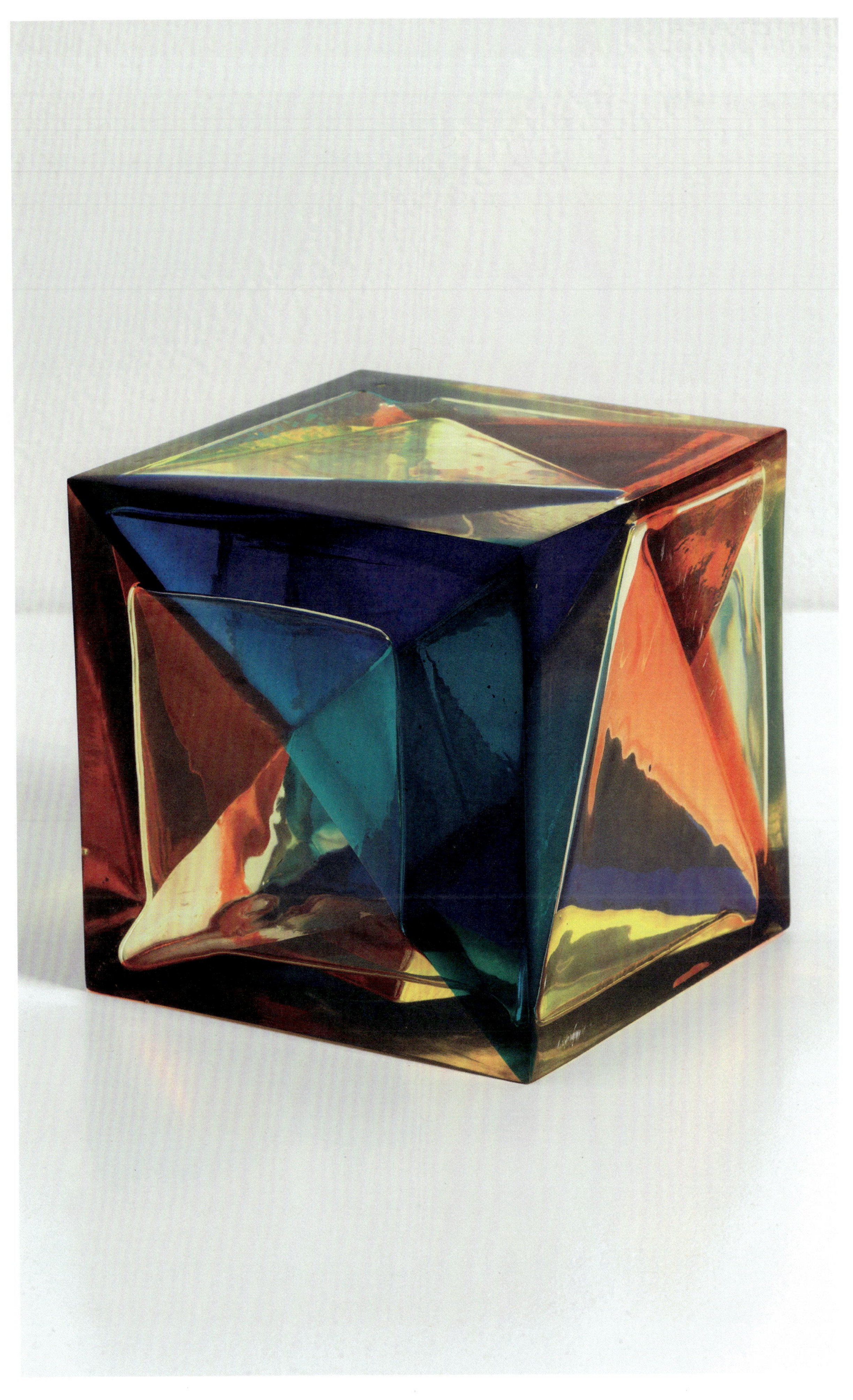

(1911–1989)

Refractional #184
1983
Polyester resin
8.75 × 3 × 2 inches
22.2 × 7.6 × 5.1 cm

     LEO AMINO

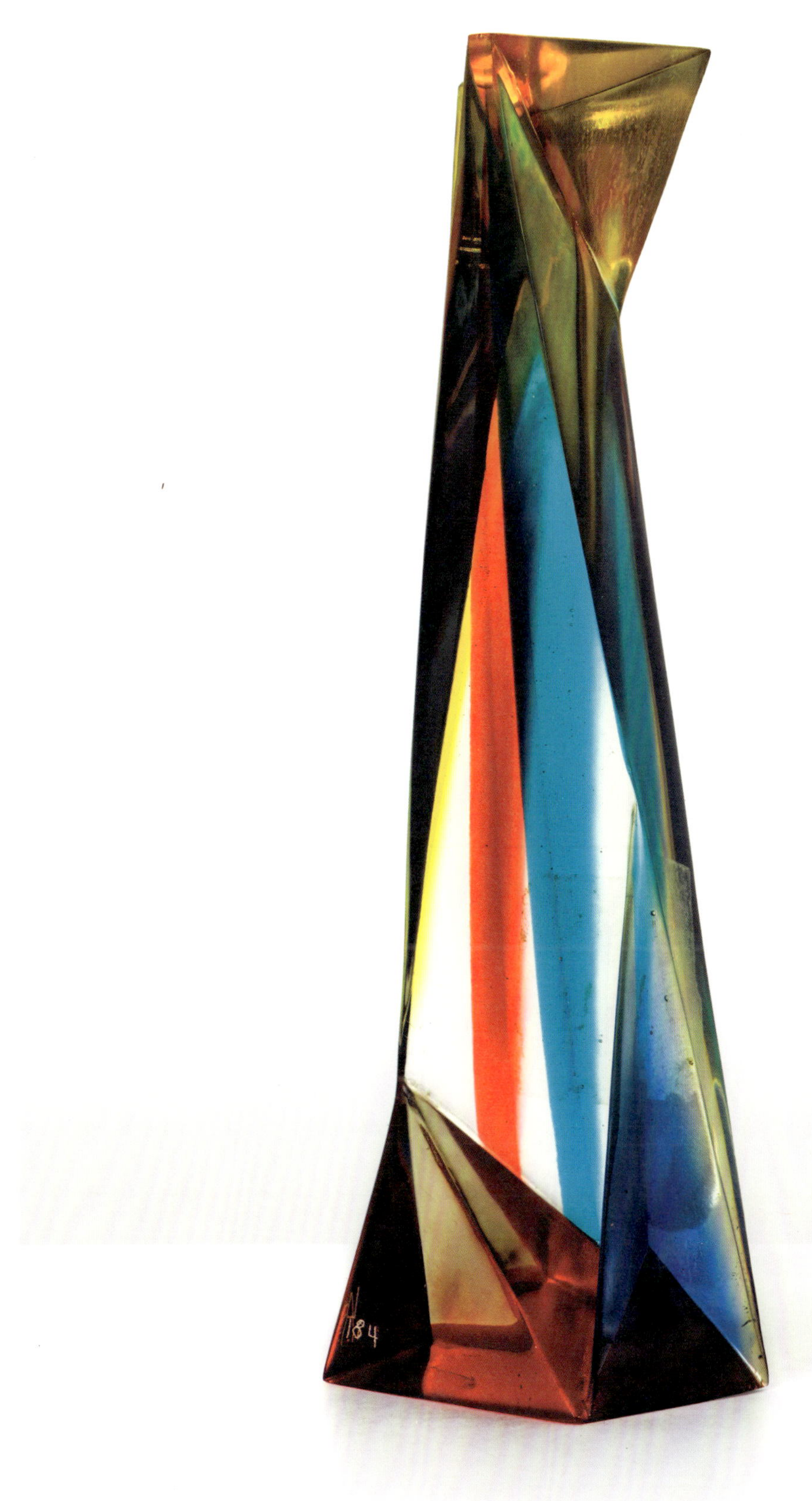

(1911–1989)

Refractional #187
1983
Polyester resin
7.75 × 4.9 × 4 inches
19.7 × 12.5 × 10.2 cm

LEO AMINO

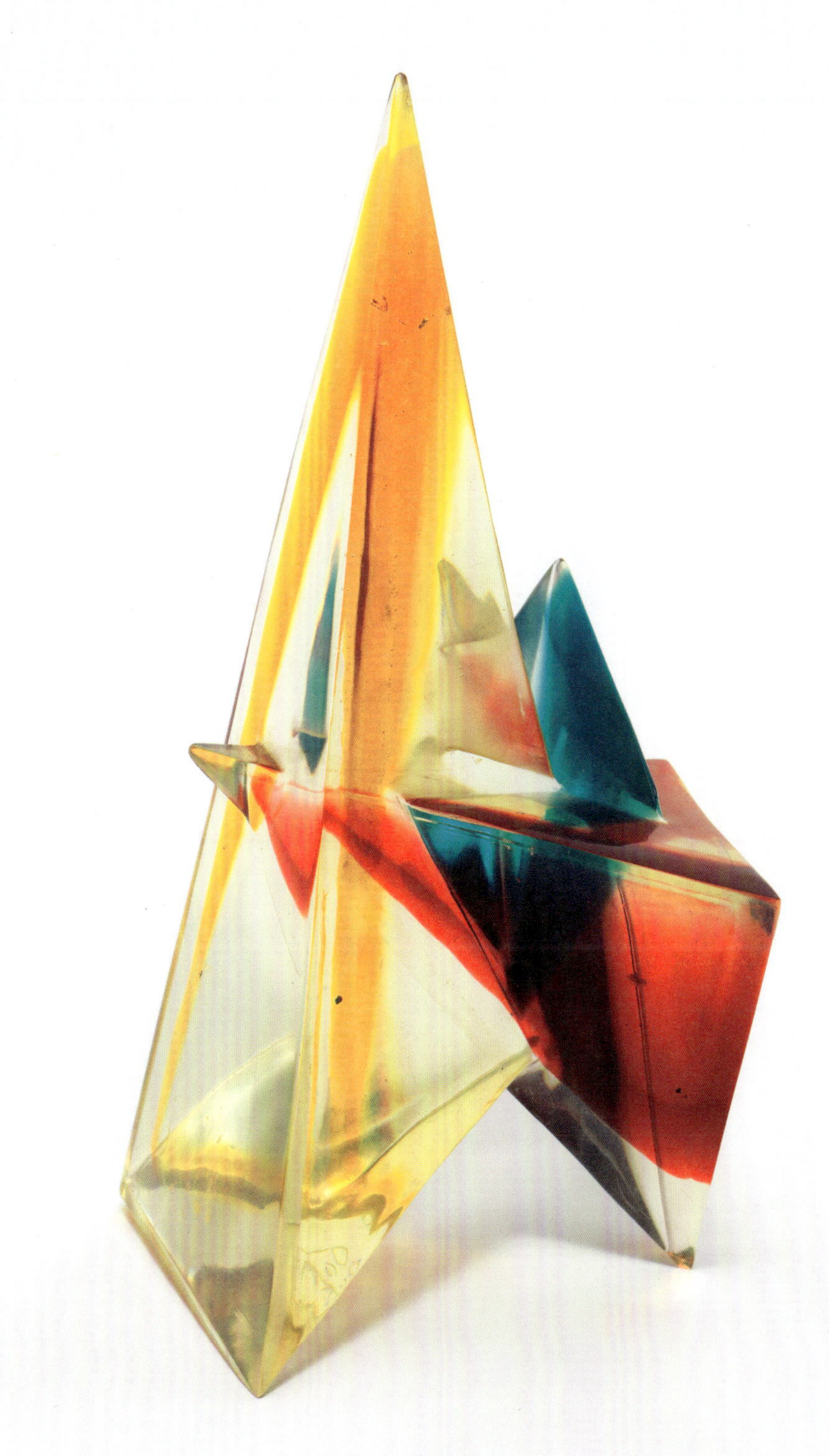

(1911–1989)

MINORU NIIZUMA

(1930–1998)

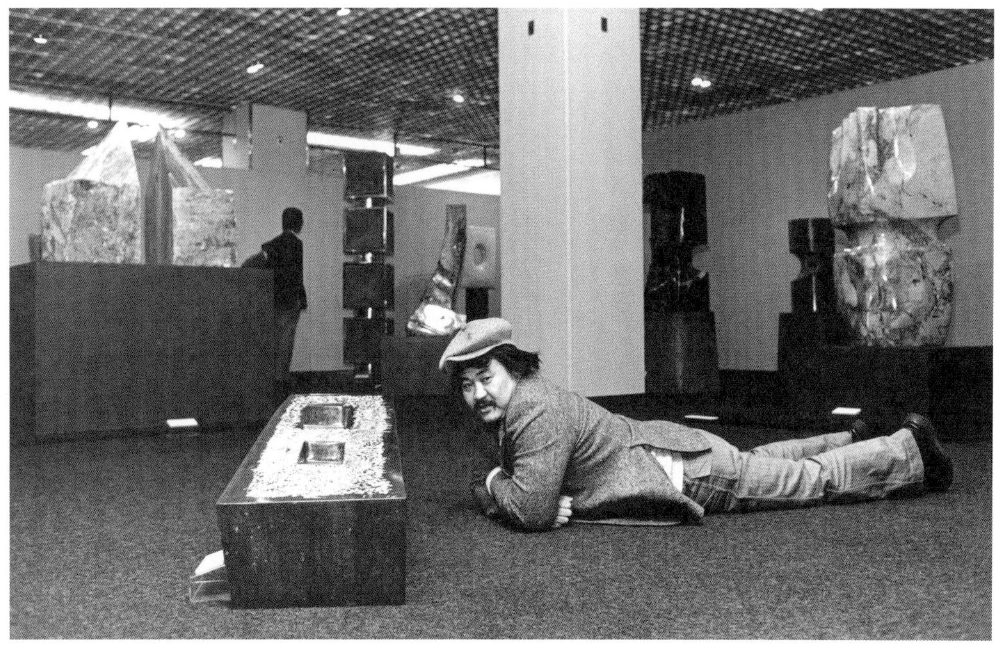

Niizuma at solo show, Umeda Museum of Modern Art, Osaka, 1977.

MINORU NIIZUMA

Born 1930 in Tokyo, Japan, Minoru Niizuma immigrated to the United States in the postwar period, following his education at Tokyo National University of Fine Arts and Music, and his subsequent local success exhibiting with the Modern Art Association in Tokyo. Settling in New York in 1959, Niizuma joined the Brooklyn Museum Art School in 1964 as a teacher, while simultaneously entering the outer orbit of the emerging artistic cluster that came to be affiliated with the term "Minimalism," though Niizuma's work defied that classification. In the next year, Niizuma came to be featured in the 1965–1966 exhibition *The New Japanese Painting and Sculpture*, which travelled from the San Francisco Museum of Modern Art to five other U.S. institutions, including the Museum of Modern Art, New York. By 1973, Niizuma had shown at two Whitney Annuals, the 1967 Pittsburgh International, and at the Solomon R. Guggenheim Museum, where he showed twice more in the mid-1980s.

Throughout his life, Niizuma worked in series, mostly focusing on refining and iterating a single form over the course of several years. His *Castle of the Eye* series came to be widely collected institutionally, the first of the series residing in the permanent collection of the Museum of Modern Art, New York, with others in the Hirshhorn Museum and Sculpture Garden and the Guggenheim. Institutional and commercial collections, particularly sculpture gardens, became an important means of exposing his work to the public for Niizuma: his works equally sit in museum collections and the collections of many large corporations.

Following his six years at the Brooklyn Museum, Niizuma was named an adjunct professor at Columbia, where he taught from 1972 through 1984, before becoming the director of the Stone Institute of New York in 1983. During the early 1980s, he began a pivot that would carry him into the last twenty years of his life and work, when he traveled to Portugal as part of the Evora Symposium.

The immense array of marble and stone available in the European nation brought Niizuma back time and time again, and he received five solo exhibitions in Portugal over the span of five years, and exhibited work in the *5th International Biennial of Sculpture*, Caldas da Rainha, Portugal. His deep engagement with Portugal eventually resulted in Niizuma working directly with Portuguese president Mario Soares to build artistic exchange between Portugal and Japan.

Niizuma passed away in 1998.

 MINORU NIIZUMA

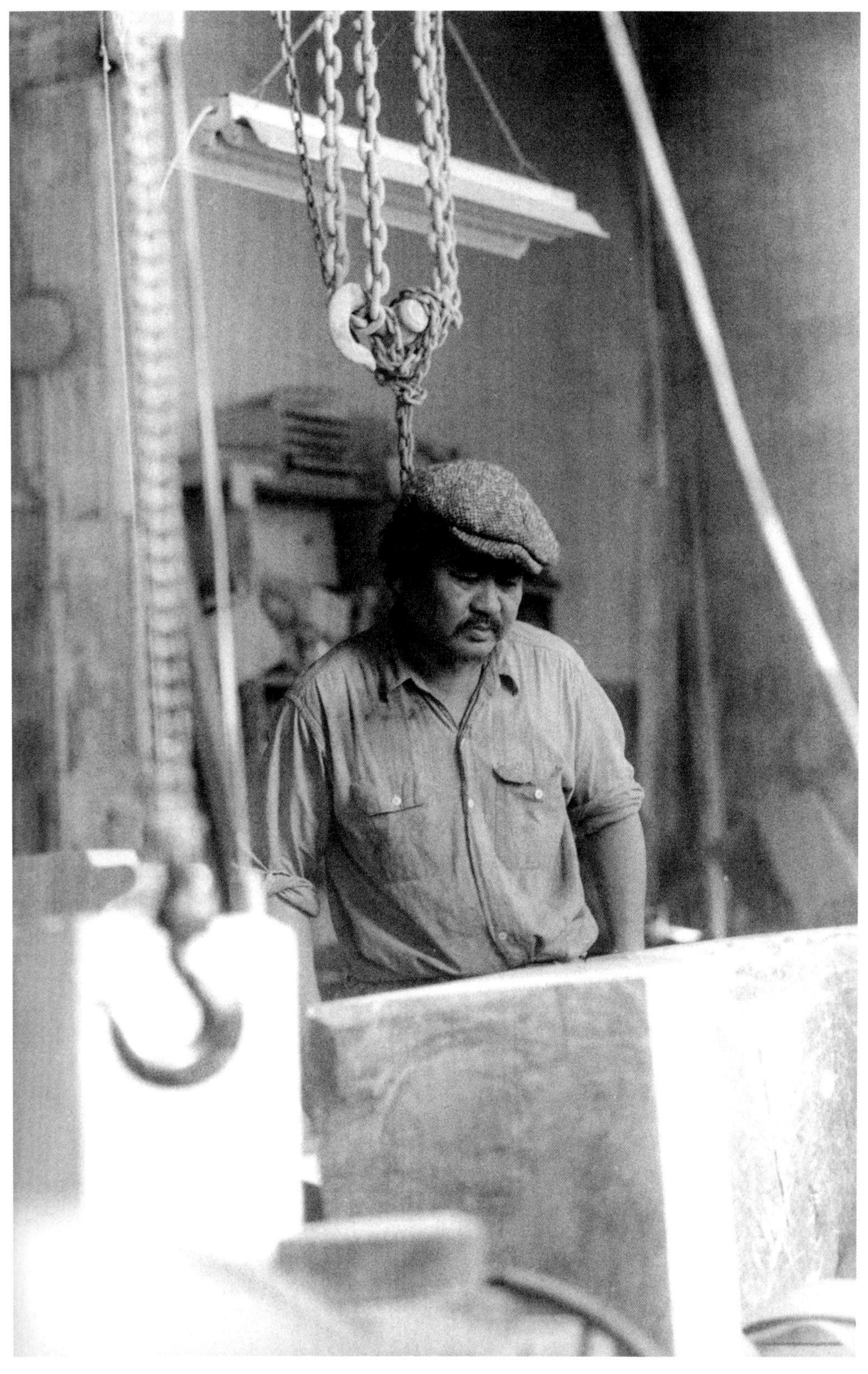

Niizuma in studio, early 1970s, West 168th Street, New York.

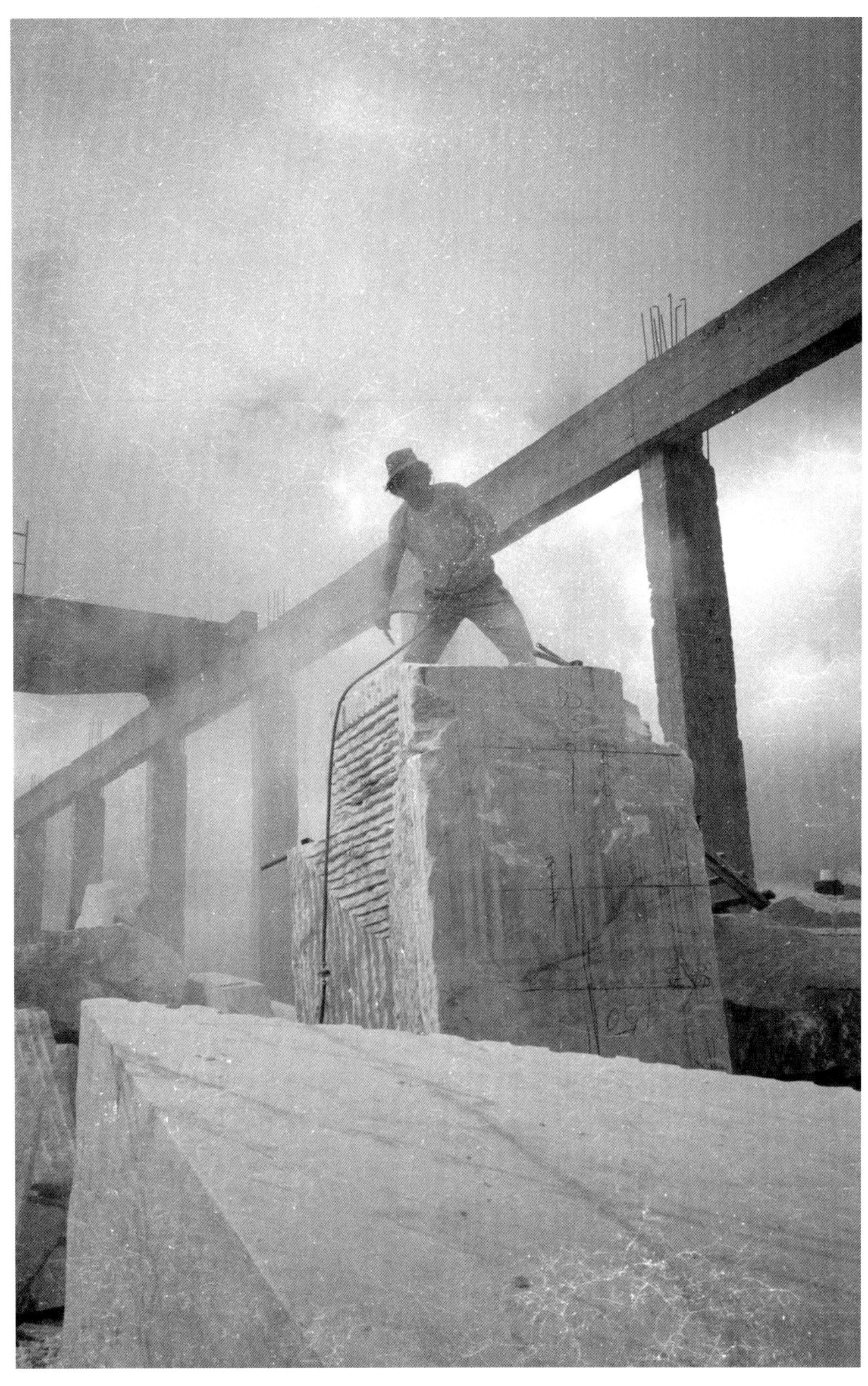

Niizuma at work onsite in Portugal, Vila Viçosa, 1989.

MINORU NIIZUMA

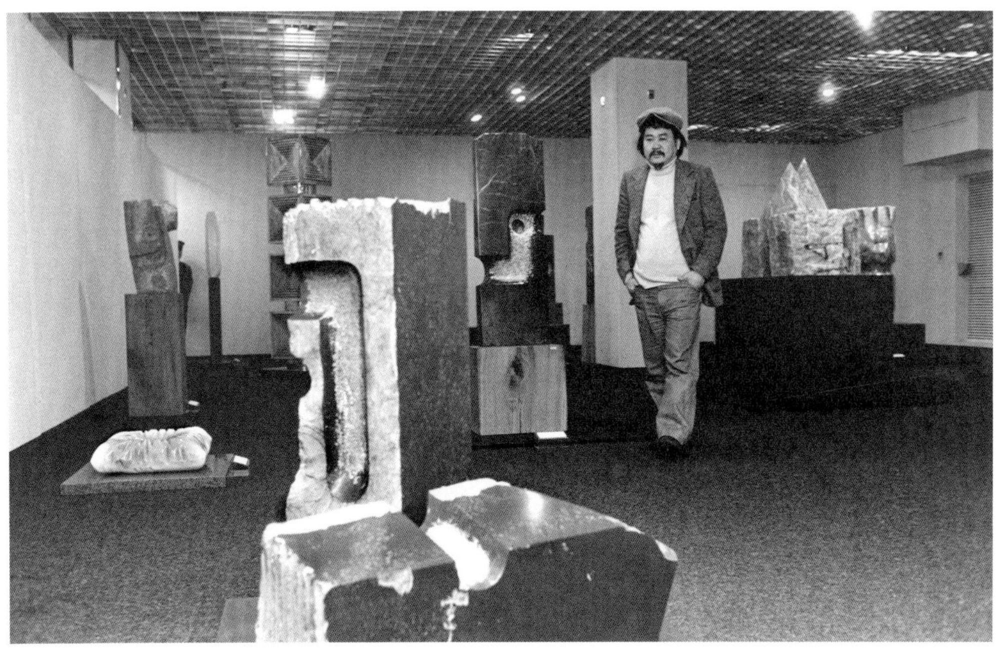

Niizuma at solo show, Umeda Museum of Modern Art, Osaka, 1977.

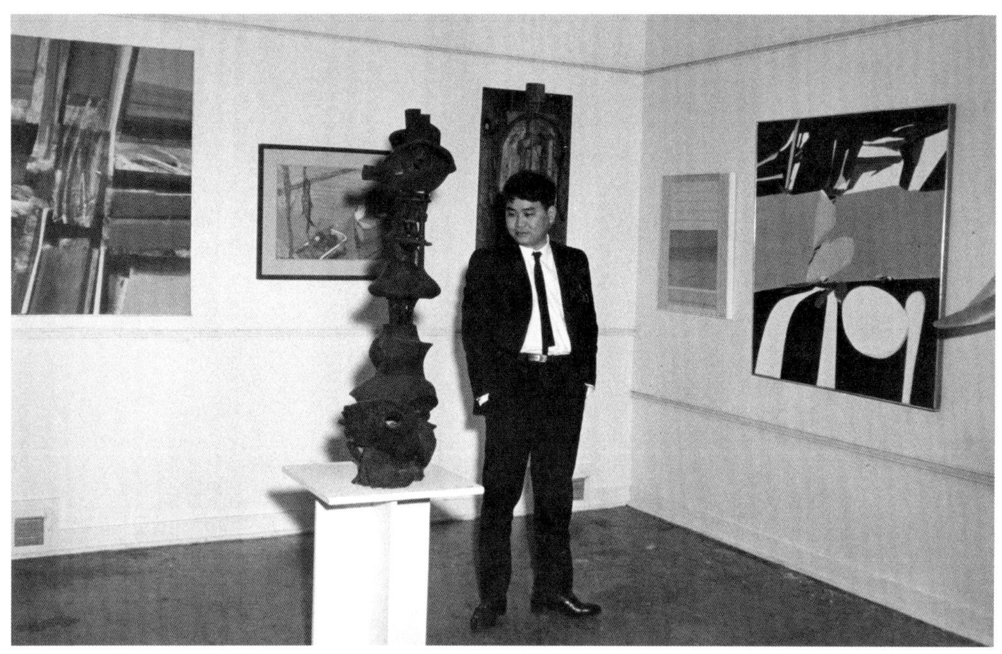

Niizuma in Japan, c. 1956.

     MINORU NIIZUMA

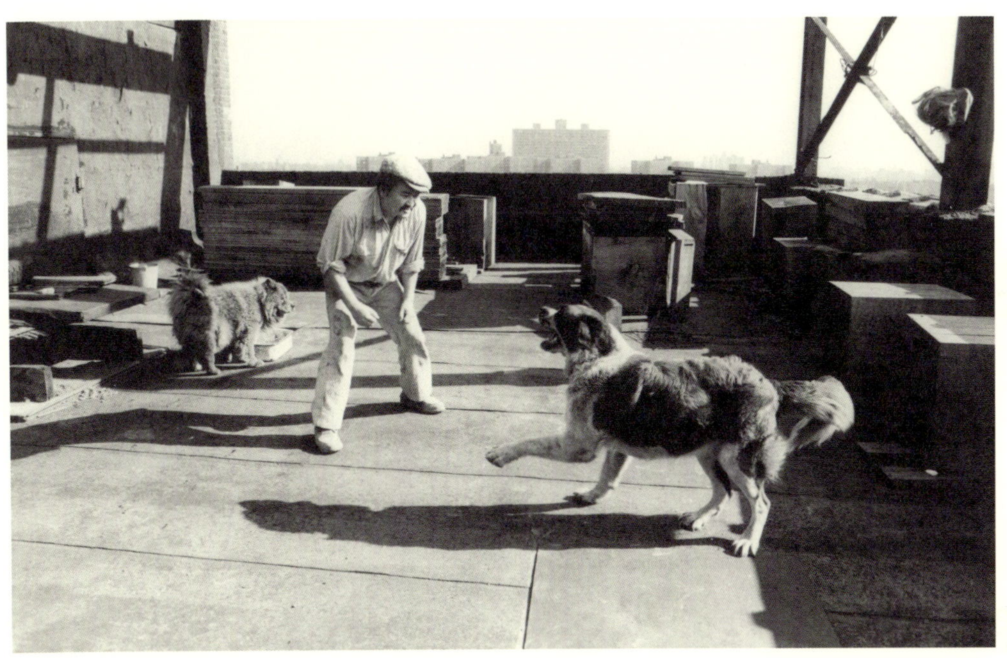

Niizuma in open air studio II, c. 1975, West 168th Street, New York.

A Journey Through Sculpture
by Arata Niizuma

MINORU NIIZUMA

Touch is one of the most important sensations when we want to experience something. When it comes to art, we are rarely afforded such luxury. In museums and galleries, paintings and prints are observed from a safe distance. Sculpture is unique in that the material and texture are a significant component of the artwork. Whether I am running my fingers across the names at the Vietnam memorial in Washington, D.C., or feeling the cold, hard steel of a di Suvero piece at Storm King, touching these pieces shapes how I experience them. Touching my father's sculptures is similarly an integral part of my experience of his work — feeling their rough grooves as well as their smooth, polished curves. It is one thing to see the shimmer of a finely polished surface and a totally different experience when I put my hand on it.

I grew up surrounded by my father's stone sculptures. I've climbed on top of them, polished them, cleaned them, and helped stage them. In one of my earlier memories from around age 7 or 8, my father and I designed and created a piece together. From this experience, I learned how to use various hand and power tools. More importantly, my father showed me all the small details and subtle nuances that he would consider when making a stone sculpture.

Most of my father's sculptures have both rough and smooth features — his take on the relationship between man and nature. When I touch the rougher parts, I'm reminded of the more physical work that goes into stone carving — one that involves chisels, hammers, pneumatic drills, and, of course, some blood and sweat, too. I am reminded that these sculptures are carved from giant blocks of marble or granite, and are very much from this Earth. Seeing and touching these stone pieces brings me back to nature, which is something that my father wanted the viewer to feel. He always felt as though his job was not to completely transform the stone, but to work with the stone. He wanted to give life to the stone and bring life out of the stone.

My father has made hundreds, if not thousands of pieces of various sizes. Some are small pieces that can fit in an apartment, while others exist as giant monuments. Many are public works that

(1930–1998)

can be found within a drive from New York City — a visitor's center in Vermont, the sculpture trail at Williams College, the sculpture garden at the New Orleans Museum of Art. Most, however, are displayed internationally across Europe and Asia. Much of my adult life has been spent searching for these sculptures — to make sure that they actually exist and, perhaps, to touch and experience them for myself. I have spent countless hours locating his many works that were installed before I was born or have moved locations since they were first installed. Although I had seen these sculptures in photographs, books, and newspaper clippings, I felt I needed to find these pieces for myself, in order to deepen my relationship with both my father and his work.

In 2019, after a decade of research, I made a pilgrimage to Lisbon, Evora, and St. Margarethen — three cities where my father would have experiences that would greatly influence his career. My journey to Portugal to visit Lisbon and Evora lasted seven days — there I discovered a different set of my father's works each day. On one day, I stood in awe in front of a 25-foot-tall *Castle of the Eye* in the Jardim de Belém. On another day, I visited the Parque do Monteiro-Mor and watched the ducks swim around a pink *Castle of the Eye* in the Lago do Niizuma. I watched a visitor at the Gulbenkian Museum playfully stand a book atop one of my father's pieces, while others looked on with curiosity. I spent a full day in Evora admiring my father's piece, as well as other works made during the 1981 Evora symposium. On my final day, I sipped wine with friends, surrounded by roughly thirty sculptures in the Minoru Niizuma Sculpture Garden at the Bacalhoa Winery-Museum. I've always known that these sculptures existed in and around Lisbon, but I did not know how beautiful these pieces were or how amazed I would be upon experiencing them.

After Lisbon, I also visited St. Margarethen, a small town around 60 kilometers outside of Vienna, Austria. My father participated in his first sculpture symposium in this area; it was organized by Karl Prantl in 1965. About this symposium, my father wrote that "no forklifts or electric powered equipment were used to move the stones. Stones were moved by all the participants in

　　　　　　　　MINORU NIIZUMA

the symposium lending a hand." He thoroughly appreciated the camaraderie and knowledge gained from working with fellow stone sculptors at these symposia. These experiences, along with direct encouragement from his friend Isamu Noguchi, pushed him to teach sculpture at Columbia University and the Brooklyn Museum Art School for many years.

Every time I encounter one of my father's sculptures, whether on this trip or otherwise, I make sure to touch the piece and reflect for a moment. When I was in Lisbon, I imagined him standing right where I was, directing the installation of the pieces. I wondered what he would have thought, knowing that I came to see these pieces twenty-five years later. I am still developing my understanding and appreciation for his work — there are many sculptures around the world that I have yet to discover. Whether it's a *Castle of the Eye* at the University College of Dublin or the many public pieces in Porto, I want to see, and especially touch them for myself. My next journey is likely to Ponta Delgada, in the Azores, where my father has three towering pieces overlooking Milicias beach. I hope that by finding and experiencing these sculptures, I am able to connect with my father in new and more profound ways.

(1930–1998)

Born 1930, Tokyo, Japan
Died 1998, New York, NY

Education

1955 Tokyo National University of Fine Arts and Music

Teaching

1964–1970 Instructor, Brooklyn Museum Art School
1972–1984 Adjunct Professor, Columbia University School of the Arts
1983–1998 Director, Stone Institute of New York

Selected Solo & Two-Person Exhibitions

1993	Galeria Valentim De Carvalho, Lisbon, Portugal
	Centro Cultural São Lourenço, Almancil, Portugal
1992	Park Ryu Sook Gallery, Seoul, South Korea
1989	Mekler Gallery, Los Angeles, CA
	Galerie Nichido, Tokyo, Japan
	Fondation Veranneman, Kruishoutem, Belgium
1988–89	Blue Hill Art and Cultural Center, Pearl River, NY
1988	Galeria Quadrum, Lisbon, Portugal
1986	Gallery Art Point, Tokyo, Japan
	Centro Cultural São Lourenco, Almancil, Portugal
	Mekler Gallery, Los Angeles, CA
	Gulbenkian Museum, Lisbon, Portugal
1985	Galleria Glide, Guimaraes, Portugal
1984	Vorpal Gallery, San Francisco, CA
	Designer's Emporium, Honolulu, HI
1983	Mekler Gallery, Los Angeles, CA
1982	Elaine Benson Gallery, Bridgehampton, NY
	Rosenberg Fine Art Gallery, Toronto, Canada
1979	Gimpel and Weitzenhoffer Gallery, New York, NY
	Contemporary Sculpture Center, Tokyo, Japan
	Contemporary Sculpture Center, Osaka, Japan
1977	Umeda Museum of Modern Art, Osaka, Japan
	Gimpel and Weitzenhoffer Gallery, New York, NY
	Guild Hall Museum, East Hampton, NY
1976	Center for International Arts, New York, NY
	Seibu Museum of Art, Tokyo, Japan
1974	Gimpel and Weitzenhoffer Gallery, New York, NY
1973	Gimpel and Weitzenhoffer Gallery, New York, NY
	Gimpel-Hanover and Andre Emmerich Galerie, Zurich, Switzerland
1972	Gimpel and Weitzenhoffer Gallery, New York, NY
1971	Rockefeller University, New York, NY
1968	Howard Wise Gallery, New York, NY
1967	Flair Gallery, Cincinnati, OH
1966	Howard Wise Gallery, New York, NY

Selected Group Exhibitions

1997	*Asian Traditions/Modern Expressions*, Zimmerli Art Museum, New Brunswick, NJ
1993	*5th International Biennial of Sculpture*, Caldas da Rainha, Portugal
1992	Kouros Gallery, New York, NY/Kouros Sculpture Center, Ridgefield, CT
1991	Kua Chun Museum, Kua Chun, South Korea
1989	*Japanese Sculpture*, Fukushima Prefectural Museum of Art, Japan
1987–88	Solomon R. Guggenheim Museum, New York, NY
1983–84	Solomon R. Guggenheim Museum, New York, NY
	Neuberger Museum of Art, Purchase, NY
1982	*World Stone Sculpture*, Kunsthaus Zug, Switzerland

　　MINORU NIIZUMA

1981	*The 2nd Henry Moore Grand Prize Exhibition*, Hakone Open-Air Museum, Japan
1980	*Paintings and Sculptures by Candidates for Art Awards*, American Academy of Arts and Letters, New York, NY
1977	*The Grand Prize of the Hakone Open-Air Museum. The Third Exhibition*, Hakone Open-Air Museum, Japan
1975	*13th Biennial*, Middelheim Open-Air Museum of Sculpture, Antwerp, Belgium
1973–74	*Japanese Artists in the Americas*, The National Museum of Modern Art, Kyoto and Tokyo, Japan
1973	Solomon R. Guggenheim Museum, New York, NY
1969	*Second Flint Invitational*, Flint Institute of Arts in the DeWaters Art Center, Flint, MI
1968	*Annual Exhibition of Contemporary American Sculpture, Watercolors and Drawings*, Whitney Museum of American Art, New York, NY
	American Painting and Sculpture, Herron Museum of Art, Indianapolis, IN
1967	*Pittsburgh International Exhibition of Contemporary Painting and Sculpture*, Carnegie Institute, Pittsburgh, PA
1966	*Annual Exhibition of Contemporary American Sculpture, Watercolors and Drawings*, Whitney Museum of American Art, New York, NY
1965–1966	*The New Japanese Painting and Sculpture*
	San Francisco Museum of Modern Art, CA
	Denver Art Museum, CO
	Columbus Gallery of Fine Arts, OH
	Museum of Modern Art, New York, NY
	Baltimore Museum of Art
	Milwaukee Art Center, WI
1965	*Japanese Artists Abroad: Europe and America*, National Museum of Modern Art, Tokyo, Japan

Institutional Collections

Albright-Knox Art Gallery, Buffalo, NY
City of Dublin, Ireland
City of Evora, Portugal
City of Tokyo, Japan
Des Moines Art Center, IA
San Francisco Museum of Modern Art, CA
Fort Worth Museum, TX
Gulbenkian Museum, Lisbon, Portugal
The Hakone Museum of Modern Art, Kobe, Japan
Hirshhorn Museum and Sculpture Garden, Smithsonian Institute, Washington, DC
Hyogo Museum of Modern Art, Kobe, Japan
Iwatem-achi Sculpture Garden, Iwate, Japan
Kasama Nichido Museum of Art, Ibaraki, Japan
Museum of Modern Art, New York, NY
Museum of Modern Art, Toyama, Japan
National Museum of Art, Osaka, Japan
National Museum of Modern and Contemporary Art, Seoul, South Korea
National Museum of Modern Art, Tokyo, Japan
National Museum of Modern Art, Kyoto, Japan
New York University, New York, NY
Oklahoma Museum, Oklahoma City, OK
Seibu Museum of Art, Tokyo, Japan
Solomon R. Guggenheim Museum, New York, NY

Private Collections

JPMorgan Chase, New York, NY
Citi, New York, NY
General Mills Corporation, Minneapolis, MN
IBM, Zurich, Switzerland
Sanwa Bank, New York, NY
Suntory, Osaka, Japan

(1930–1998)

MINORU NIIZUMA

SELECTED WORKS

Thunderstorm II
1972
Ramello Rosso Italian marble
8 × 16 × 6 inches
20.3 × 40.6 × 15.2 cm

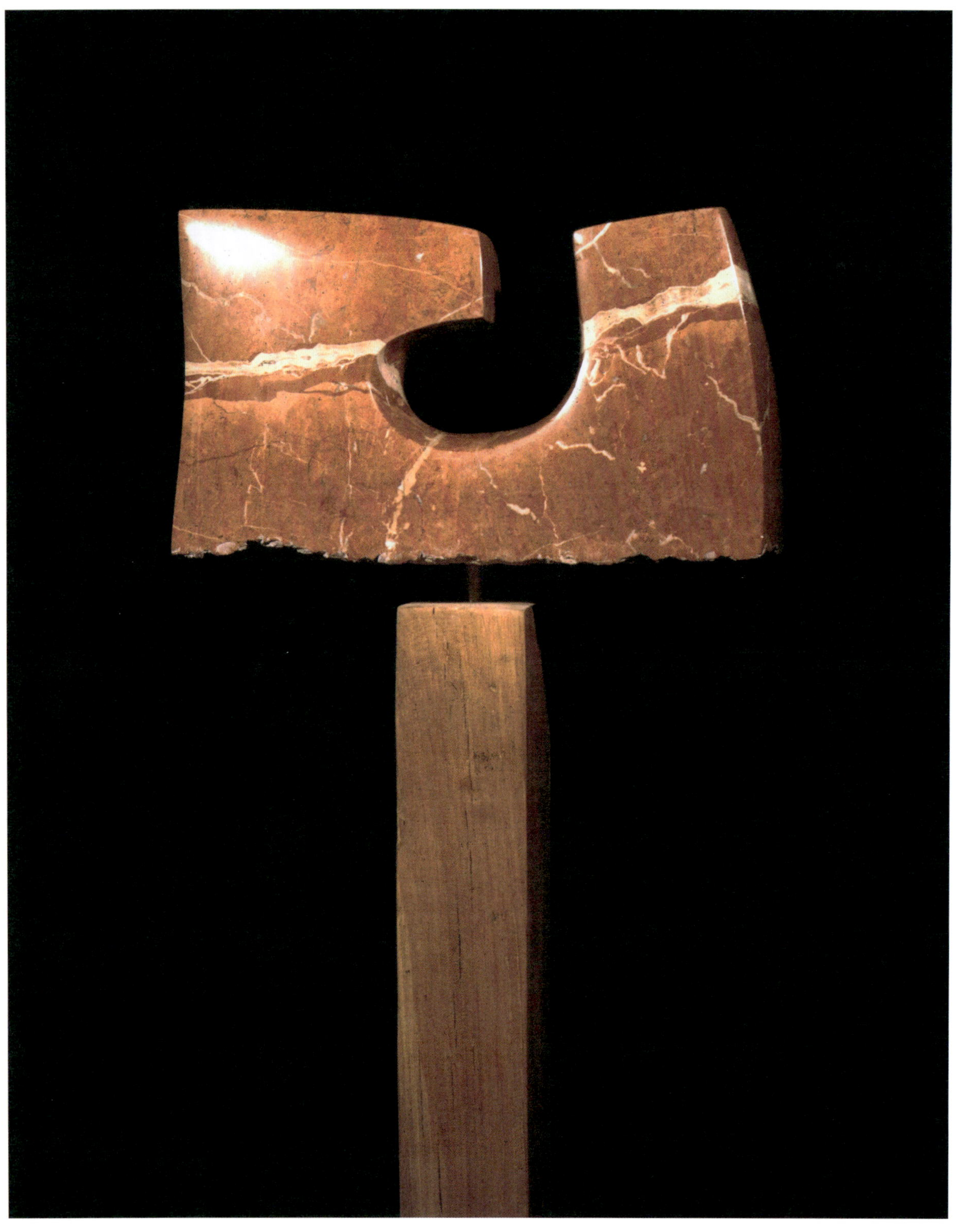

MINORU NIIZUMA

Rondo
1973
Carrara Italian marble
31.9 × 24 × 7.9 inches
81 × 61 × 20 cm

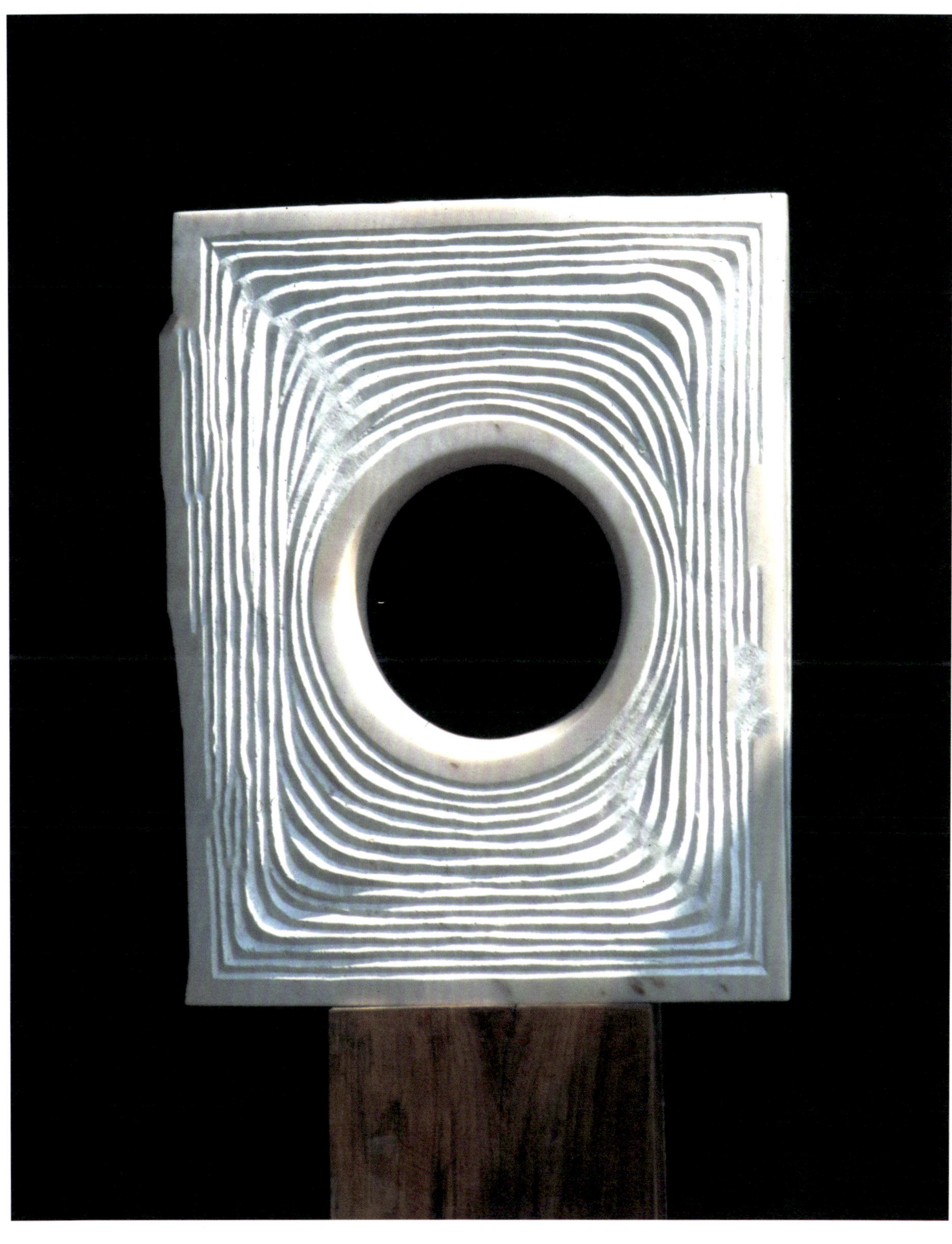

Crenel
1975
Verona red marble
39 × 19 × 19 inches
99.1 × 48.3 × 48.3 cm

MINORU NIIZUMA

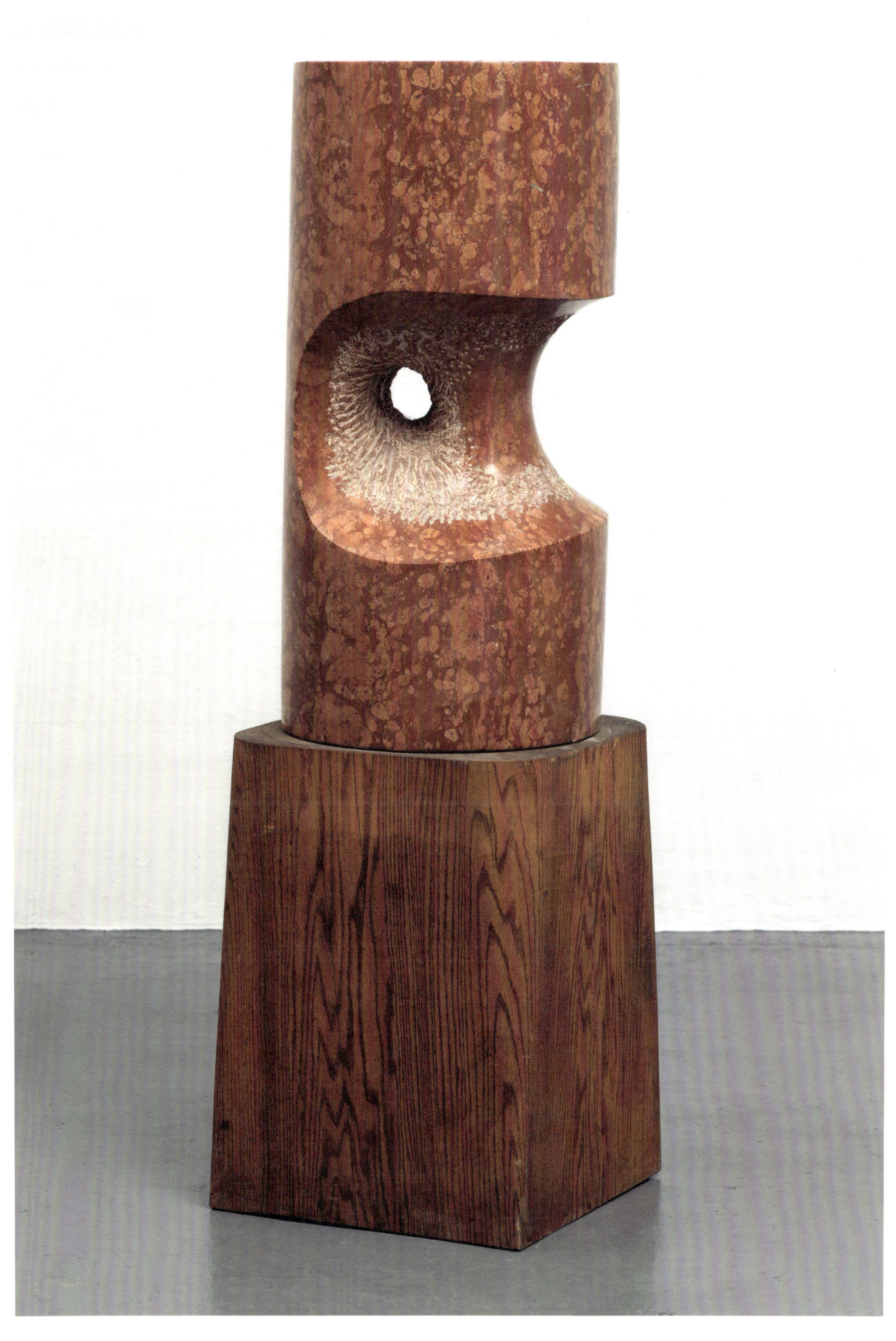

(1930–1998)　　117

Nest
1975
Gray marble
13 × 12 × 11 inches
33 × 30.5 × 27.9 cm

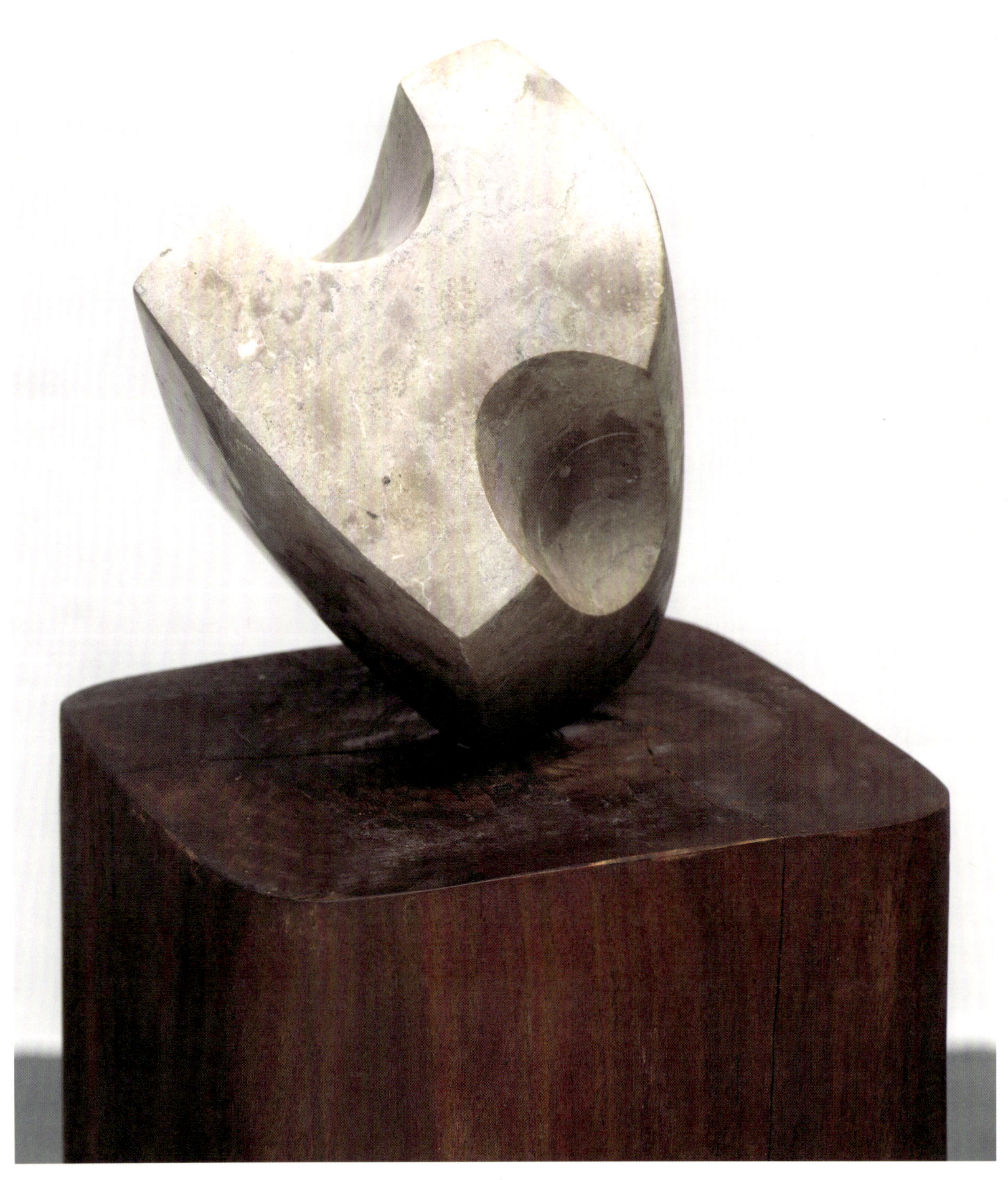

                    MINORU NIIZUMA

Nest
1975
Belgian black marble
11 × 10 × 10 inches
27.9 × 25.4 × 25.4 cm

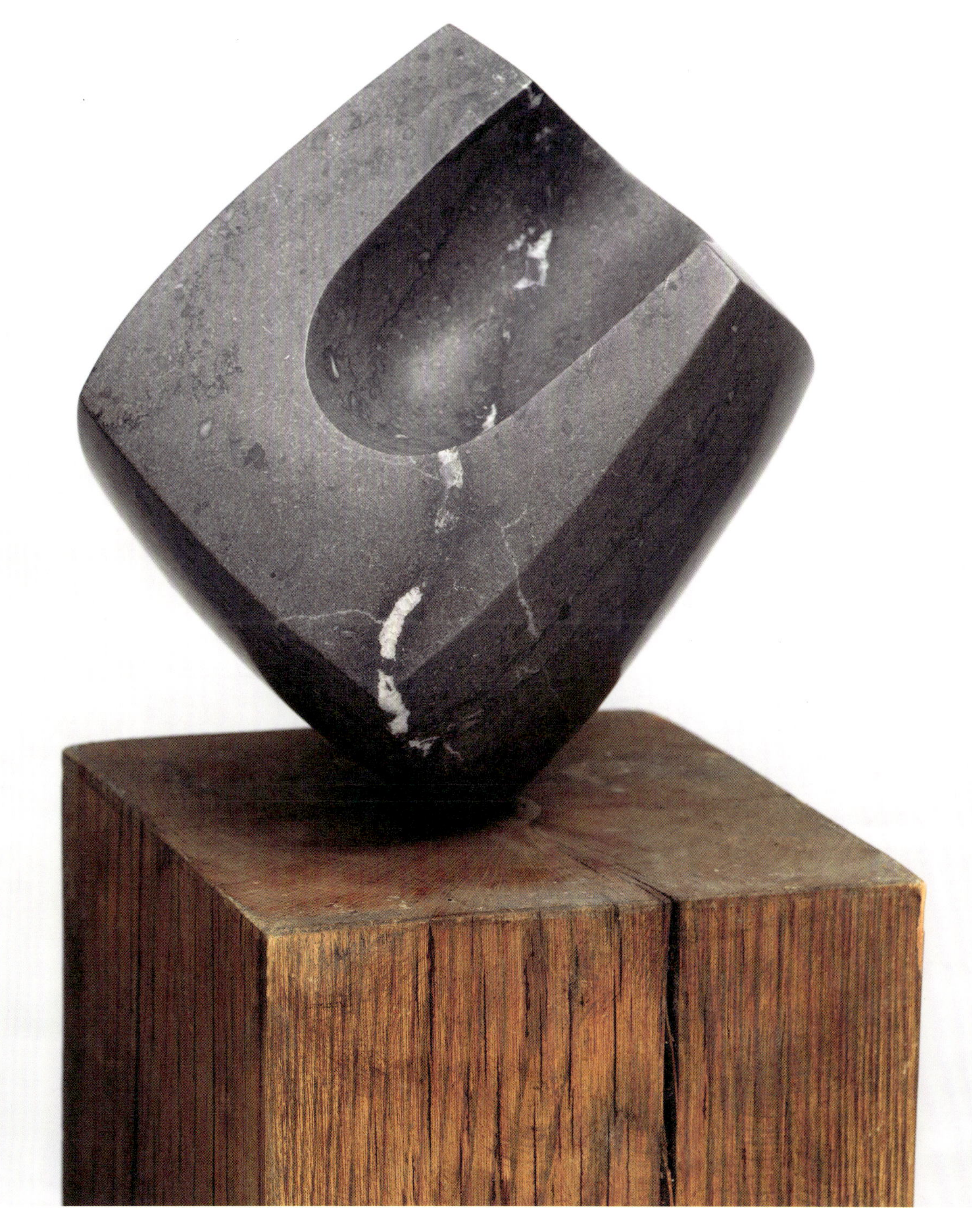

Castle of the Eye
1975
Carrara Italian marble with granite base
Washington, D.C.
171 × 38 × 38 inches
434 × 96.5 × 96.5 cm

MINORU NIIZUMA

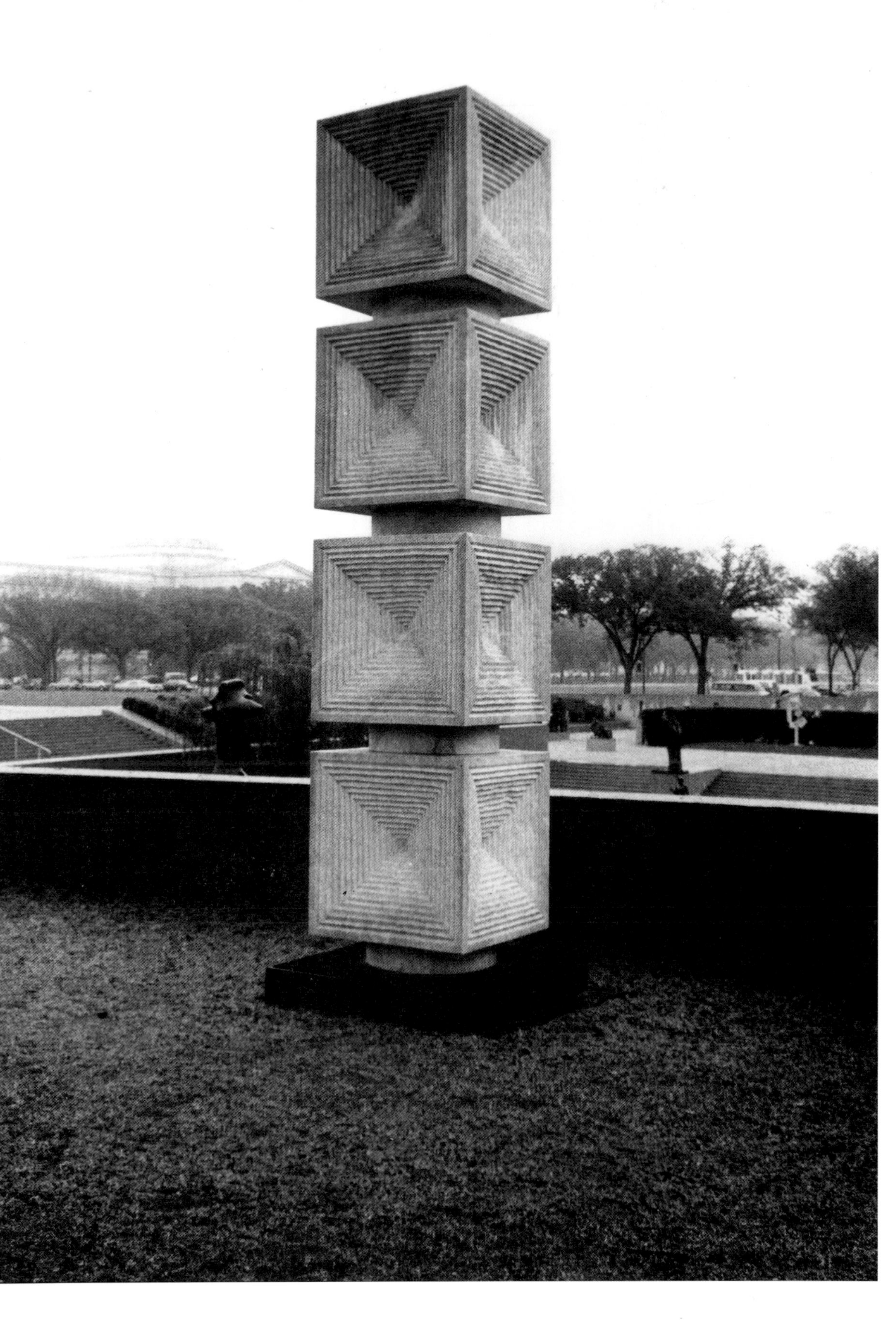

(1930–1998)   121

Water in the Mountain
1976
English Burlington slate
35.8 × 11 × 11 inches (91 × 28 × 28 cm)
29 × 11 × 11 inches (74 × 28 × 28 cm)

MINORU NIIZUMA

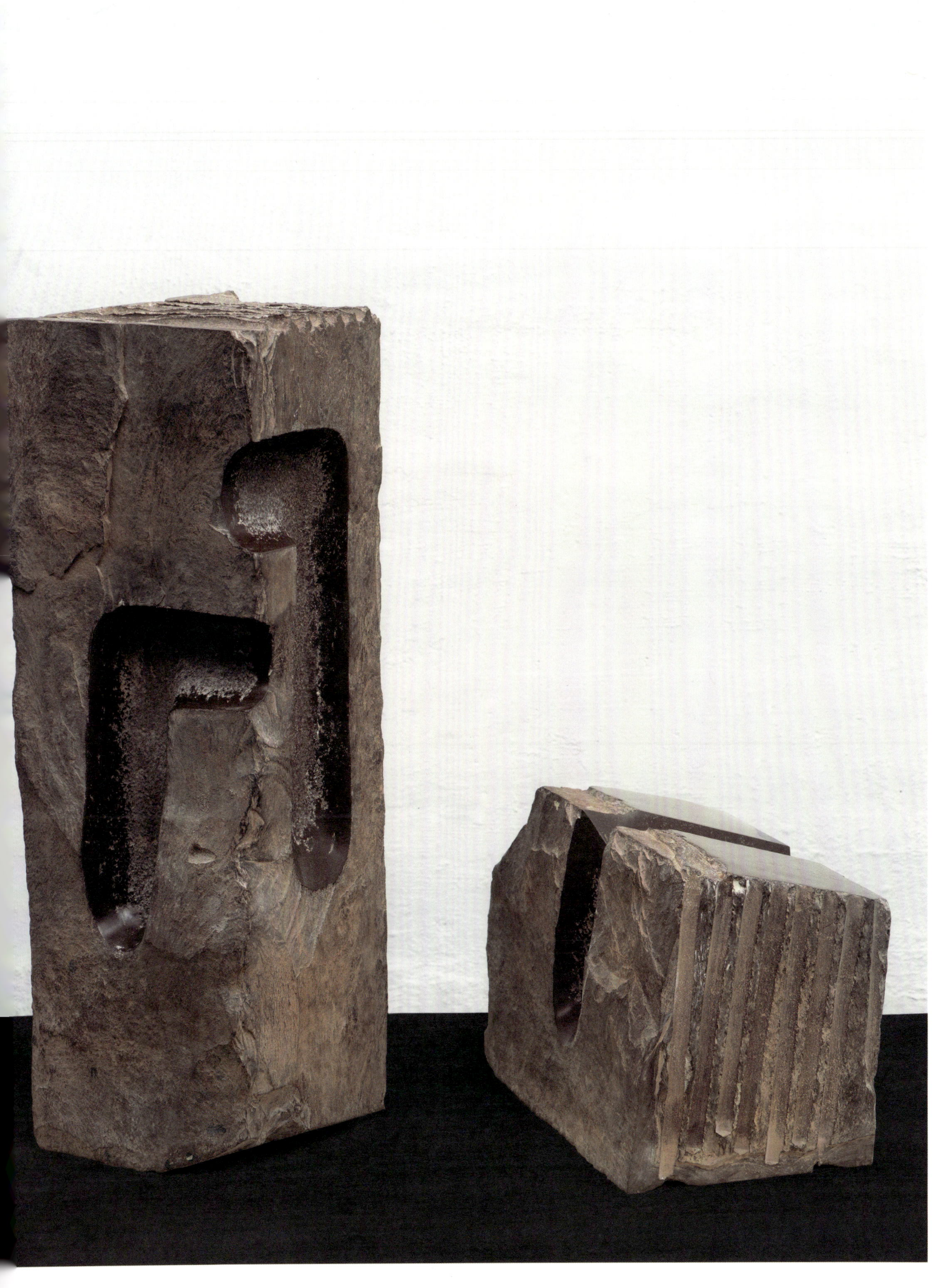

(1930–1998)   123

Crenel II
1976
Purple marble
25.75 × 12.75 × 12.75 inches
65.4 × 32.4 × 32.4 cm

 MINORU NIIZUMA

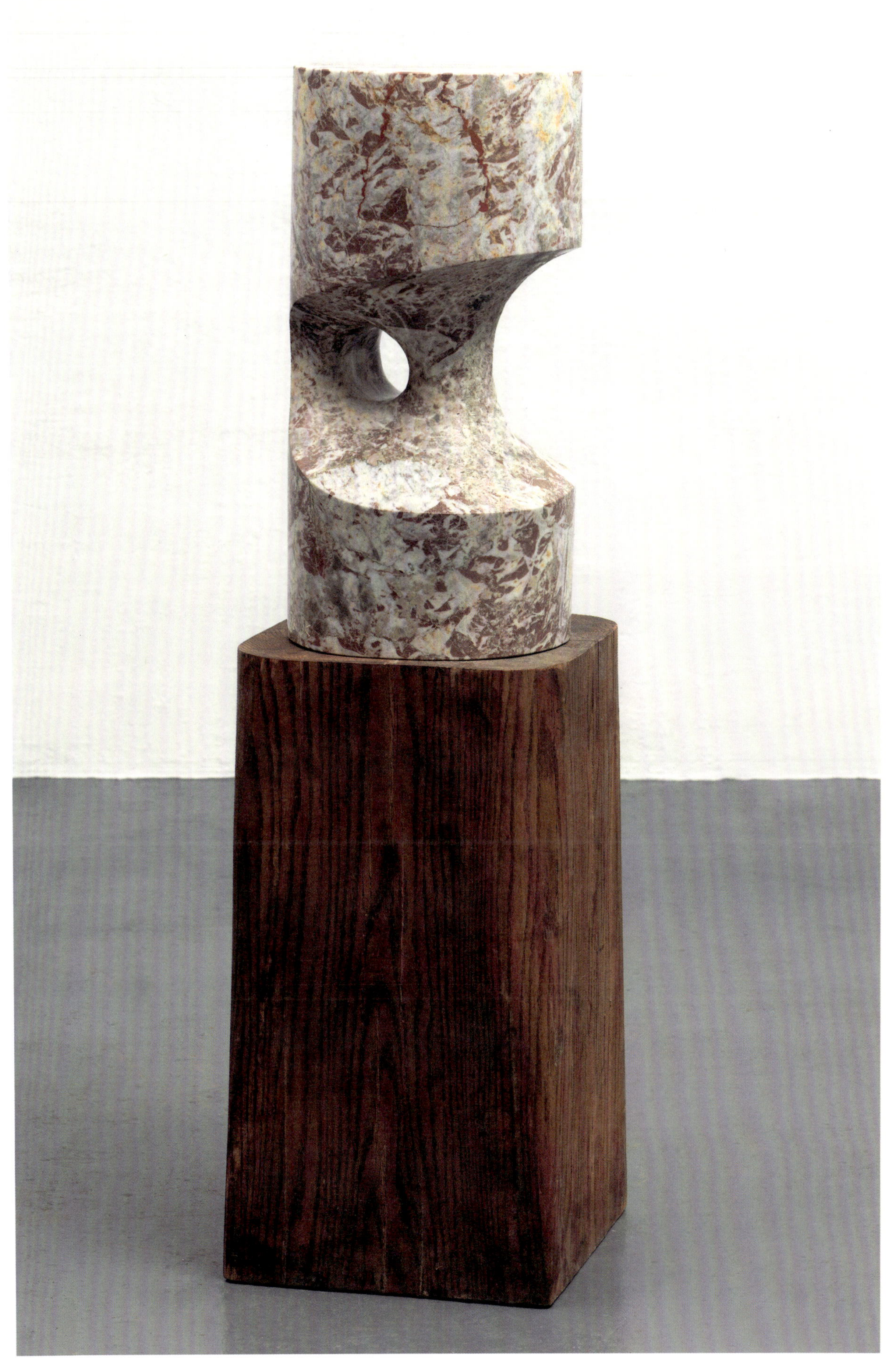

Menkaura Pyramid
1977
Verde Antico Vermont marble
13 × 15 × 19 inches (each)
33 × 38.1 × 48.3 cm

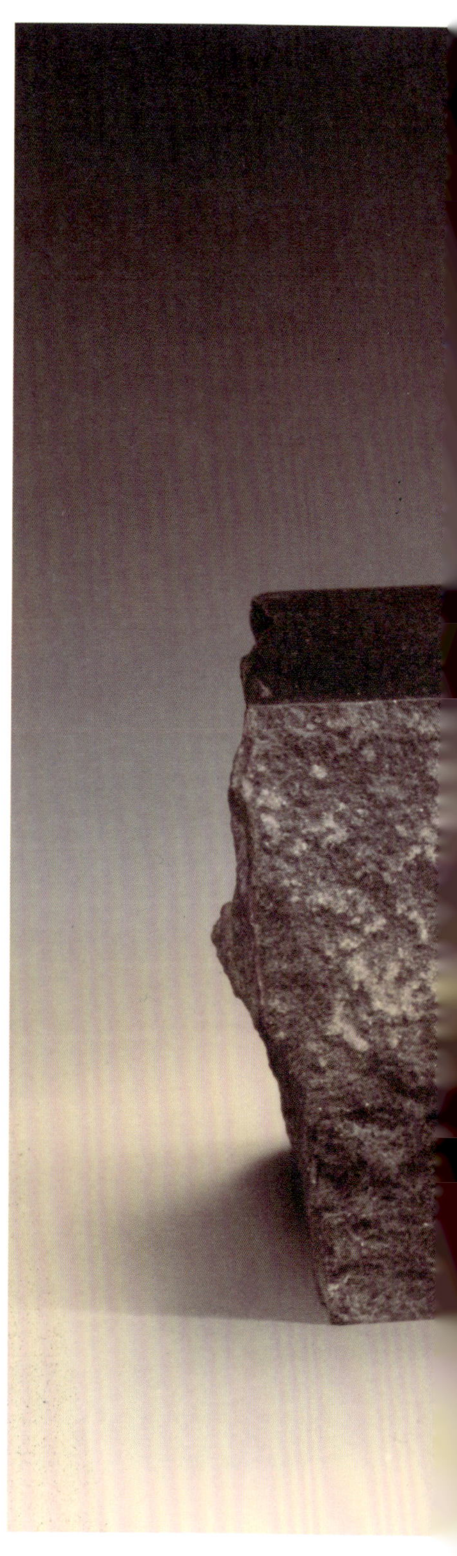

 MINORU NIIZUMA

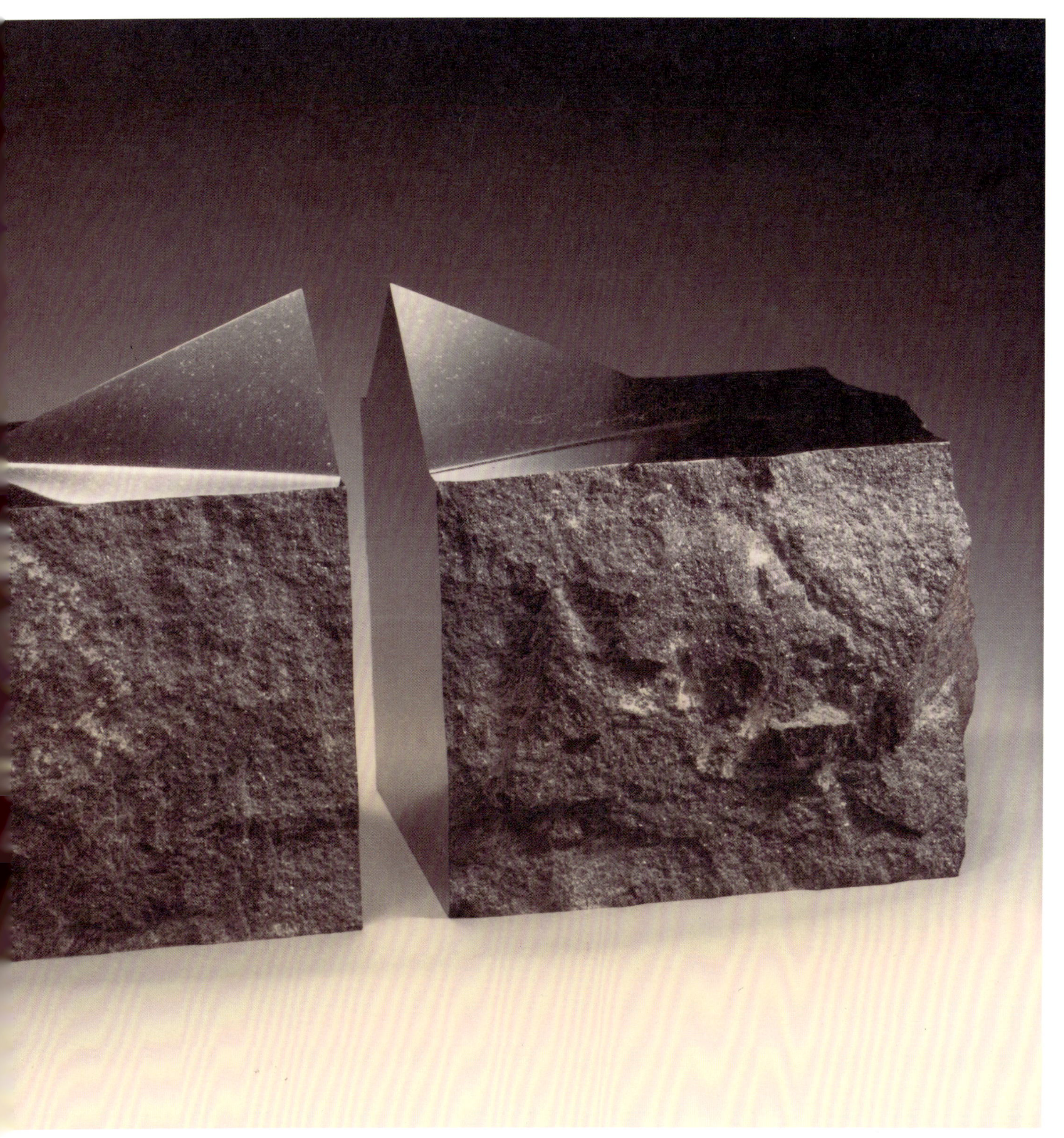

(1930–1998)

Mountainous
1979
Belgian Black marble
9.1 × 9.4 × 9.8 inches
23 × 24 × 25 cm

 MINORU NIIZUMA

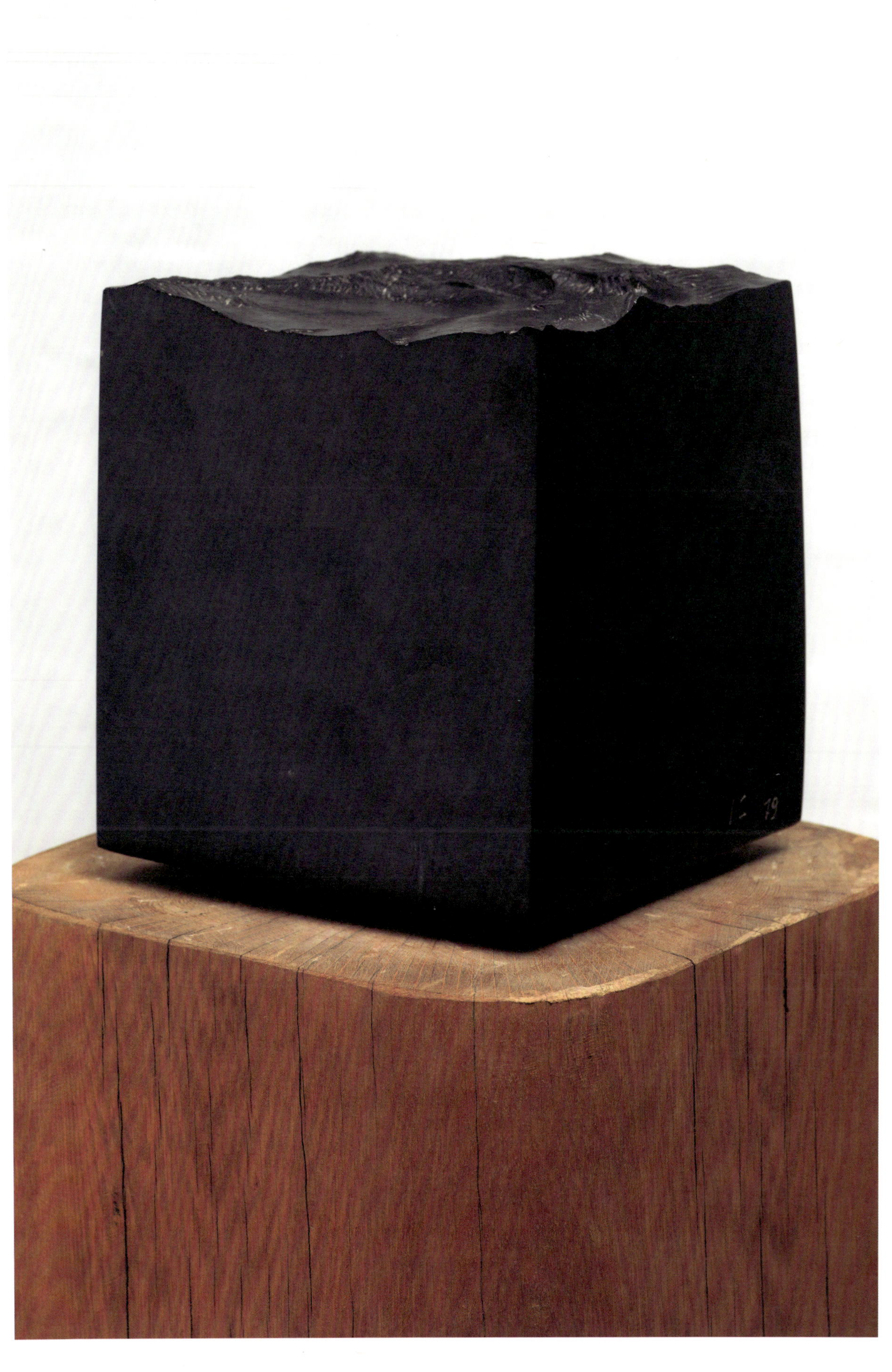

(1930–1998)

Castle of the Eye
1981
Portuguese Vila Viçosa marble
Evora, Portugal
5.5 × 5.5 × 11 feet
167.6 × 167.6 × 335.3 cm

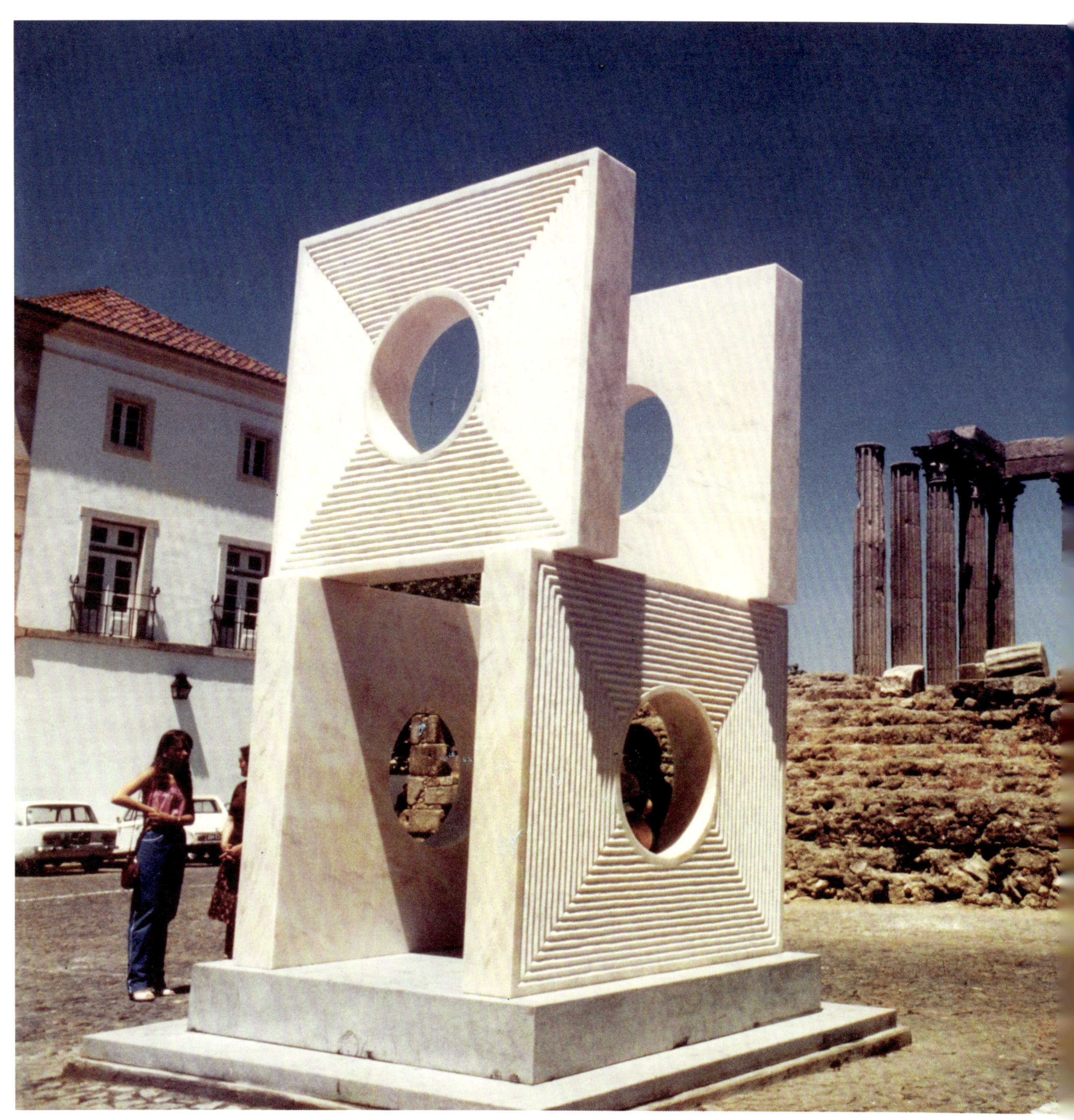

 MINORU NIIZUMA

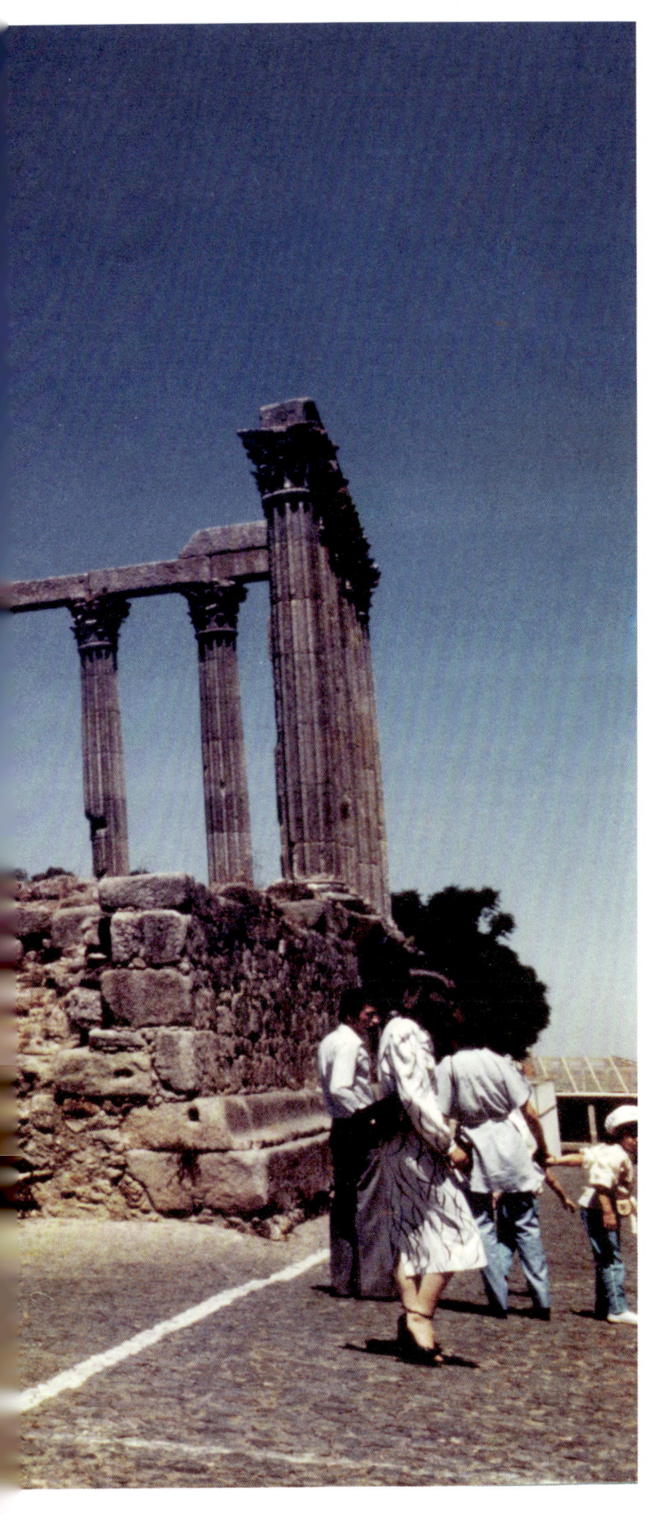

Unknown
1982
Black marble
21.5 × 10 × 8 inches
54.6 × 25.4 × 20.3 cm

 MINORU NIIZUMA

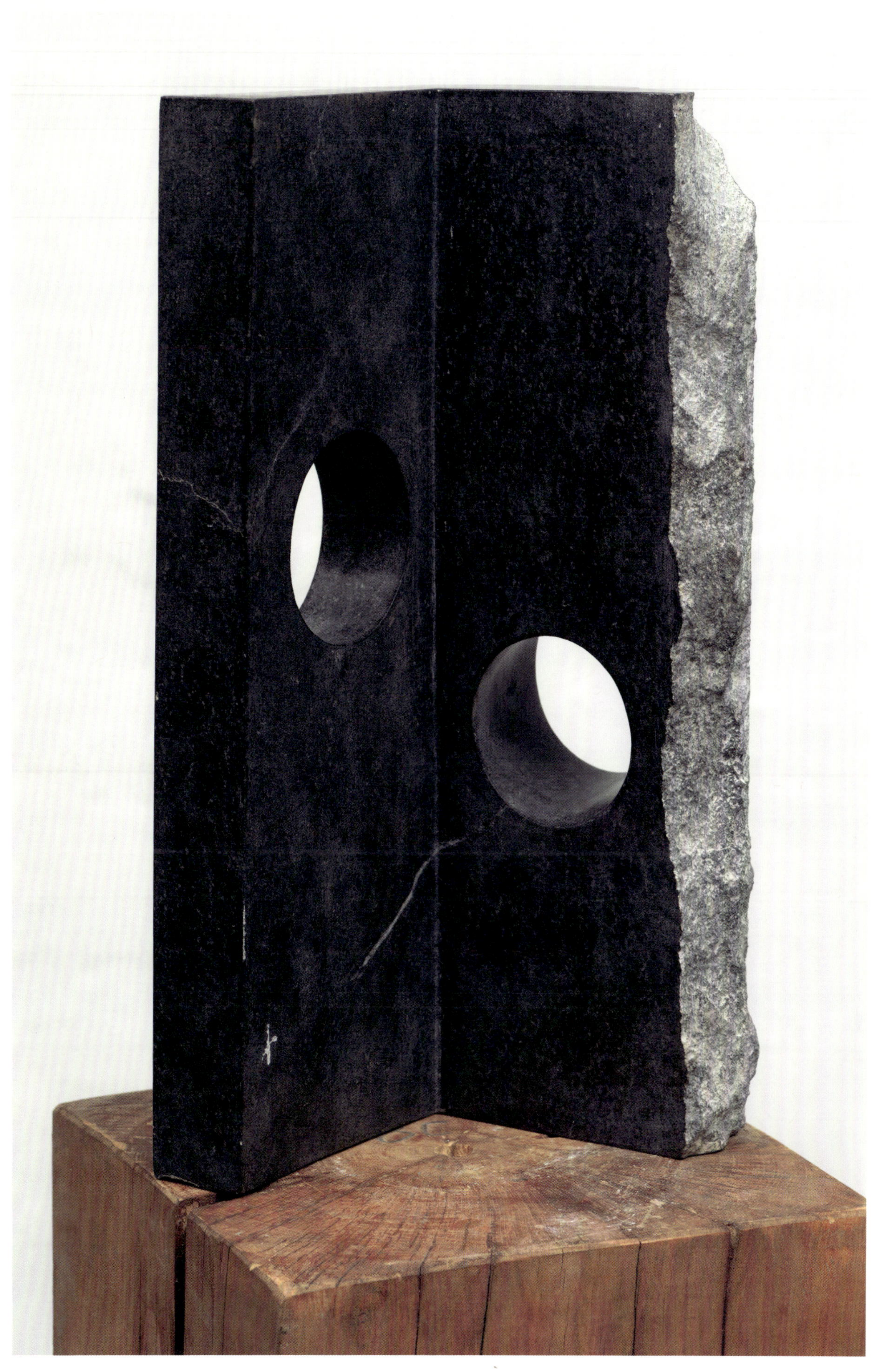

(1930–1998)

Infinity
1983
Gray Japanese granite
Numakunai, Iwate, Japan
Two pieces: 4 × 4 × 26 feet
1.25 × 1.25 × 8 m

 MINORU NIIZUMA

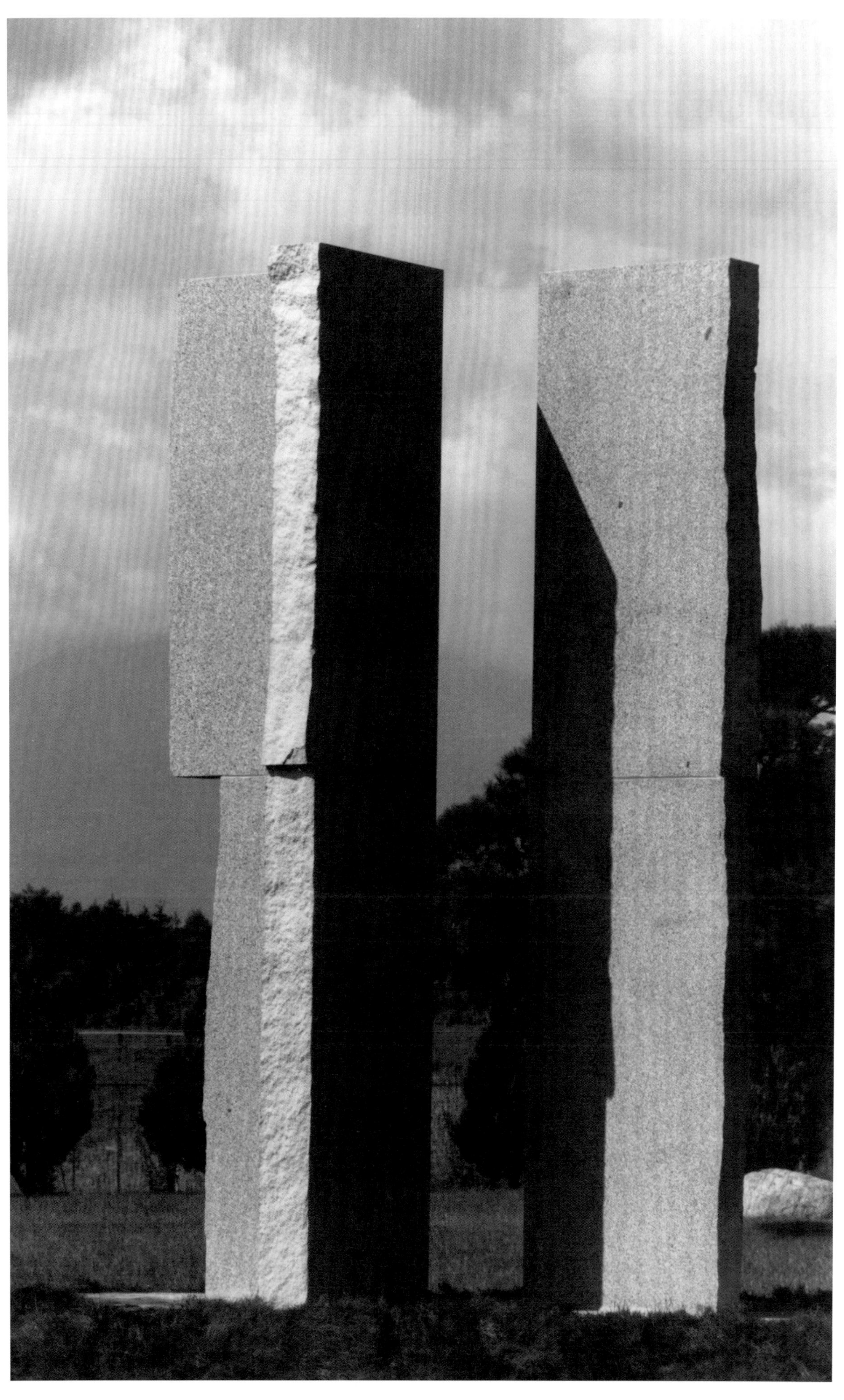

(1930–1998)

Castle of the Eye III
c. 1985
Portuguese marble
16.5 × 14 × 14 inches
41.9 × 35.6 × 35.6 cm

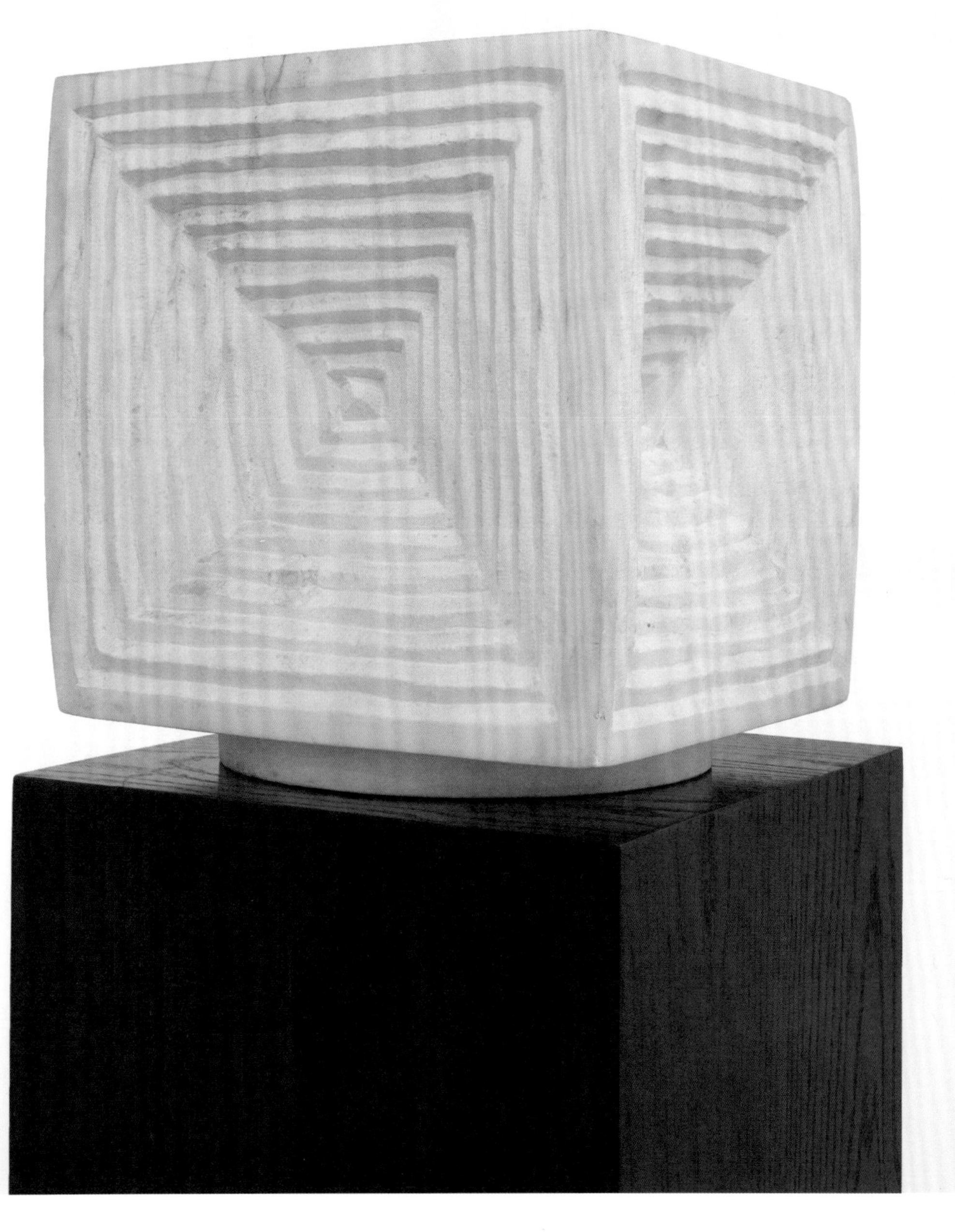

      MINORU NIIZUMA

Untitled
1985
Gray granite
Porto, Portugal
16 × 16 × 20 feet
4.9 × 4.9 × 6 m

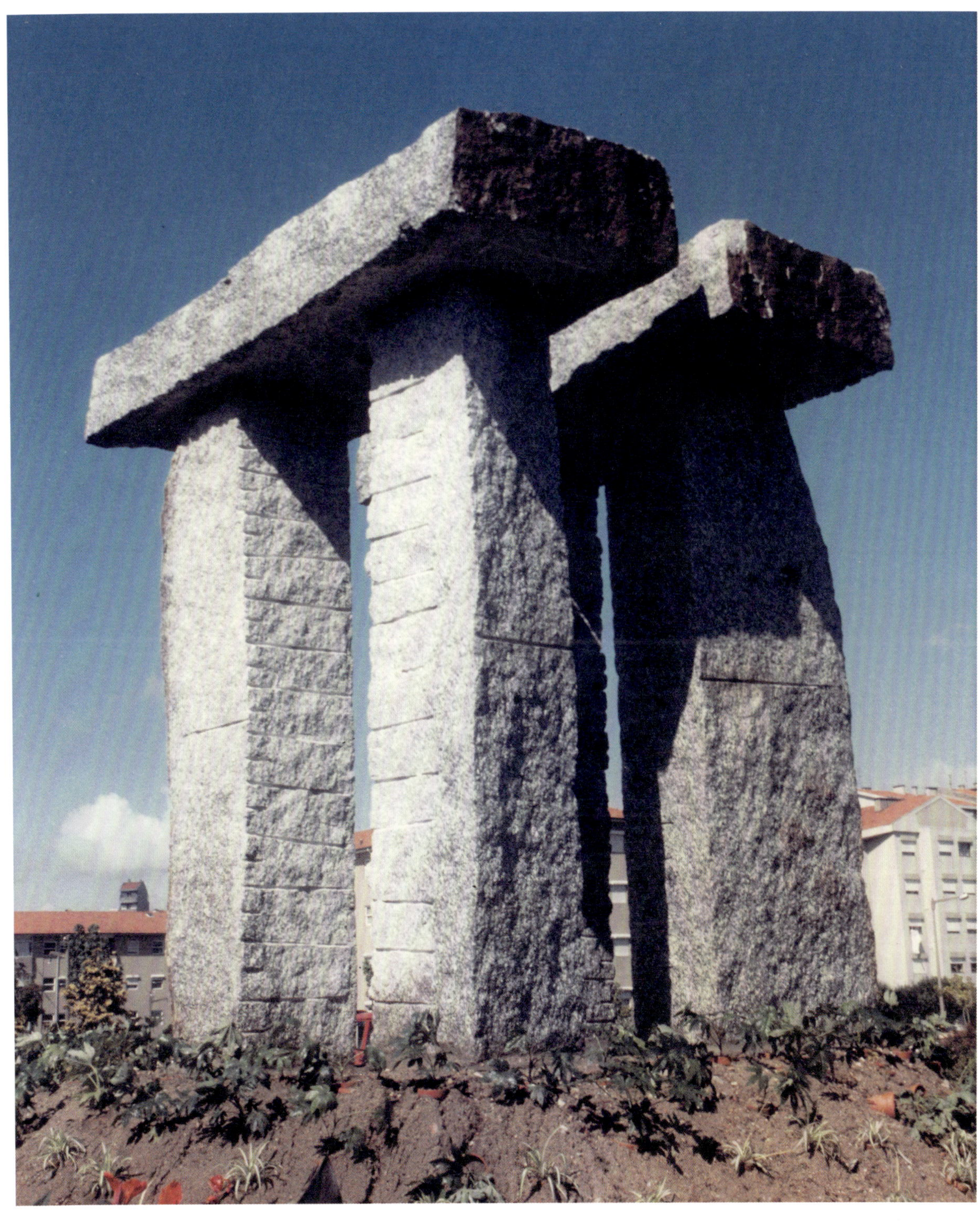

Unknown
c. 1986
Italian marble
19 × 10 × 10 inches
48.3 × 25.4 × 25.4 cm

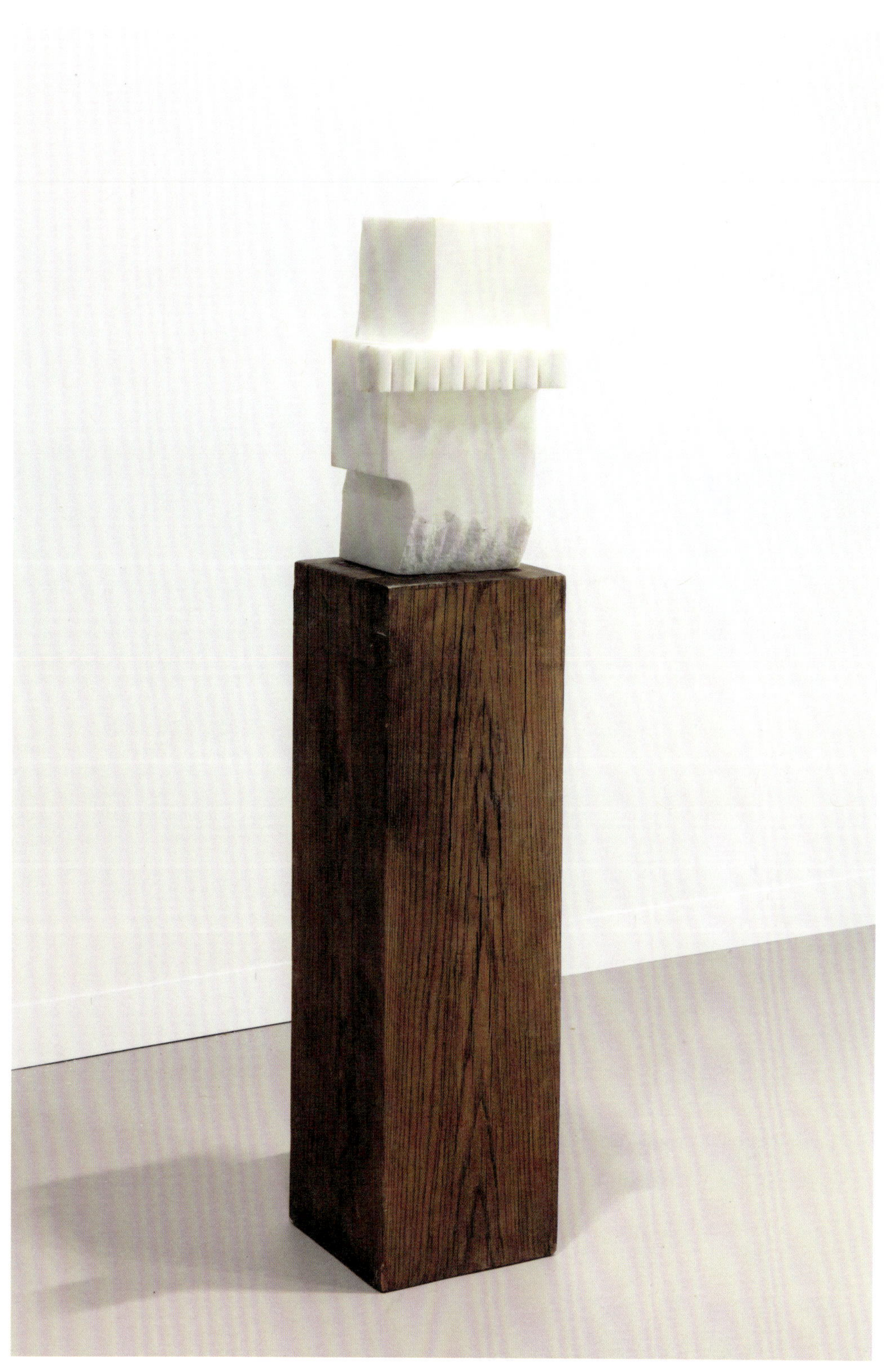

    MINORU NIIZUMA

Unknown
c. 1986
Pale pink marble
15 × 18.5 × 13.75 inches
38.1 × 47 × 34.9 cm

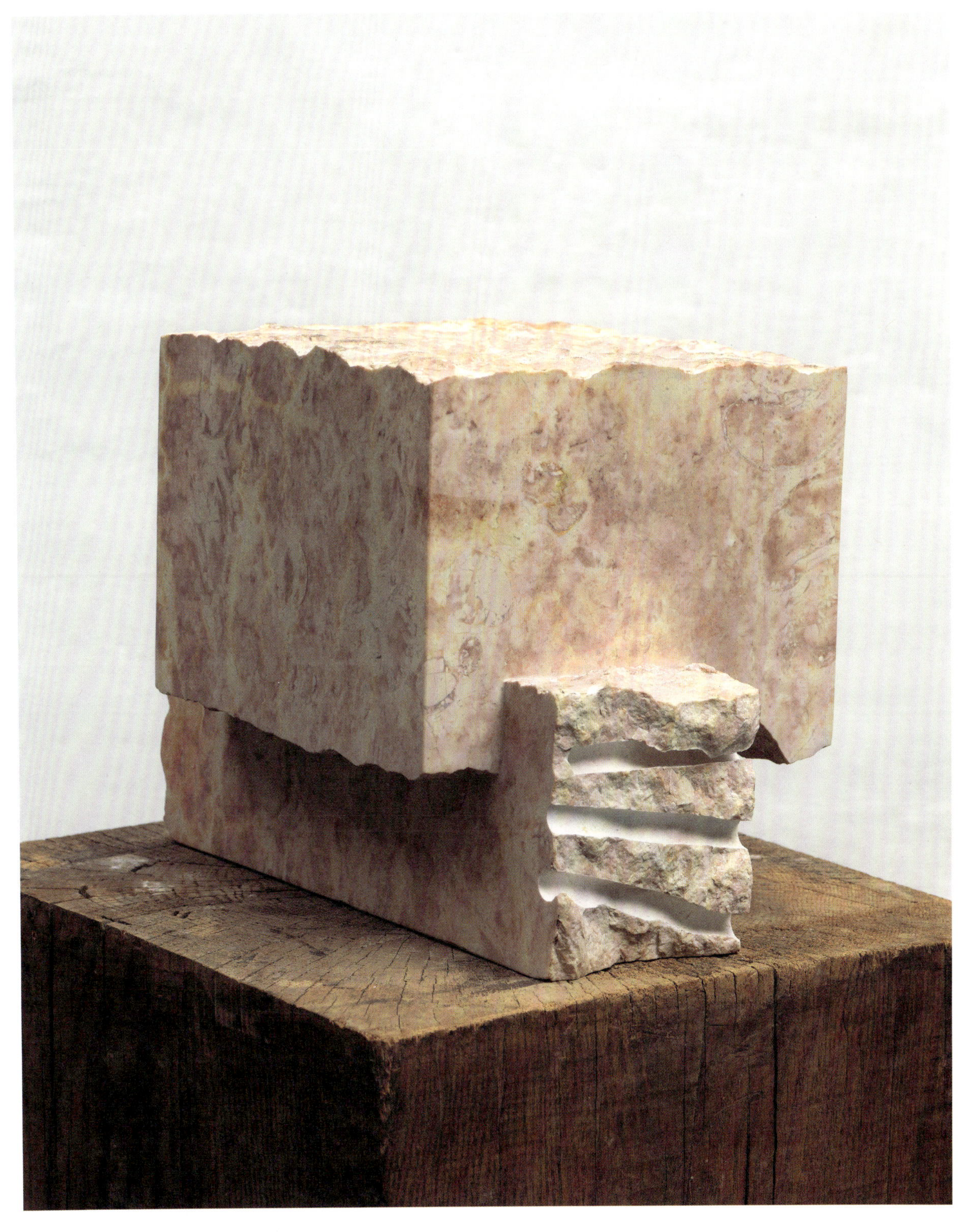

Water Fall
c. 1986
Italian marble
20 × 19.5 × 13.75 inches
50.8 × 49.5 × 34.9 cm

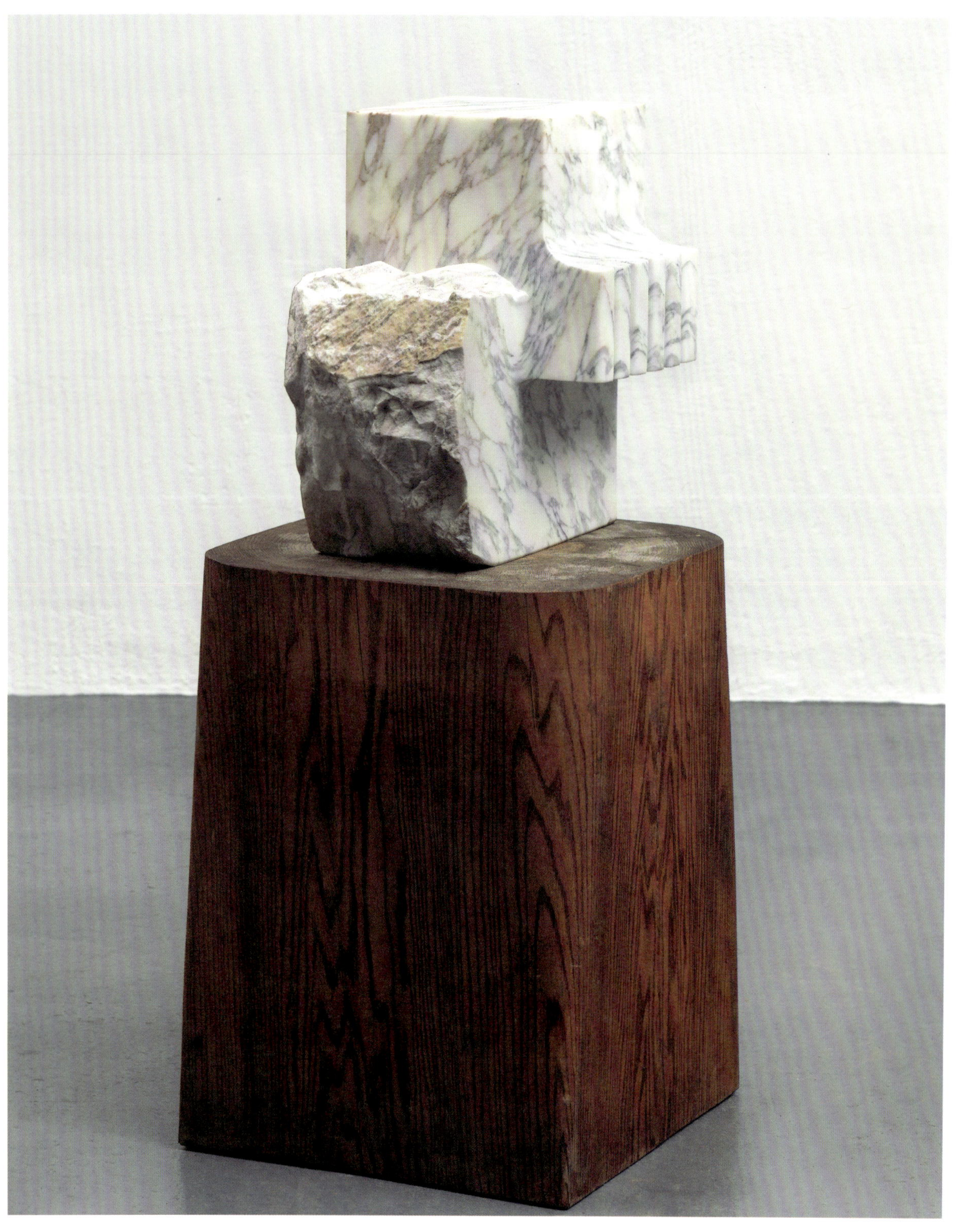

                    MINORU NIIZUMA

Unknown
c. 1986
Italian Paonazzo marble
19.5 × 13.5 × 11.75 inches
49.5 × 34.3 × 29.8 cm

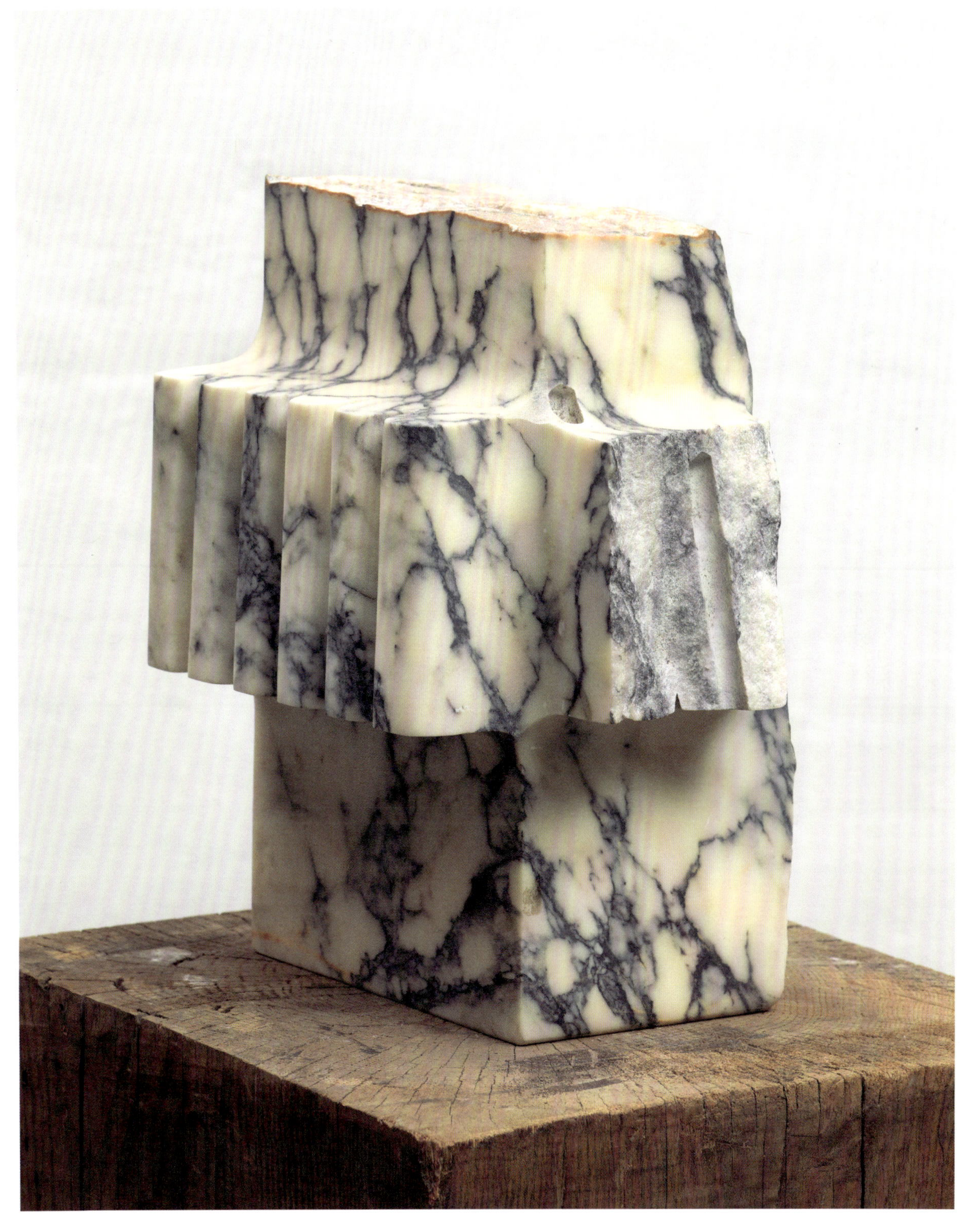

Black Mountain
1986
Portuguese black granite
54.33 × 16.54 × 15.75 inches
138 × 42 × 40 cm

  MINORU NIIZUMA

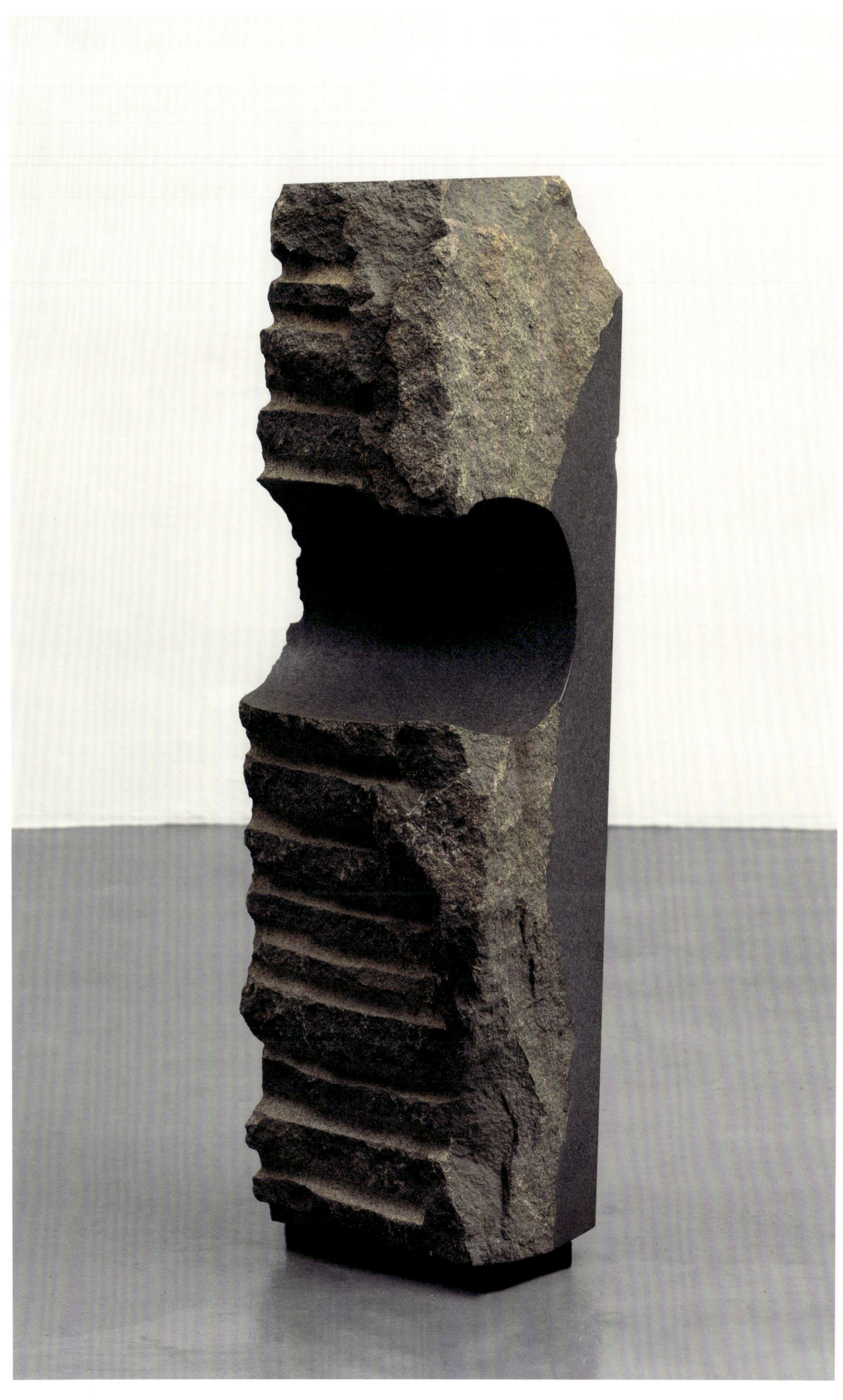

(1930–1998)   143

JOHN PAI

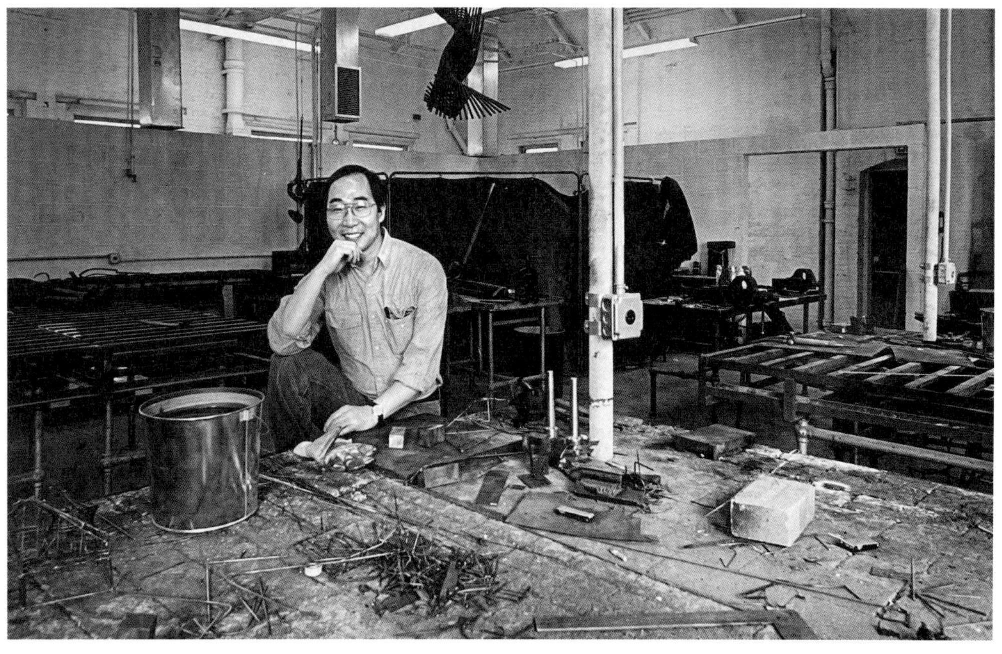

Photographed in the welding shop at Pratt Institute, where he was the youngest professor hired and then became director of the Fine Arts Program.

JOHN PAI

John Pai's childhood was defined by constant migration between places, his parents moving back and forth to Korea over the course of World War II and the Korean War. Born in Seoul in 1937, Pai immigrated to the United States at age 11, though his parents returned to Korea shortly after. He was marked as an artistic talent early on, receiving his first solo exhibition at age 15 at the Oglebay Institute in Wheeling, West Virginia.

In a short time, he rapidly rose to be the youngest ever professor at the Pratt Institute. Pai completed his BFA in industrial design at Pratt in 1962, before finishing his MFA in sculpture there in 1964. While in the midst of his undergraduate work, Pai was involved in the design and production of the Hawaii Pavilion at the 1964 World's Fair. Across his later undergraduate and graduate studies, Pai convinced the Constructivism-adjacent sculptor Theodore Roszak to take him on as an assistant, while also teaching at Pratt and Parsons. Pai proved instrumental in advocating for the creation of Pratt's fine arts division, pushing to receive his MFA in sculpture though it was not yet a degree track offered.

Within Pratt's ongoing organizational turmoil, even in the midst of his own education, Pai proved a talented educator. Pratt named him a professor in 1965 just after he finished his MFA, and promoted him to the undergraduate chair of Pratt's sculpture department in the same year. Pai continued to hold various chair positions at Pratt for almost a decade, including the director of the fine arts division. Stepping back into a standard professorship in 1972, Pai continued to mentor artists at Pratt, while simultaneously fostering the growing Korean artistic community in New York through gatherings within his home. Pai also found more time to focus on his own artistic practice, his meticulously welded forms showing extensively across Korea and within Korean-themed exhibitions. Pai participated in *Korean Drawing Now* at the Brooklyn Museum, and several exhibitions with the Seoul Whanki Foundation.

After his retirement in 2000, Pai's career further blossomed, with solo presentations at Gallery Hyundai in Seoul, and inclusion in exhibitions at the National Museum of Modern and Contemporary Art, South Korea, and the Smithsonian American Art

(B. 1937)

Museum. He is currently preparing for a solo exhibition at
the Korean Cultural Center, New York. He lives and works in
Fairfield, Connecticut.

JOHN PAI

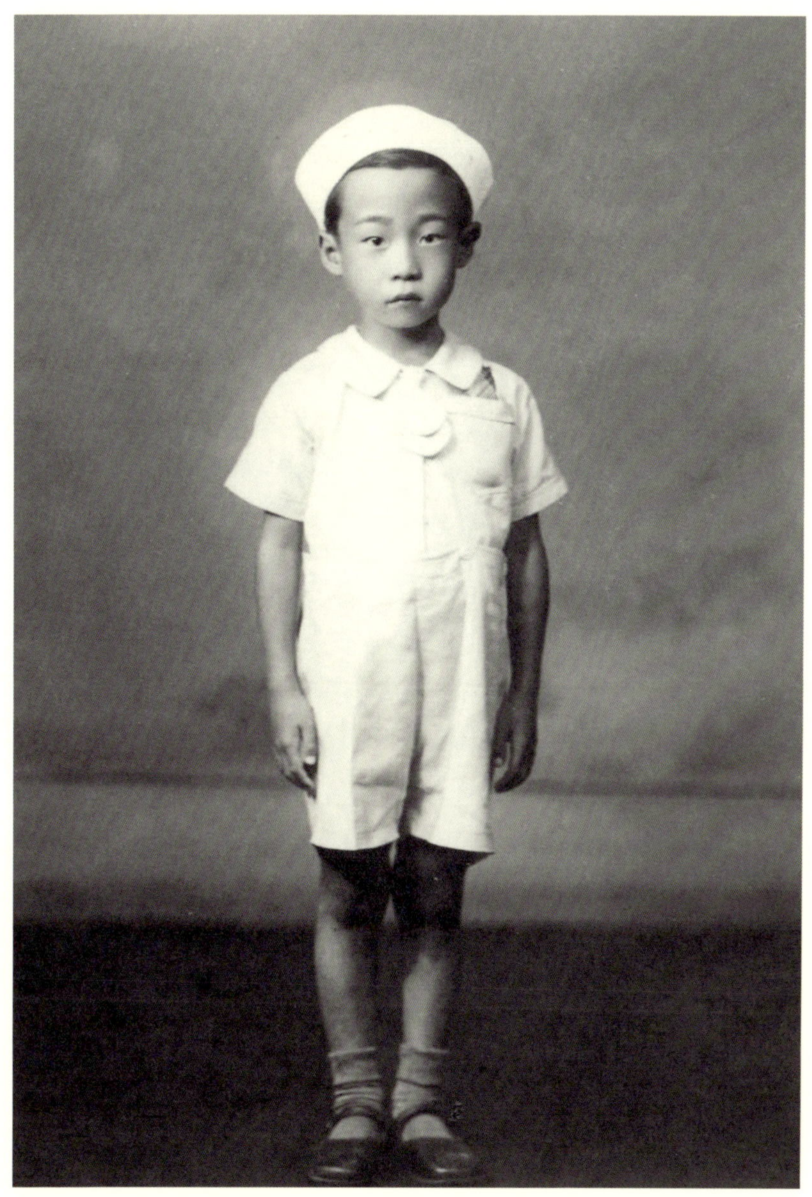

John Pai photographed in Seoul, Korea, c. early 1940s.

(B. 1937)

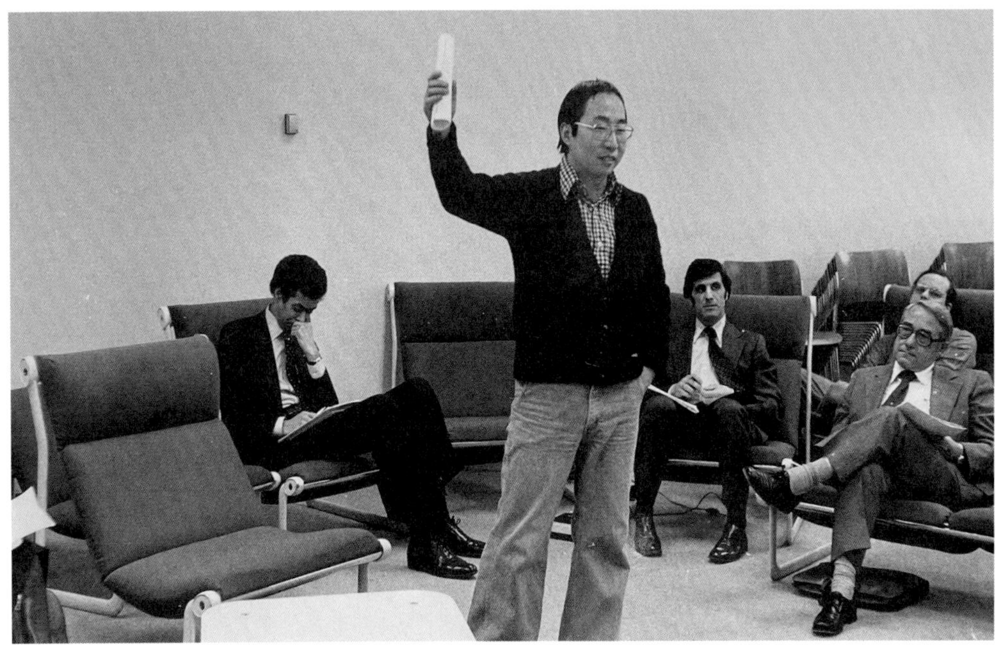

Speaking at a meeting of faculty, administration, and trustees, including the trustee John Morning. There were often meetings and discussions that took place between faculty, administration, and trustees regarding issues that revolved around revolutionary movements that were taking place.

JOHN PAI

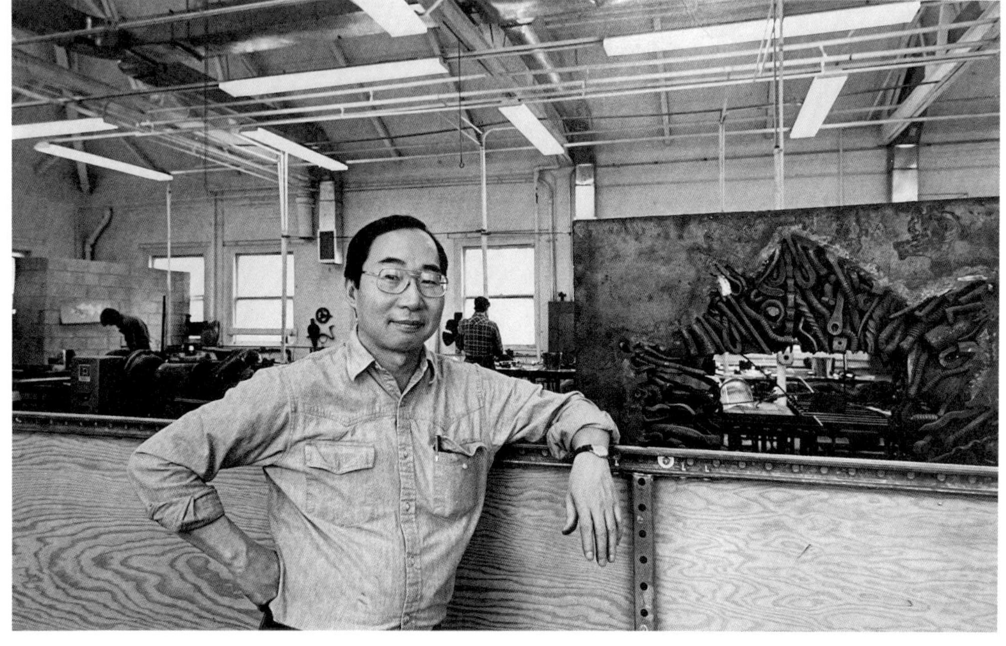

Pai in the welding shop at Pratt when he was a professor there and the director of fine arts, 1970s.

(B. 1937)

"Then I got a full, two-year fellowship to graduate school," the artist says. By 1965 Pai was head of the sculpture department. In 1972 he was named chairman of the art division, one year later he was director.

"Pratt has been a most positive experience for me," he states. "The conflicts mostly are the result of people's intensity and involvement with the place. The years of unrest—the late 60s—were really the heyday for sculpture," he recalls with a smile. "We defined the concept of sculpture on a broader basis, the modular curriculum was developed, and interdisciplinary options incorporated.

"Now people are concerned with specific skills for getting jobs. Sculptors work in a variety of jobs, but the training is the same, which is why they have the capability to do many things. You must change your head, but the technical preparation is the same. But I don't really believe opportunities have decreased that much," Pai insists, mindful of the fact that his options were many when he gave up administration for teaching.

Only the carriage house stands in his way. □ M.A.

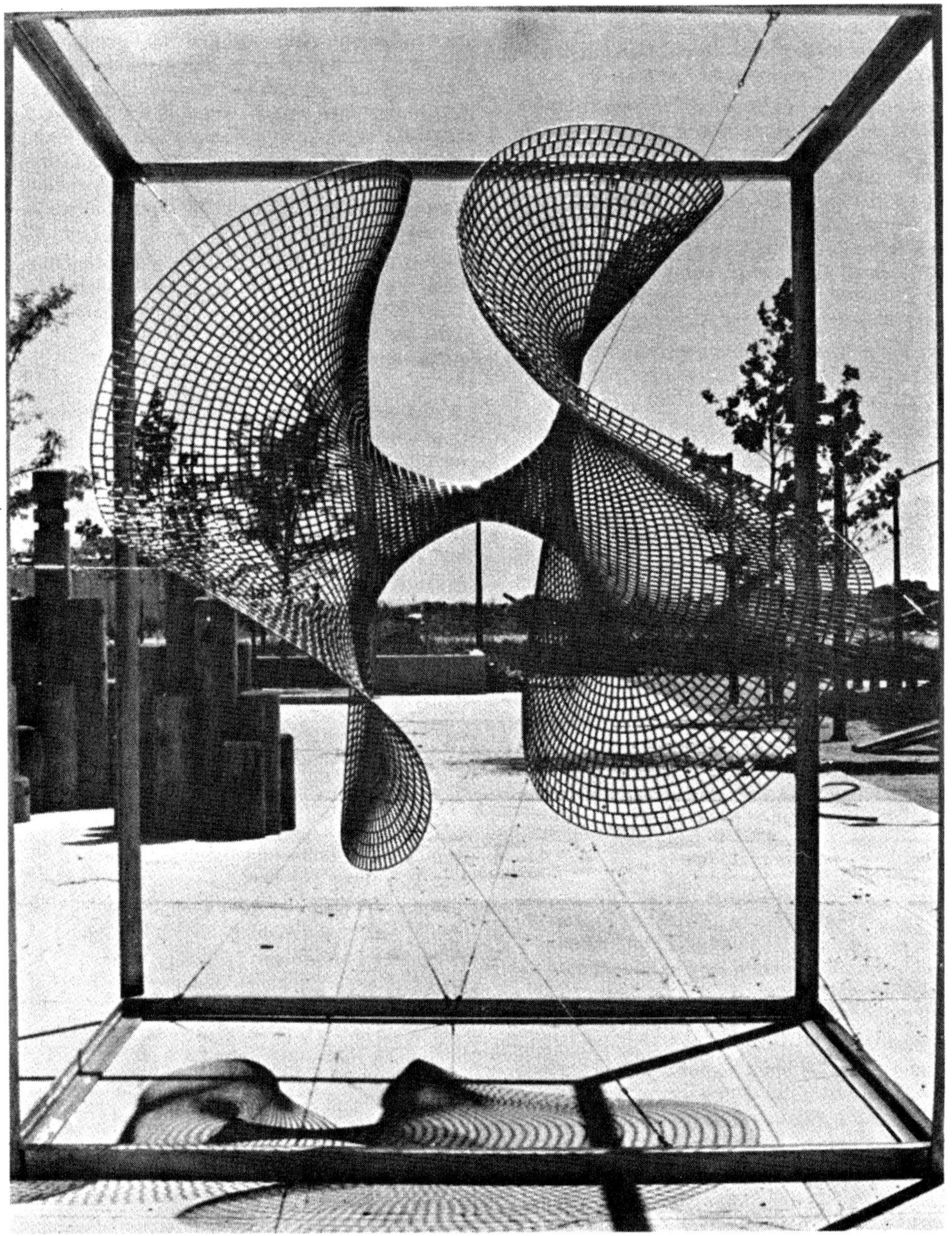

Pai's sculpture, executed during his sabbatical leave, stands on the Kingsborough Community College campus in Brooklyn. 1978 June 2. Pratt Reports. with Mon

JOHN PAI

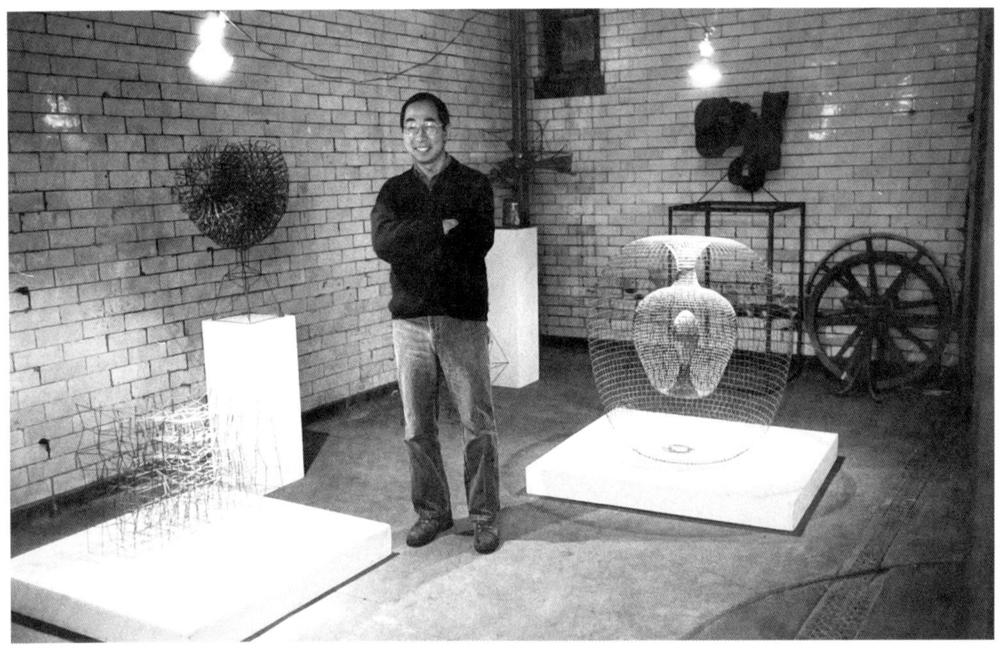

John Pai pictured with several artworks, including *Involution*, in his studio in Brooklyn.

I was working for Theodore Roszak, and had seen his show *New Images of Man* at MoMA, where he was exhibiting welded pieces. It was the style of the period to take found objects, or parts of cars, or anything that was made of steel, and weld them together. In the case of Roszak, I felt like he was partially from the Renaissance and partially from the modern world, because he was also known for designing airplanes. He had the technical know-how, he understood metallurgy, understood the process of welding. His works, to me, were almost like Renaissance drawings. But his early works, Constructivist works, were more architectonic.

I think my early work resembles Roszak's work quite a bit. And because of my interest in music – this process of working with line, plane, texture, mass – it all kind of fit in very neatly. During that period, I was busy trying to practice what I was learning. And I think a lot of the elements, like movement, gesture, almost classical concerns about formal relationships... It was a combination of things that I was taught, and also what artists were doing during that period. There was a branch of people who liked the idea of working with heavy chunks of metal, geometric, and I think the basic strength of steel. They wanted steel to look like steel. I think I was beginning to see the other side of steel – with a welding torch, you're taking something very strong and solid and you're melting it until it's liquid. That's the side that fascinated me, because it seemed to offer an incredible range of flexibility. From there, I began to experiment with what the torch can do.

I sort of like the idea of drawing, being able to sculpt the way I could draw. When the line is reduced to that scale, it's not really that different from pen and ink drawing, where the line can join other lines to create a plane. One of the things I recognized then was that there's a certain logic that you become very conscious of. For instance, how does it stand? So, you're always dealing with an orientation to gravity. [One day], I thought, what if you didn't? What if you didn't have to worry about structure all the time? So, I created a frame so that I could start anywhere inside that space.

[More recently], there are two things at play. One was the whole idea of abstraction, of breaking things down to the smallest

(B. 1937)

unit, and then building from there. And in the process, you really don't know where it's going, but each form is kind of a reaction to the ones next to it. And so, my process of working changed quite a bit. Like the very early work has a sense of direction and some degree of planning, but [now] there's a possibility of accidents and kind of almost like stream-of-consciousness building or drawing. I mean, it's a large three-dimensional drawing, but until the end, I really didn't know how it would end. So, it's almost like knitting or something, where I don't have to chop up pieces and then put them together.

      [In working this way], you have to know something about how things work, the physics and chemistry of nature. There are certain patterns of relationships, like the whole idea of symbiosis. And you think about proportions or dynamics. There are things about proportions in nature, where just a couple of degrees makes the difference between liquid and solid, and solid and gas. You learn that these abstract things dealt with in basic design describe something about the larger nature of the universe. So, I think quite a bit of my work is motivated by curiosity, and the process that I use is very flexible that way. When you do break it down to basic elements, it gives you tremendous freedom. It takes time.

      I thought, there has to be something more than surface to be concerned about. And I asked myself, what if I tried to do something without worrying about the surface at all? I thought that would give me some kind of new experience. [I would describe it as the] "persistence of forgotten things." I think it was sort of in the air, the idea of silence or nothingness. Can you have silence and nothingness with somethingness? I think, just on a personal level, there are some things that you want to forget, or try to forget, and some things just hang around. And you can never really be separated from whatever that is, and it could be something of conscience or guilt – and it affects you. It kind of made me think – I haven't gone to church in a long time – but I was always kind of struck by prayers, like saying, "Forgive us for our sins." And I thought, why should we be forgiven? It should be remembered, and it should affect you. And you should kind of bear the cross. You can't be really forgiven – what does that do for you? Anyway, that's the gist of it.

            JOHN PAI

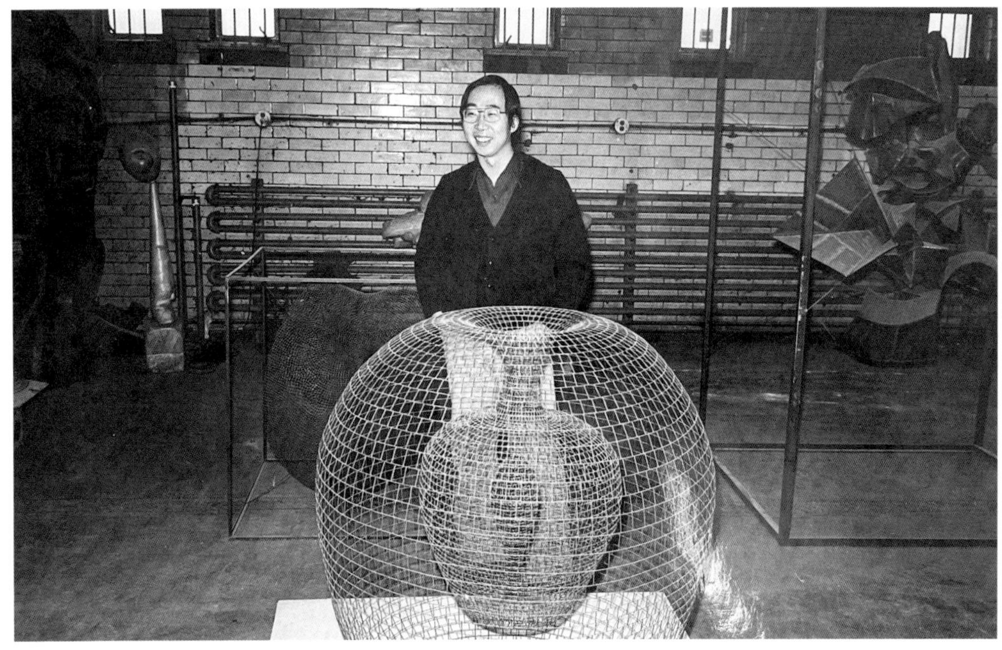

Pai in his Brooklyn studio with his work *Involution*, 1970s.

Born 1937, Seoul, Korea

Education

1964	Pratt Institute, MFA Sculpture
1962	Pratt Institute, BFA Industrial Design

Selected Solo Exhibitions

2013	Gallery Hyundai, Seoul, South Korea
2006	Gallery Hyundai, Seoul, South Korea
2003	Rodin Gallery, Seoul, South Korea
1997	Sigma Gallery, New York, NY
1994	Sigma Gallery, New York, NY
1993	Gallery Hyundai, Seoul, South Korea
1990	Souyun Yi Gallery, New York, NY
1988	Souyun Yi Gallery, New York, NY
1987	Gallery Korea, New York, NY
1987	Won Gallery, Seoul, South Korea
1982	Won Gallery, Seoul, South Korea
1982	Whanki Foundation, New York, NY
1964	Pratt Institute, New York, NY
1952	Oglebay Institute, Wheeling, WV

Selected Group Exhibitions

2015	*Art and the Measure of Liberty: The UN Turns 70*, Permanent Mission of the Republic of Korea to the United Nations, New York, NY, organized by Baik Art
2011	*American Abstract Artists 75th Anniversary*, OK Harris Works of Art, New York, NY
2010	*Floating Hours: Moon Is the Oldest Clock* National Museum of Modern and Contemporary Art, Deoksugung, Seoul, South Korea Czech National Museum of Contemporary Art, Prague, Czech Republic
2009	*The Great Hands*, Gallery Hyundai, Seoul, South Korea
2003	*Dreams and Reality: Korean–American Contemporary Art*, Smithsonian International Gallery, Washington, DC *At the Crossroad*, Gallery Korea, Korean Cultural Service, New York, NY
2001	*Whanki Museum Retrospective 1975–2001*, Whanki Museum, Seoul, South Korea
2000	*Welded Sculpture of the 20th Century*, Neuberger Museum of Art, Purchase, NY *New York 20/20*, Korean Cultural Service at the Permanent Mission of the Republic of Korea to the United Nations, New York, NY
1997	*Asian Traditions/Modern Expressions*, Zimmerli Art Museum, New Brunswick, NJ Taipei Gallery, New York, NY
1996	*Art 1996 Chicago* at the Navy Pier, Chicago, IL Gallery Hyundai, Seoul, South Korea
1991	Souyun Yi Gallery, New York, NY
1993	Whanki Museum, Seoul, South Korea
1987	Centre Nationale des Arts Plastiques, Paris, France
1982	*Transparent Structure: Endless Summer*, Thorpe Intermedia Gallery, Sparkill, NY
1981	*Korean Drawing Now*, Brooklyn Museum, New York, NY Alain Oudin Gallery, Paris, France
1980	*Art Expo, New York*, Sponsored by the Whanki Foundation, New York, NY
1977	*Four Contemporary Sculptors*, The Alternative Museum, New York, NY
1967	*Made with Paper*, Museum of Contemporary Crafts, New York, NY

    JOHN PAI

(B. 1937)

JOHN PAI

SELECTED WORKS

(B. 1937)

Untitled-Entitled 2021
1970
Welded steel
36 × 36 × 16 inches
91.4 × 91.4 × 40.6 cm

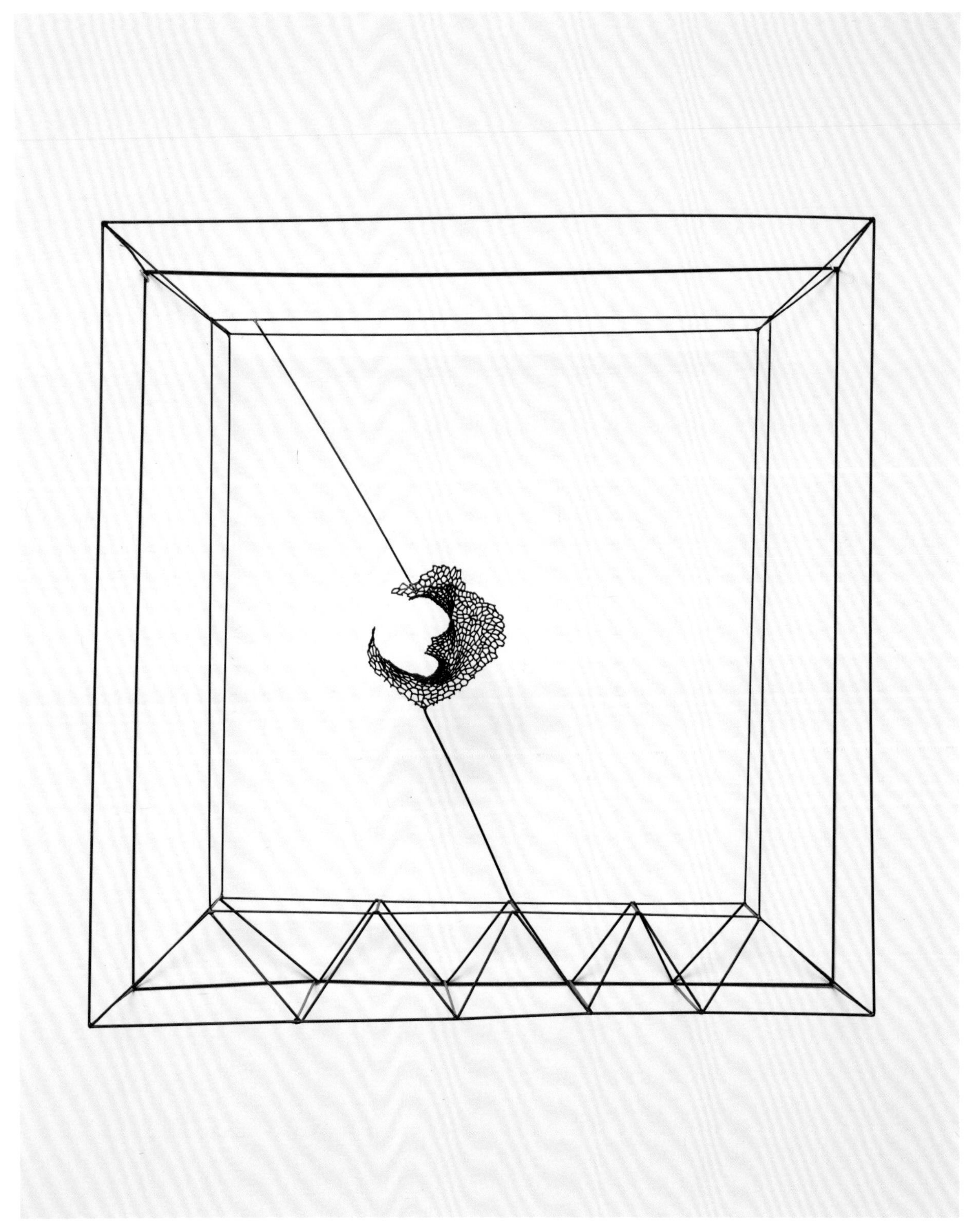

JOHN PAI

Involution
1974
Welded steel
40 × 40 × 40 inches
101.6 × 101.6 × 101.6 cm

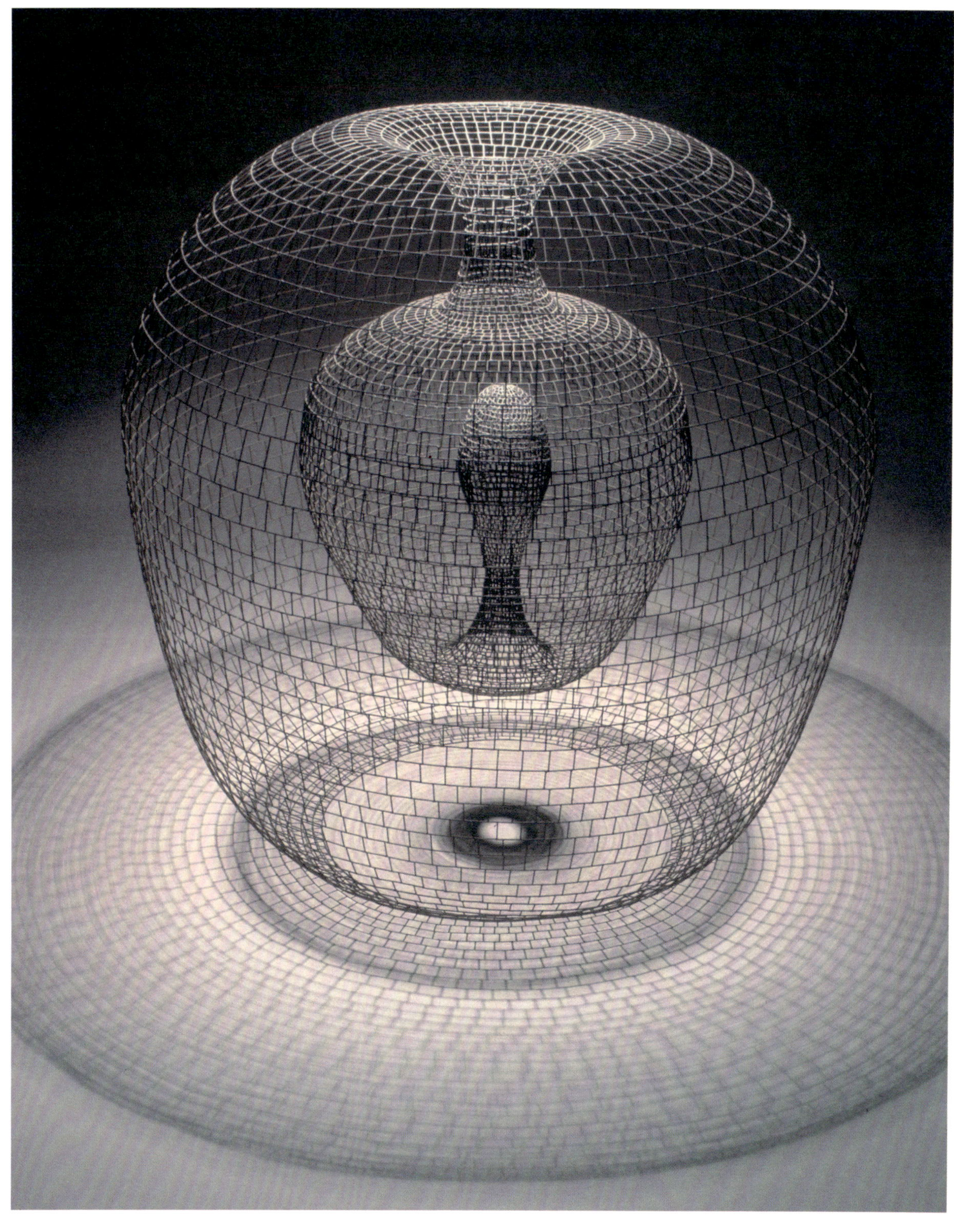

(B. 1937)

Convolution
1976
Welded steel
47 × 45 × 45 inches
119.4 × 114.3 × 114.3 cm

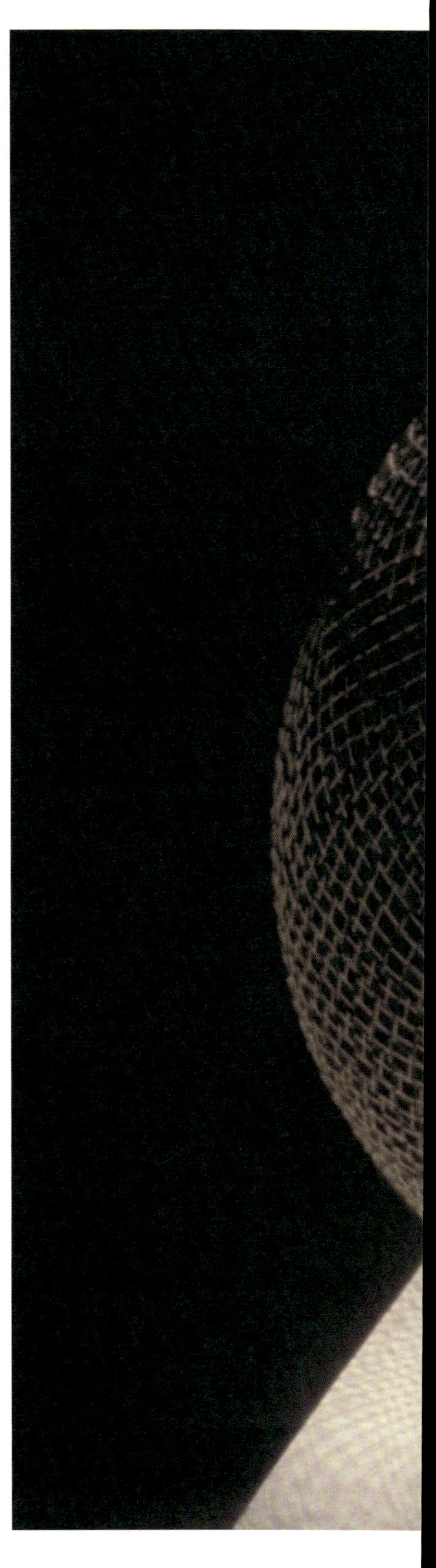

JOHN PAI

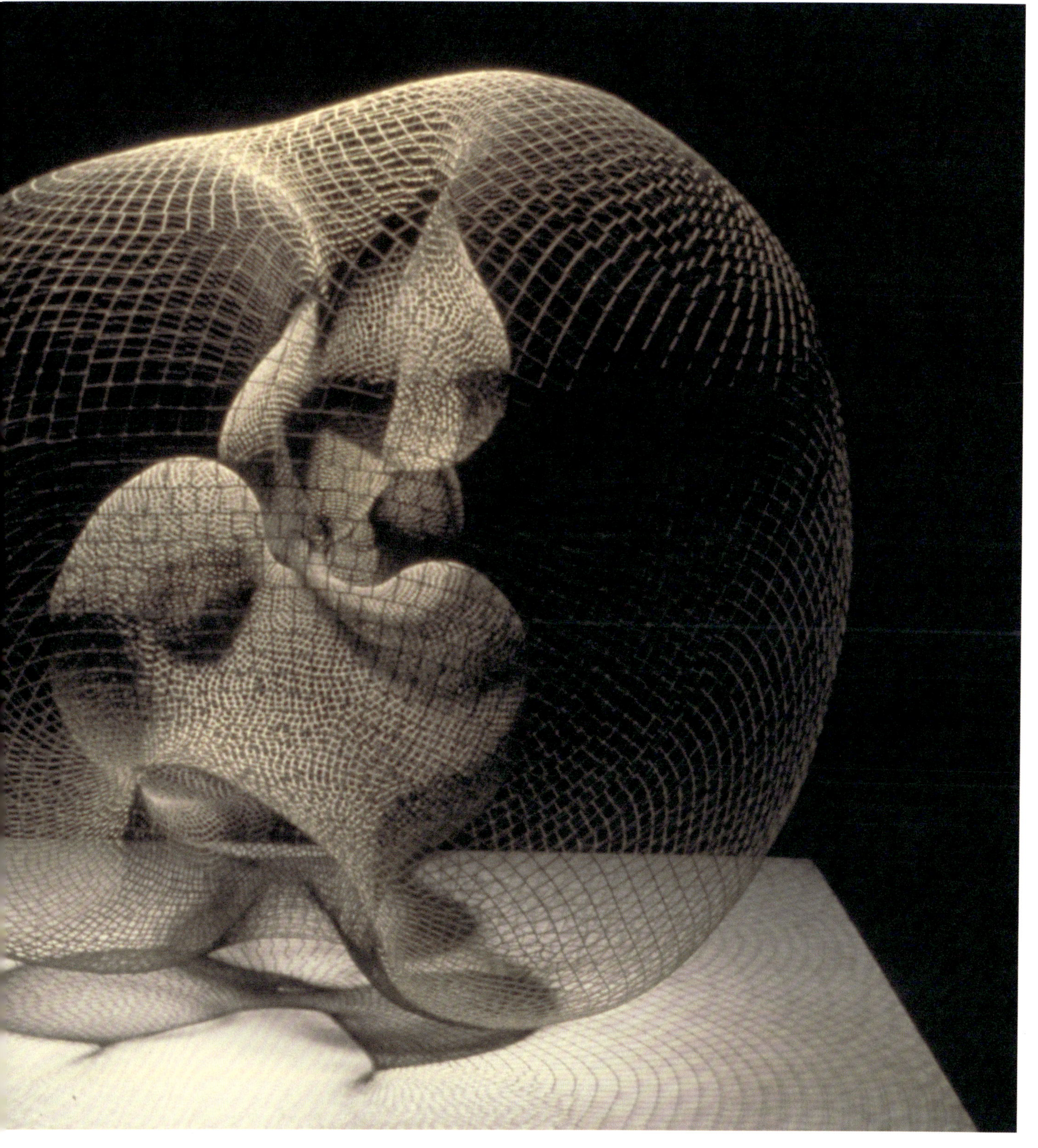

(B. 1937)

Persistence of Forgotten Things
1977
Welded steel
69 × 23 × 23 inches
183 × 61 × 61 cm

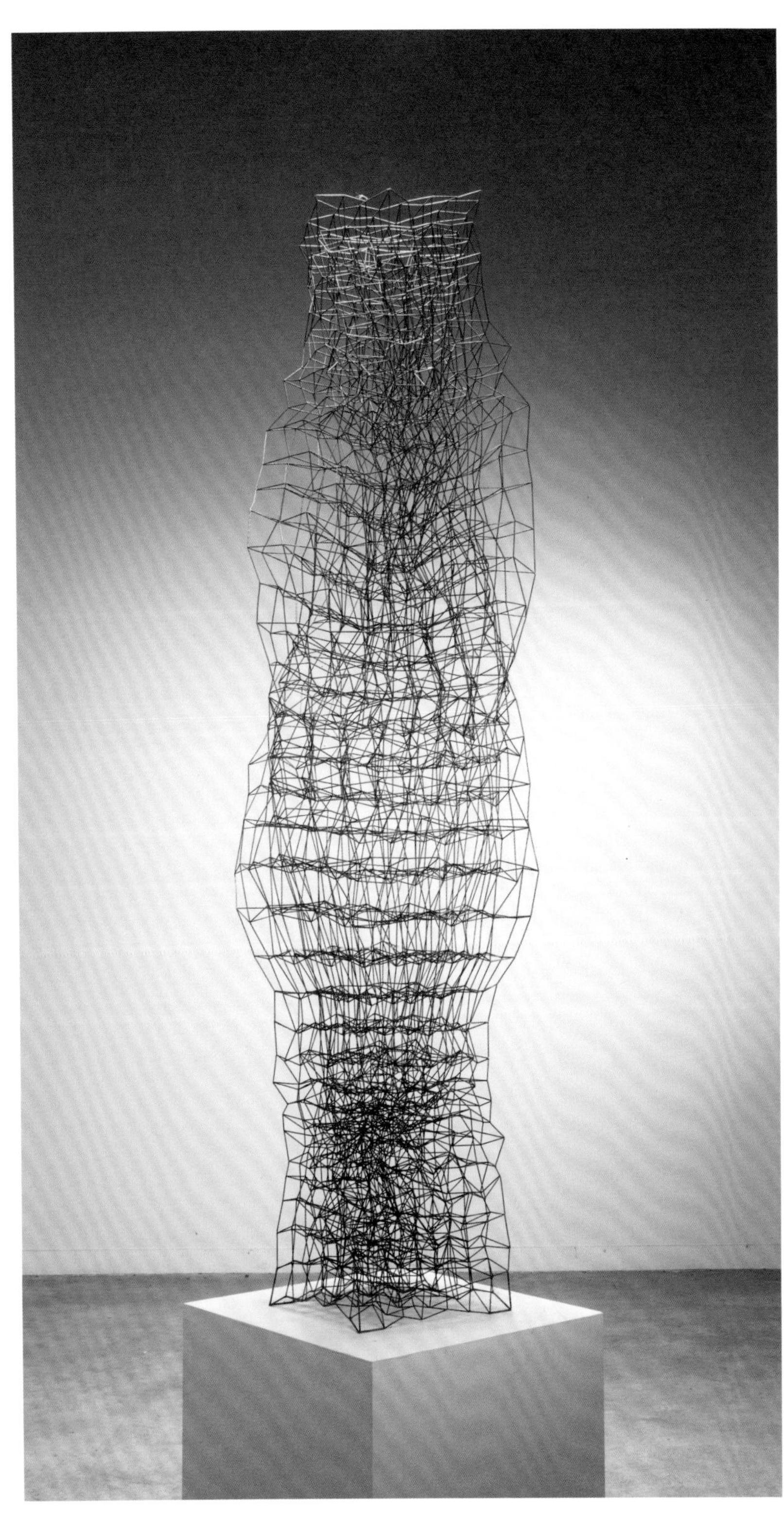

JOHN PAI

Slice of Wave to Go
1980
Welded steel
23.5 × 32 × 30.5 inches
59.7 × 81.3 × 77.5 cm

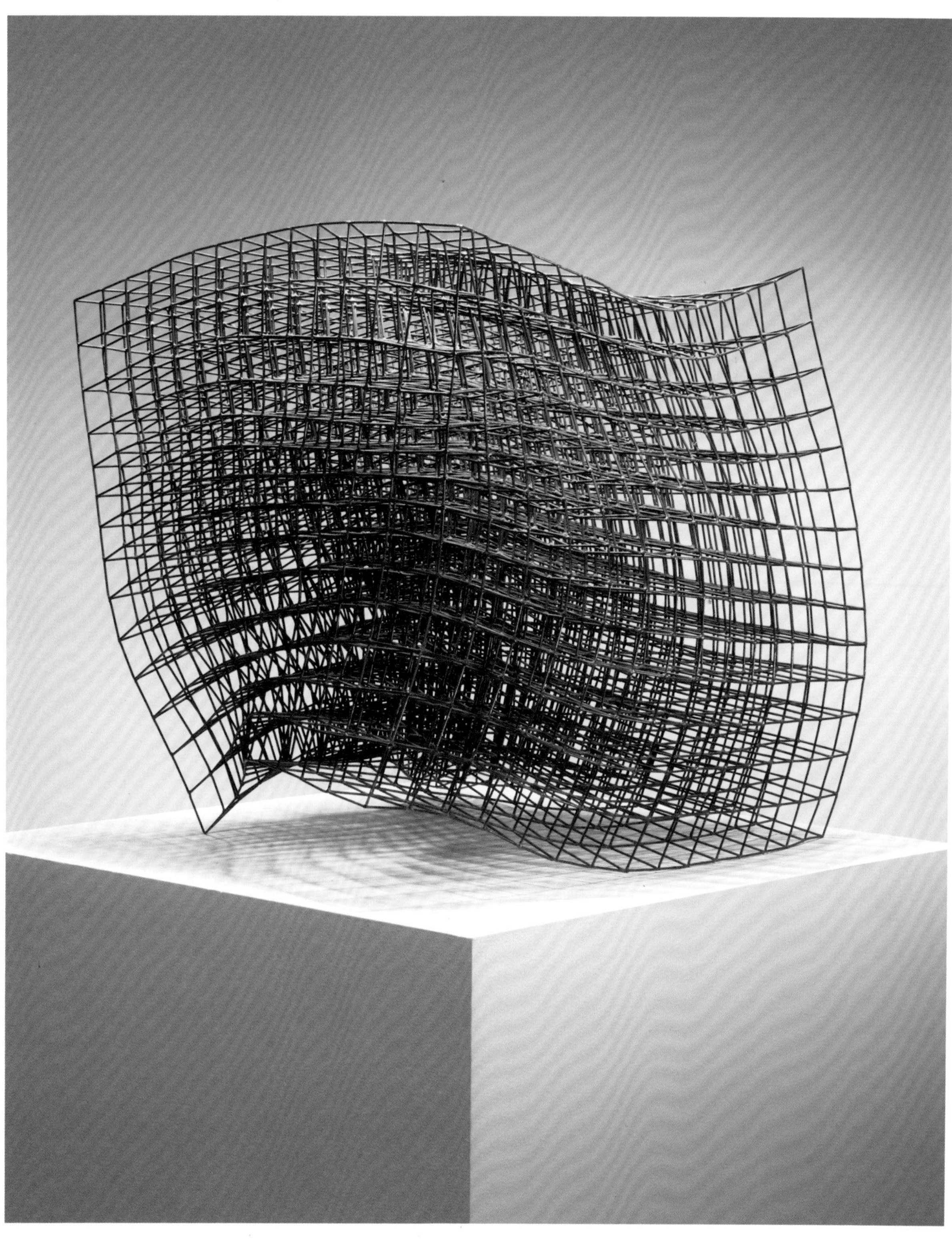

Great Barrington
1985
Welded steel
28 × 41 × 35 inches
71.1 × 104.1 × 88.9 cm

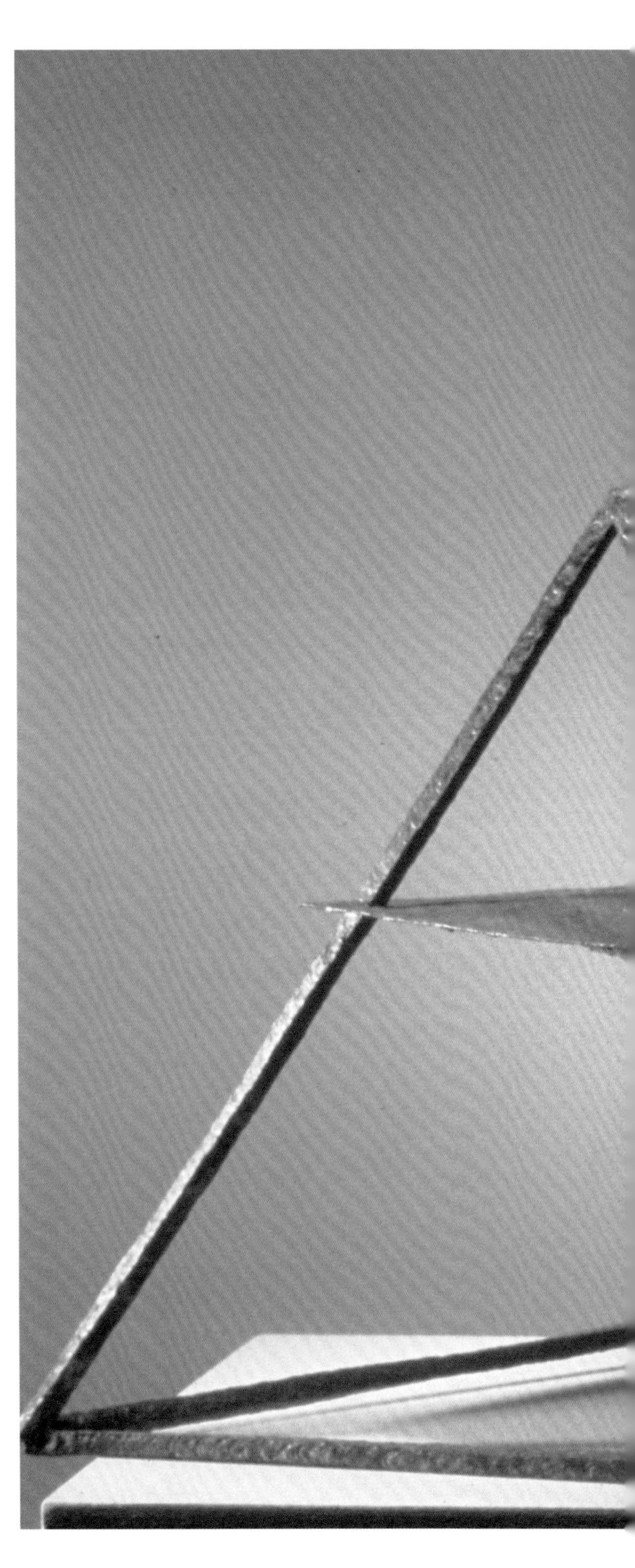

JOHN PAI

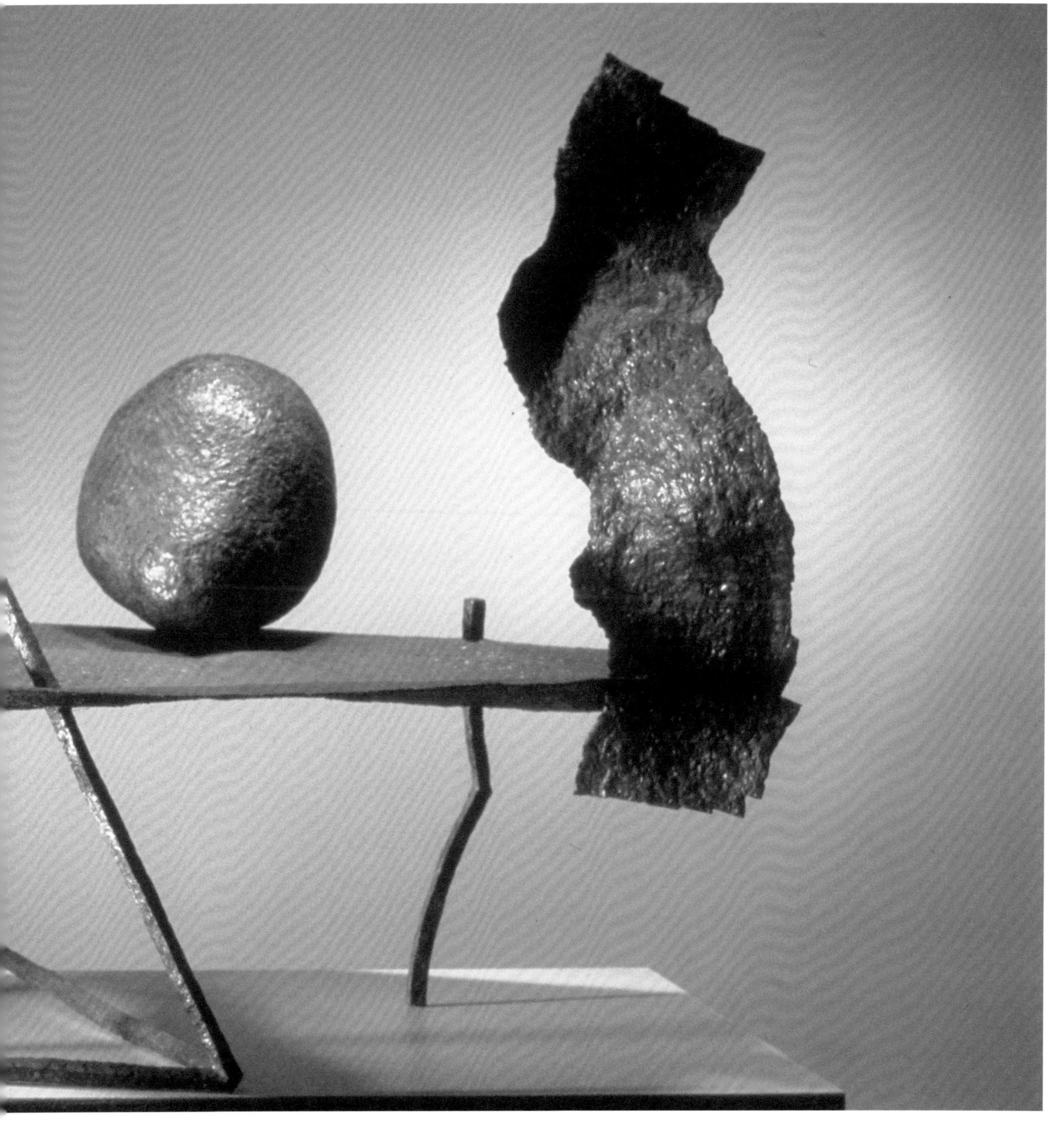

(B. 1937)

Dawn of Night
1985
Welded steel
36.5 × 20 × 10 inches
92.7 × 50.8 × 25.4 cm

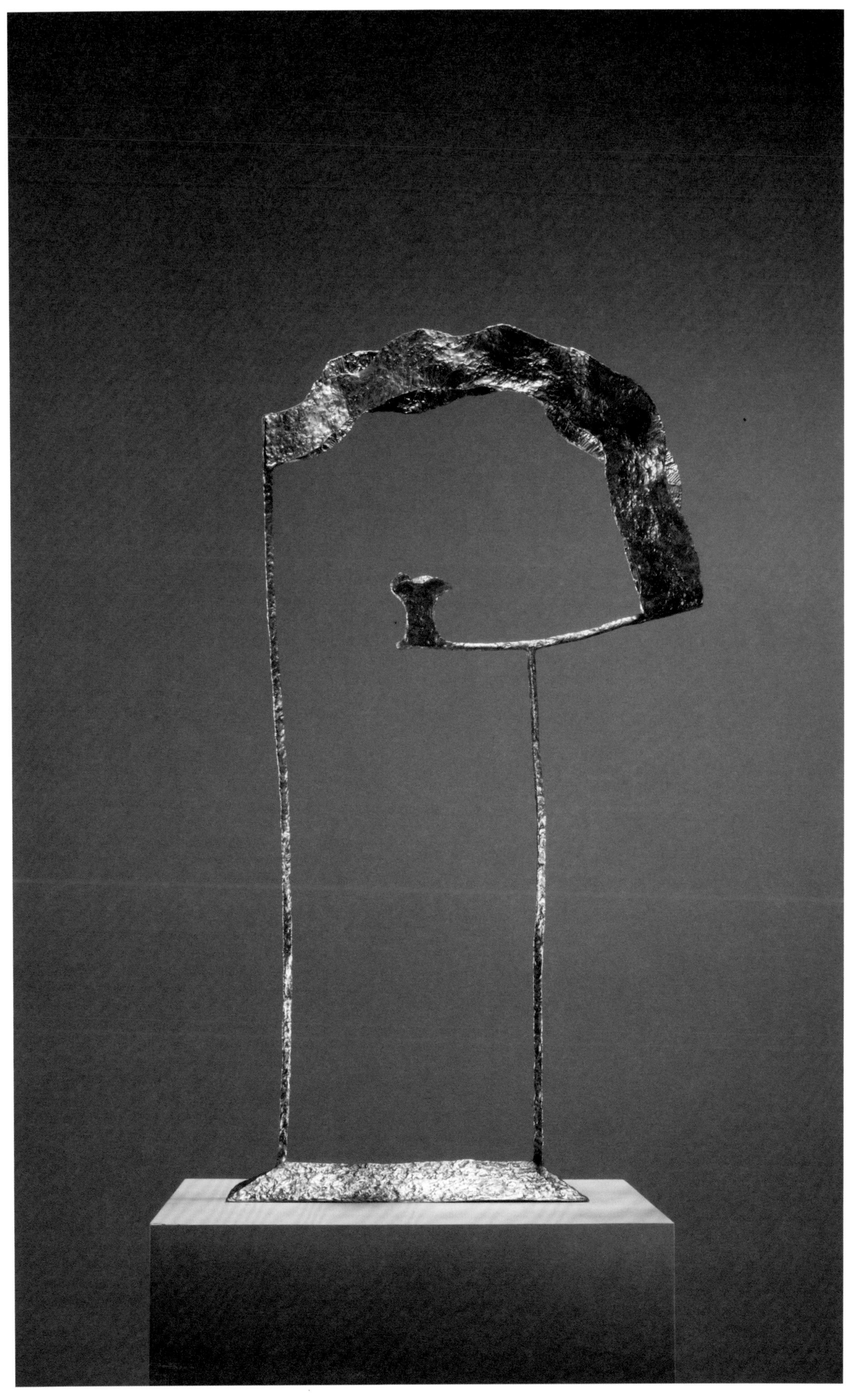

(B. 1937)   171

The Vigil
1986
Welded steel
42.13 × 26 × 24 inches
107 × 66 × 61 cm

JOHN PAI

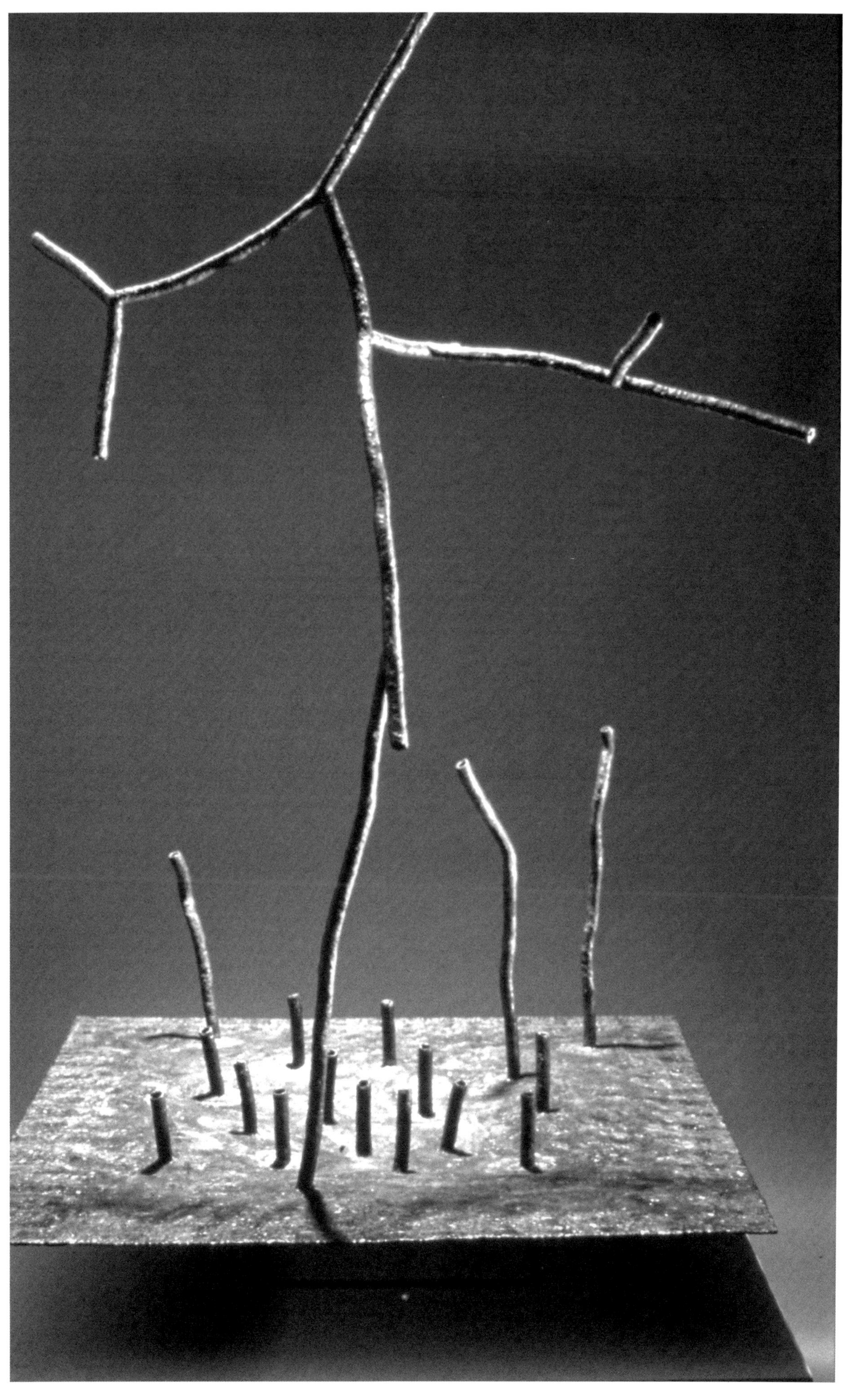

(B. 1937)

Forgotten Rule
1990
Welded steel
36 × 40 × 15 inches
91.4 × 101.6 × 38.1 cm

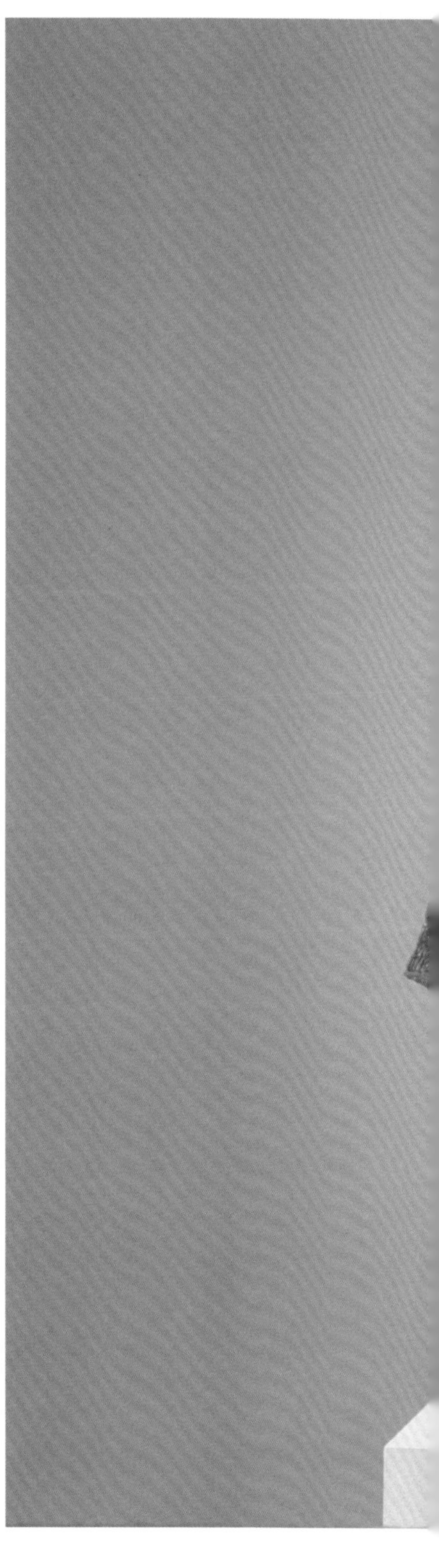

JOHN PAI

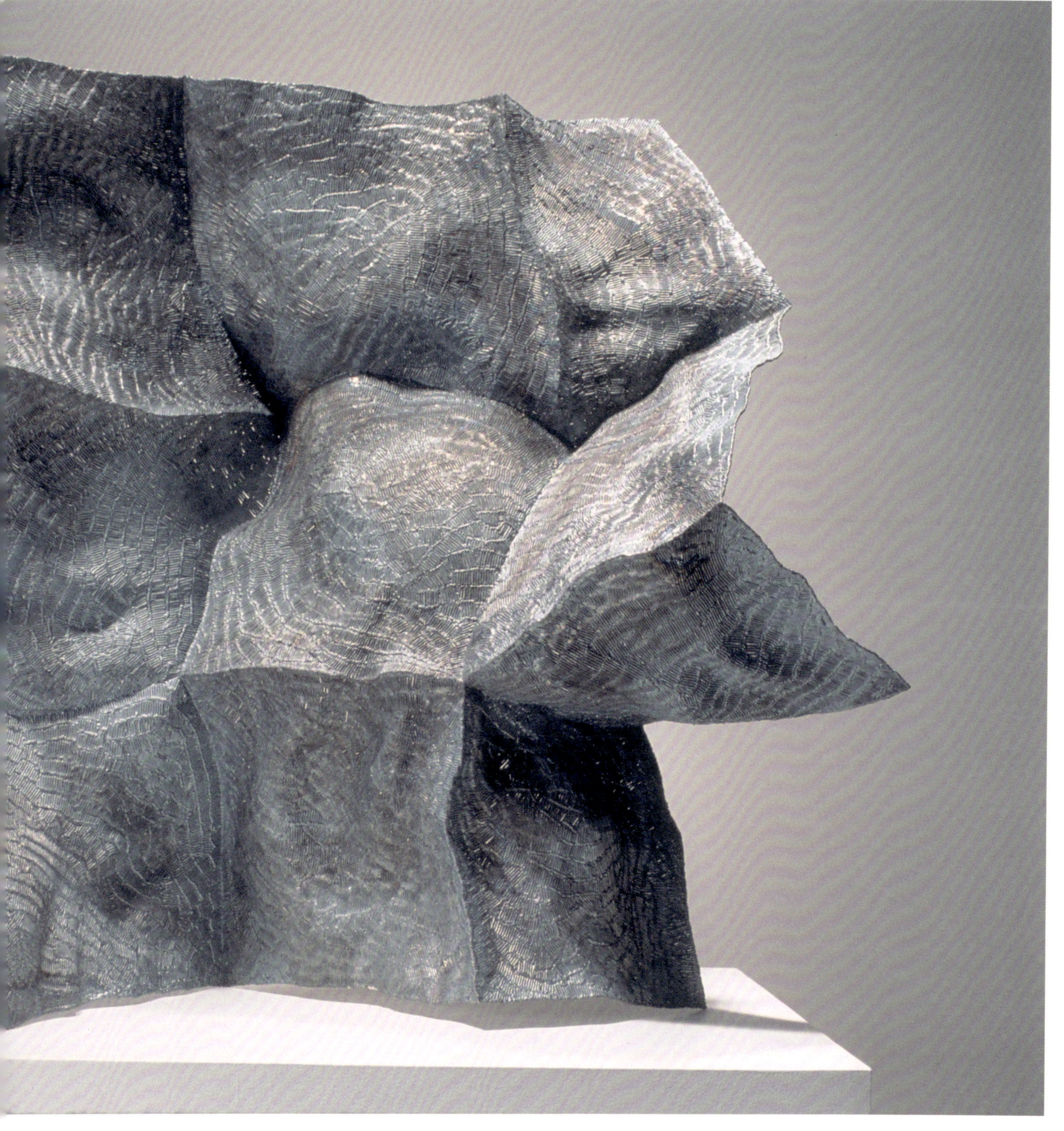

(B. 1937)

Weigh of the Way
1996
Welded steel
46 × 46 × 46 inches
116.8 × 116.8 × 116.8 cm

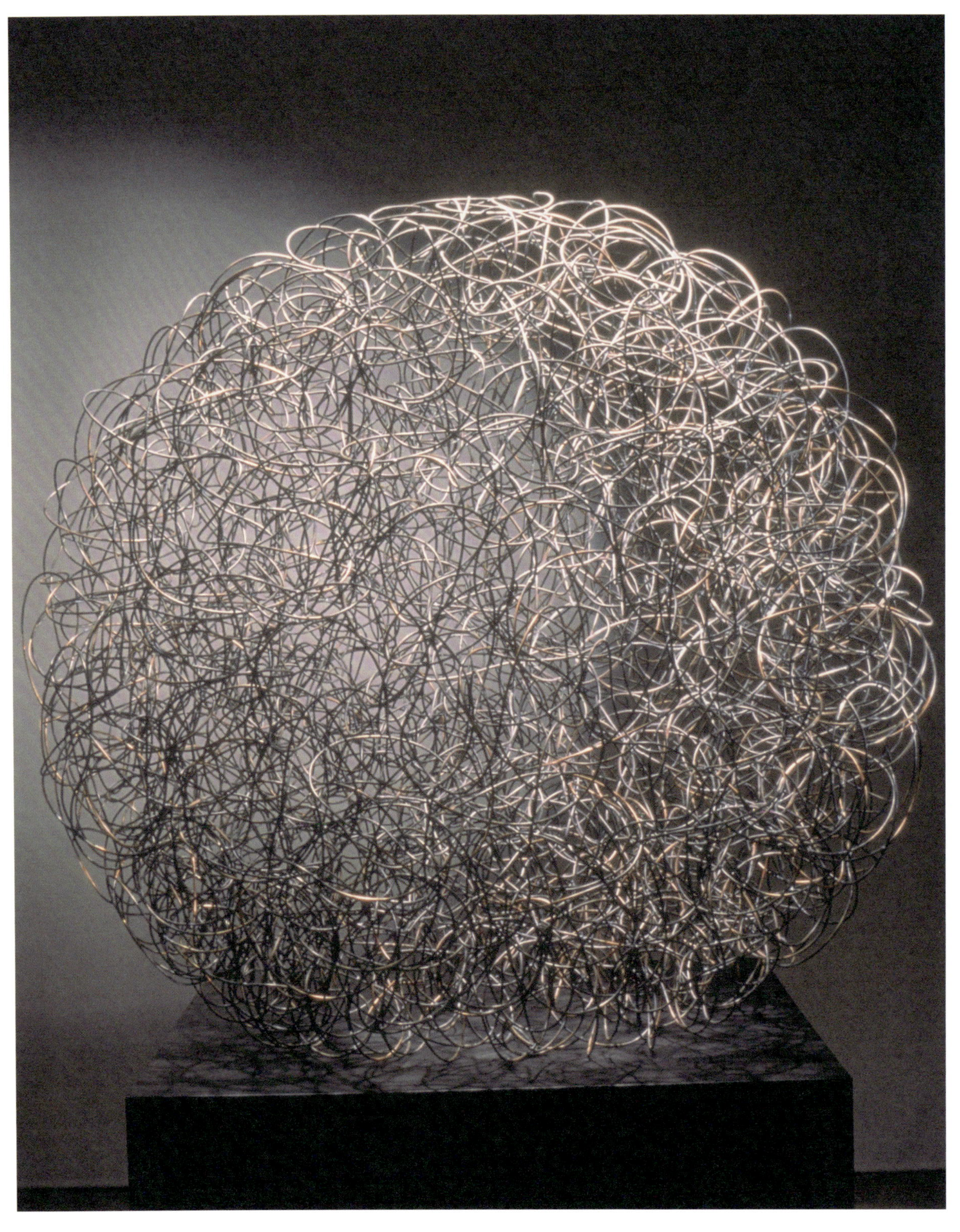

JOHN PAI

Rooster That Became A Tree
2002
Welded steel
108 × 102 × 78 inches
274 × 259 × 198 cm

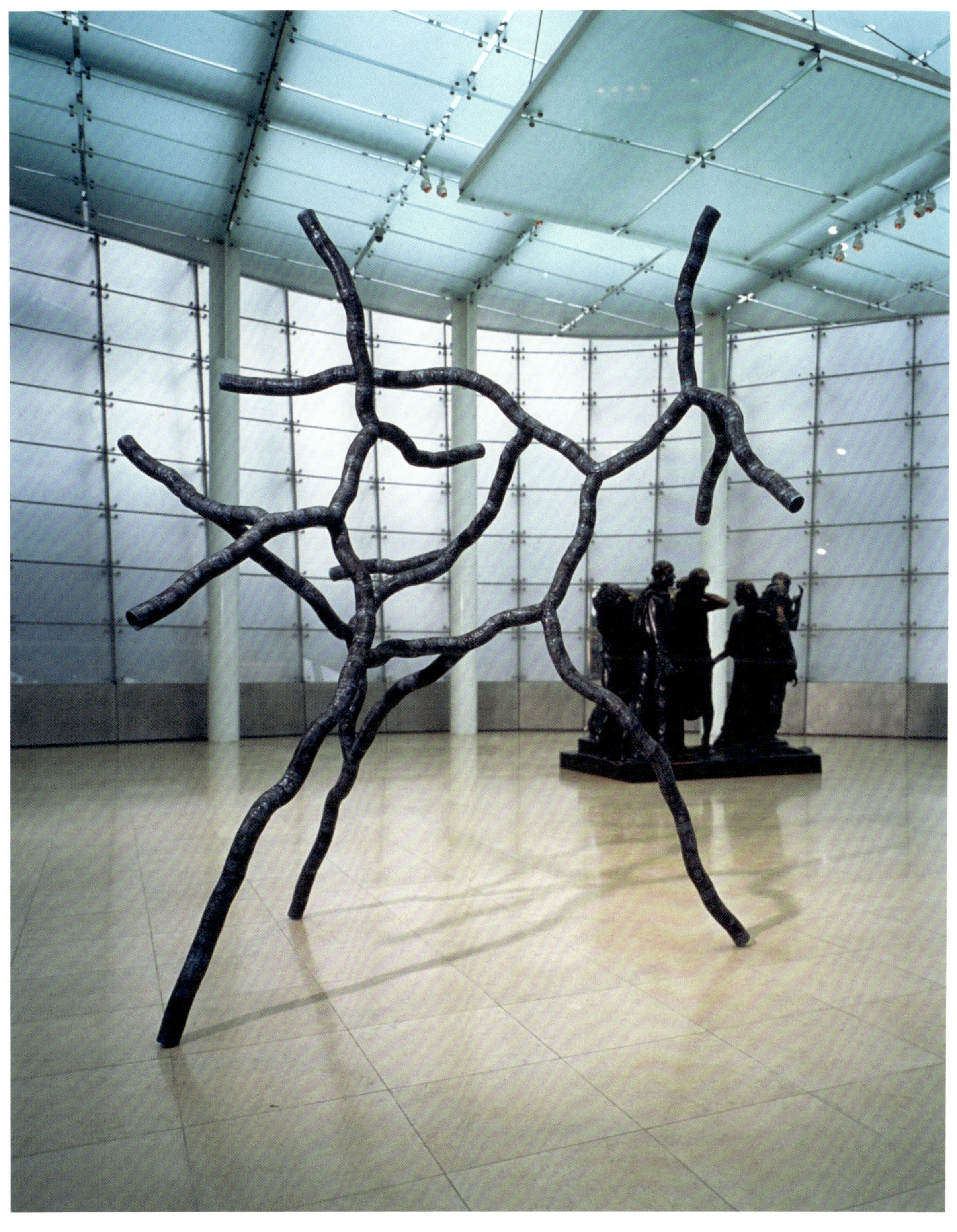

Eternal Moment
2011
Welded steel
52 × 31 × 31 inches
132.1 × 78.7 × 78.7 cm

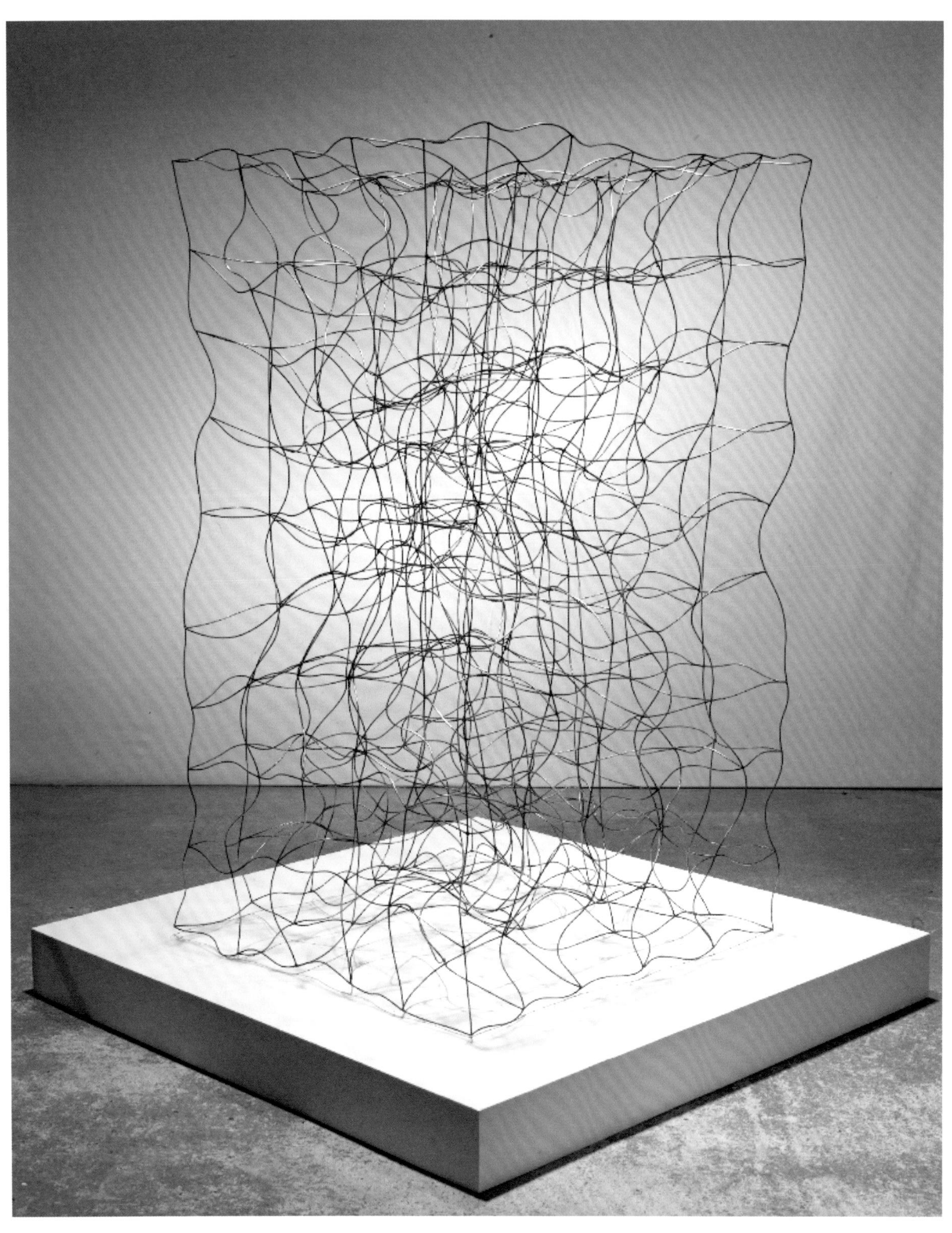

JOHN PAI

Choices, Choices
2012
Welded steel
106 × 58 × 36 inches
269.2 × 147.3 × 91.4 cm

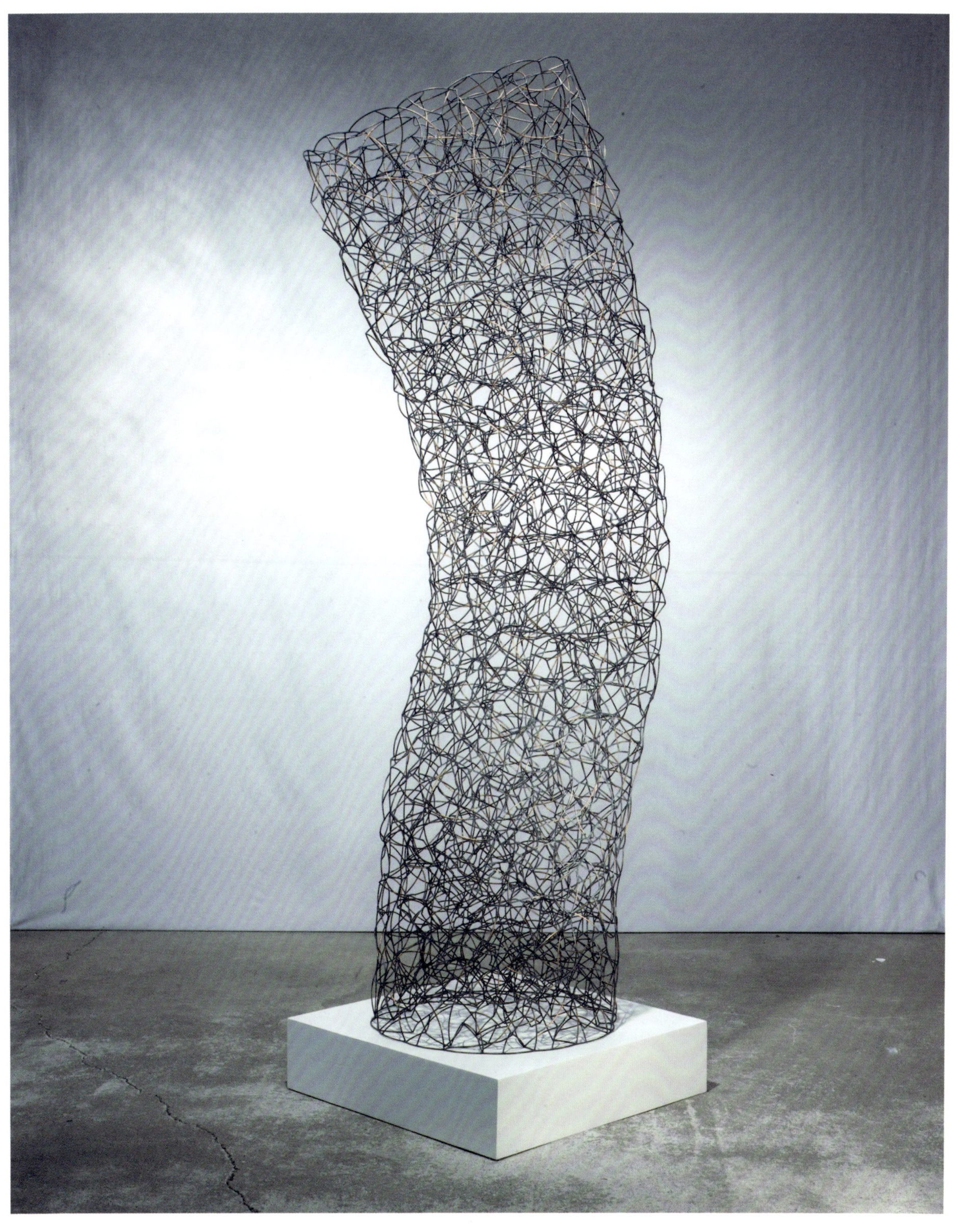

(B. 1937)

Notes from the Stars
2007
Stainless steel
31 feet
9.5 m

JOHN PAI

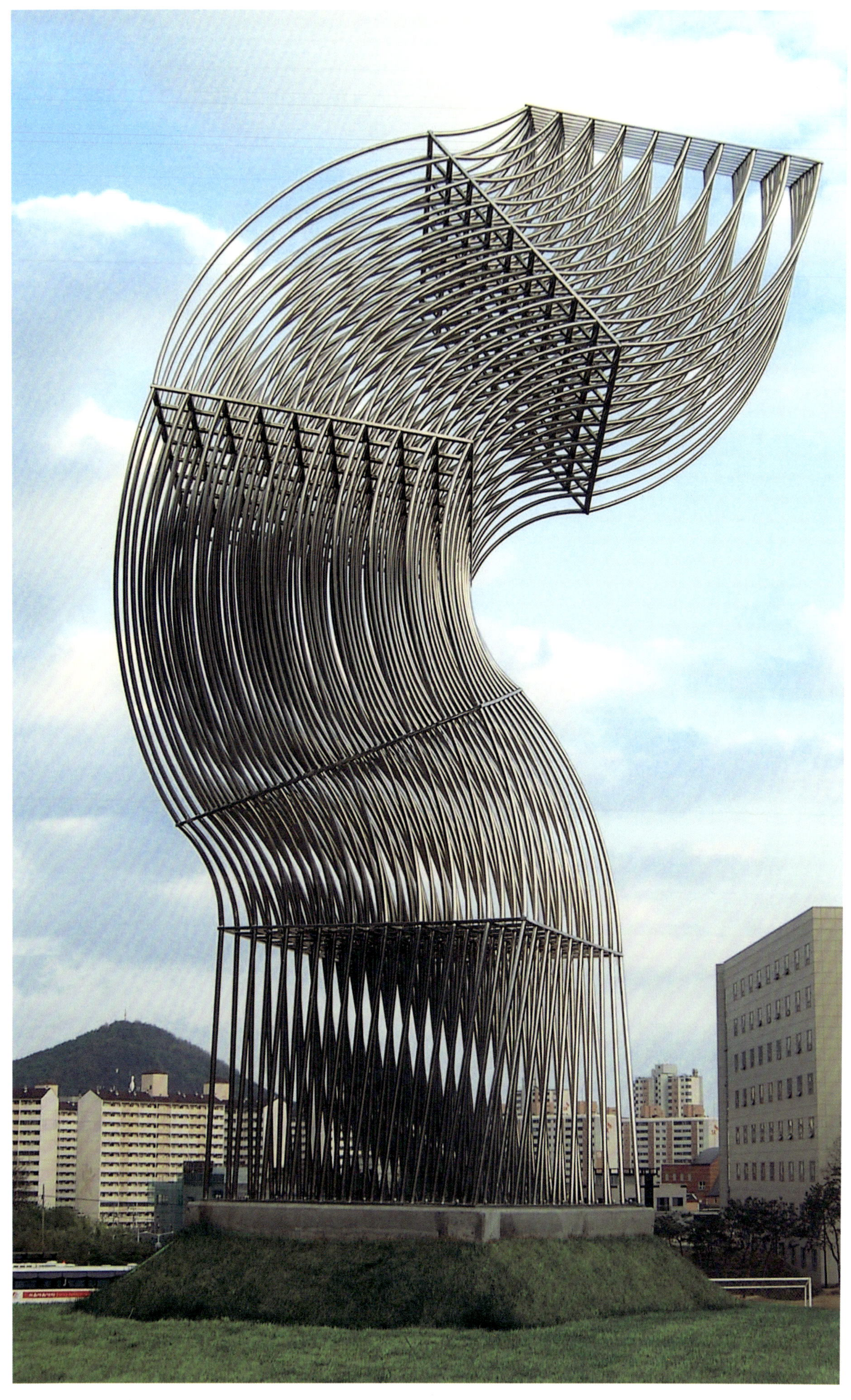

(B. 1937)

In Stillness They Dance
2009
Welded steel
83 × 25 × 25 inches
210.82 × 63.5 × 63.5 cm

JOHN PAI

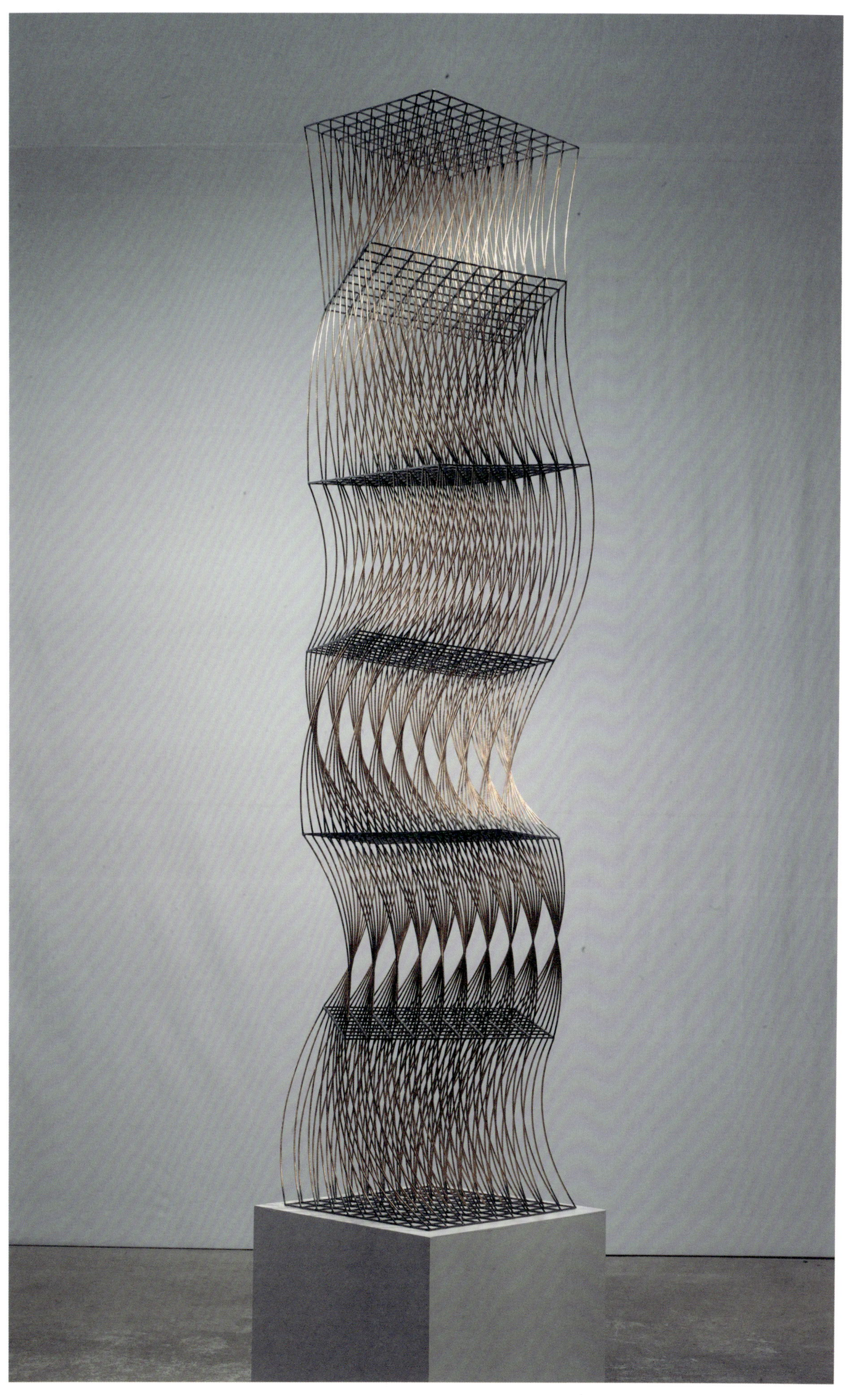

(B. 1937)

Pas de Deux
2010
Welded steel
14 × 17.5 × 14.5 inches
35.6 × 44.5 × 36.8 cm

JOHN PAI

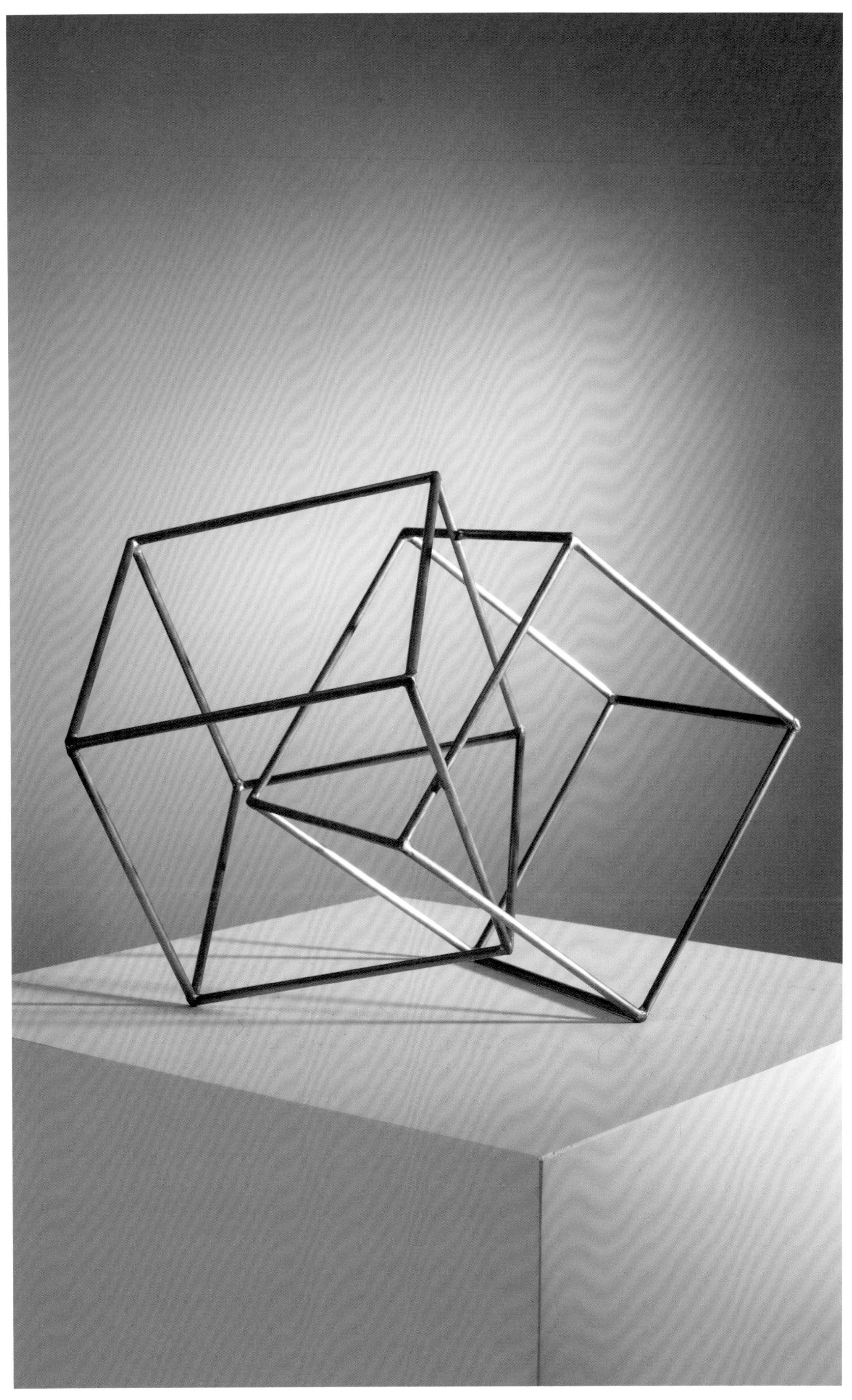

(B. 1937)

Lost in Finite Space
2011
Welded steel
52 × 46 × 35 inches
132.1 × 116.8 × 88.9 cm

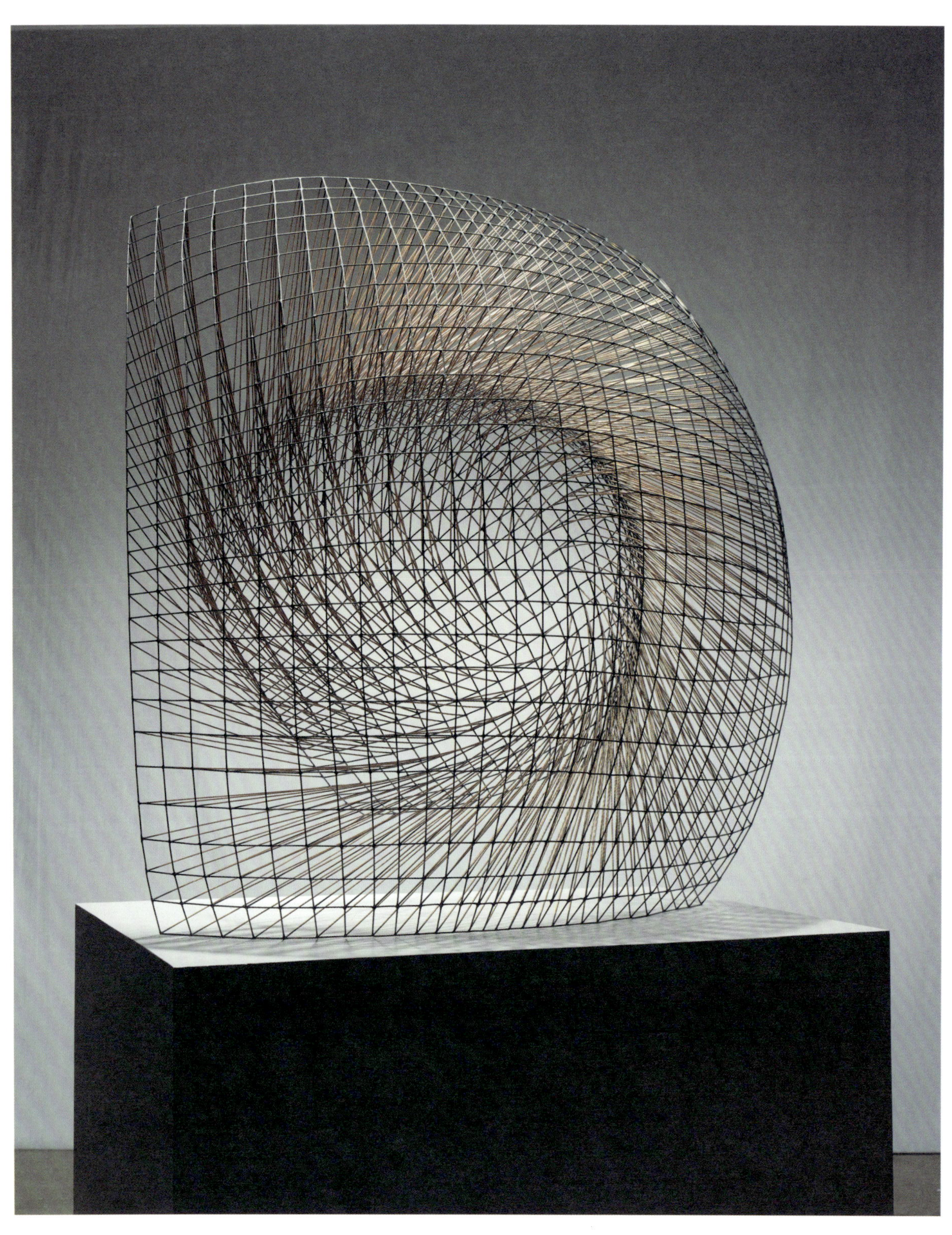

　　　　JOHN PAI

Concerto for a Flea
2012
Welded steel
30.5 × 28 × 30 inches
77.5 × 71.1 × 76.2 cm

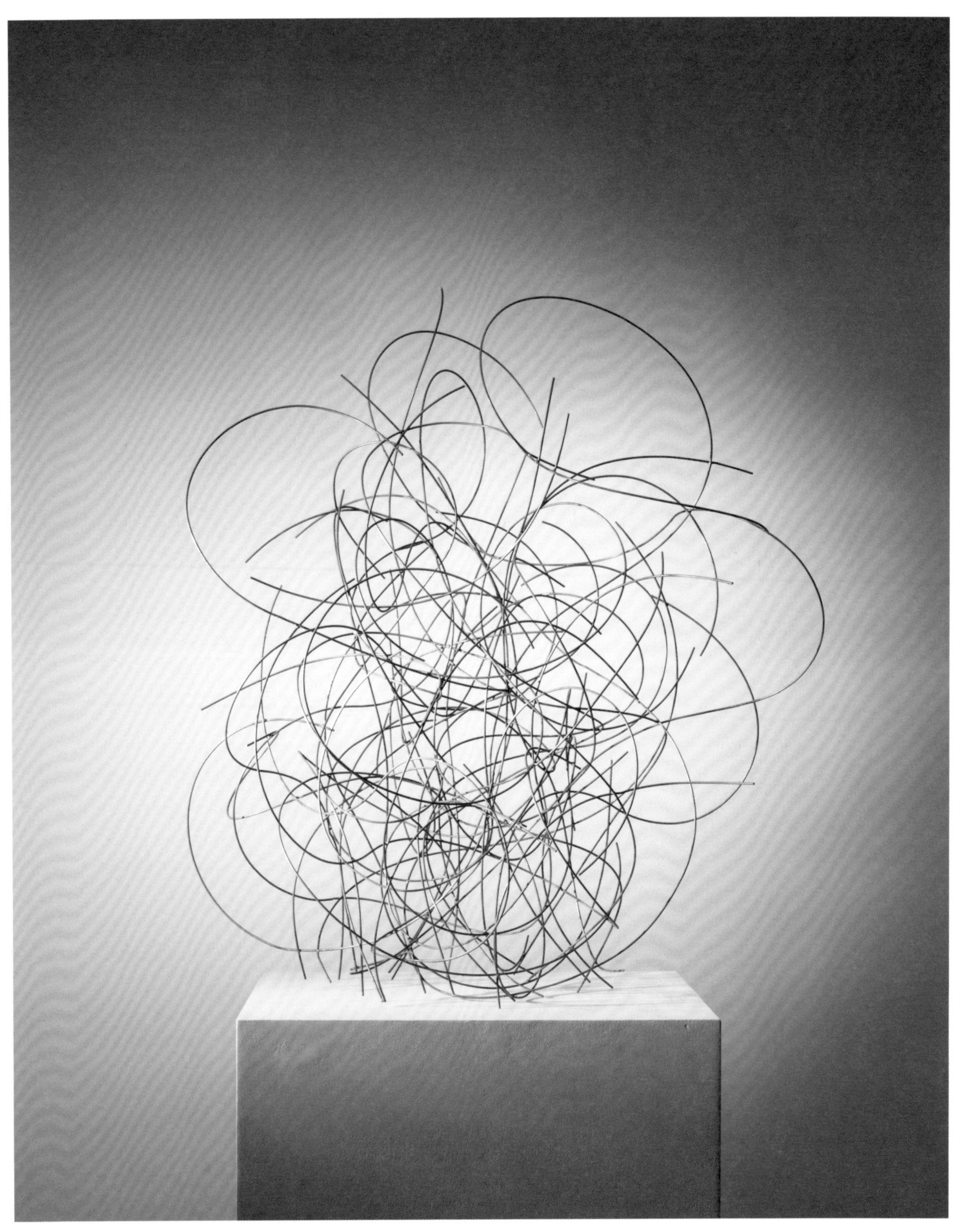

Shared Destinies
2014
Welded steel
70 × 28 × 23 inches
177.8 × 71.1 × 58.4 cm

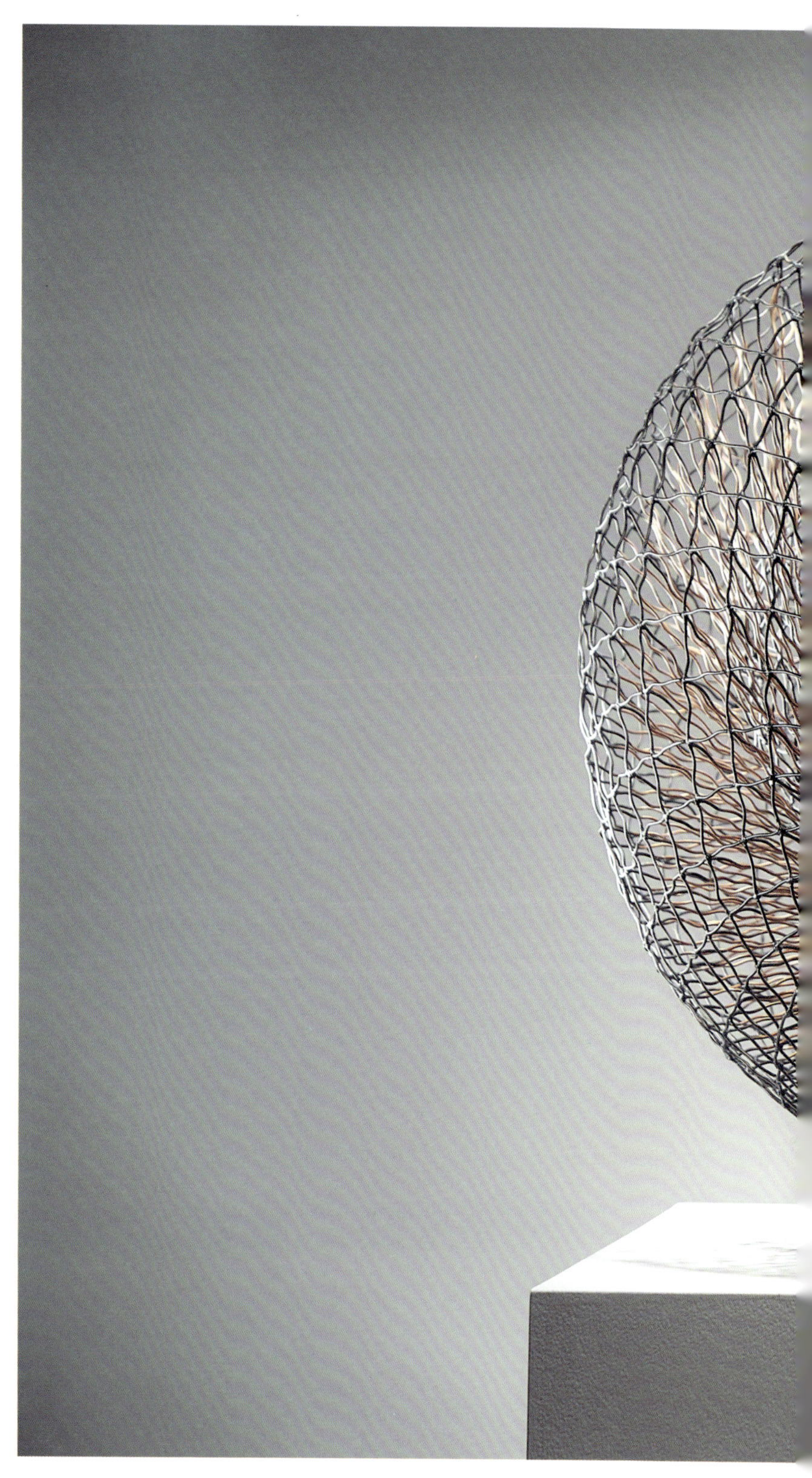

JOHN PAI

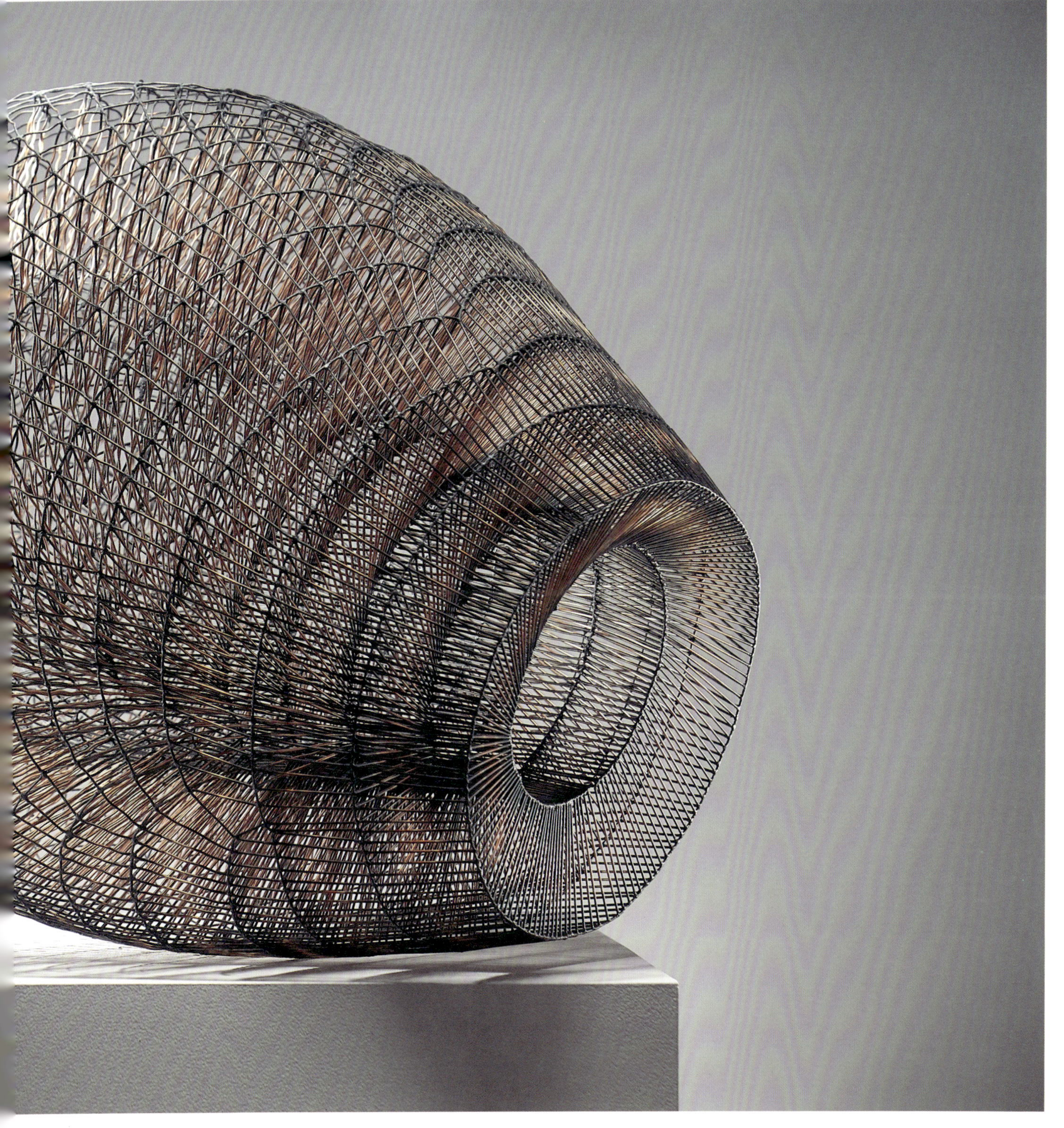

(B. 1937)

Sylvia's Dream
2021
Welded Steel
16 × 21 × 16 inches
40.6 × 53.3 × 40.6 cm

JOHN PAI

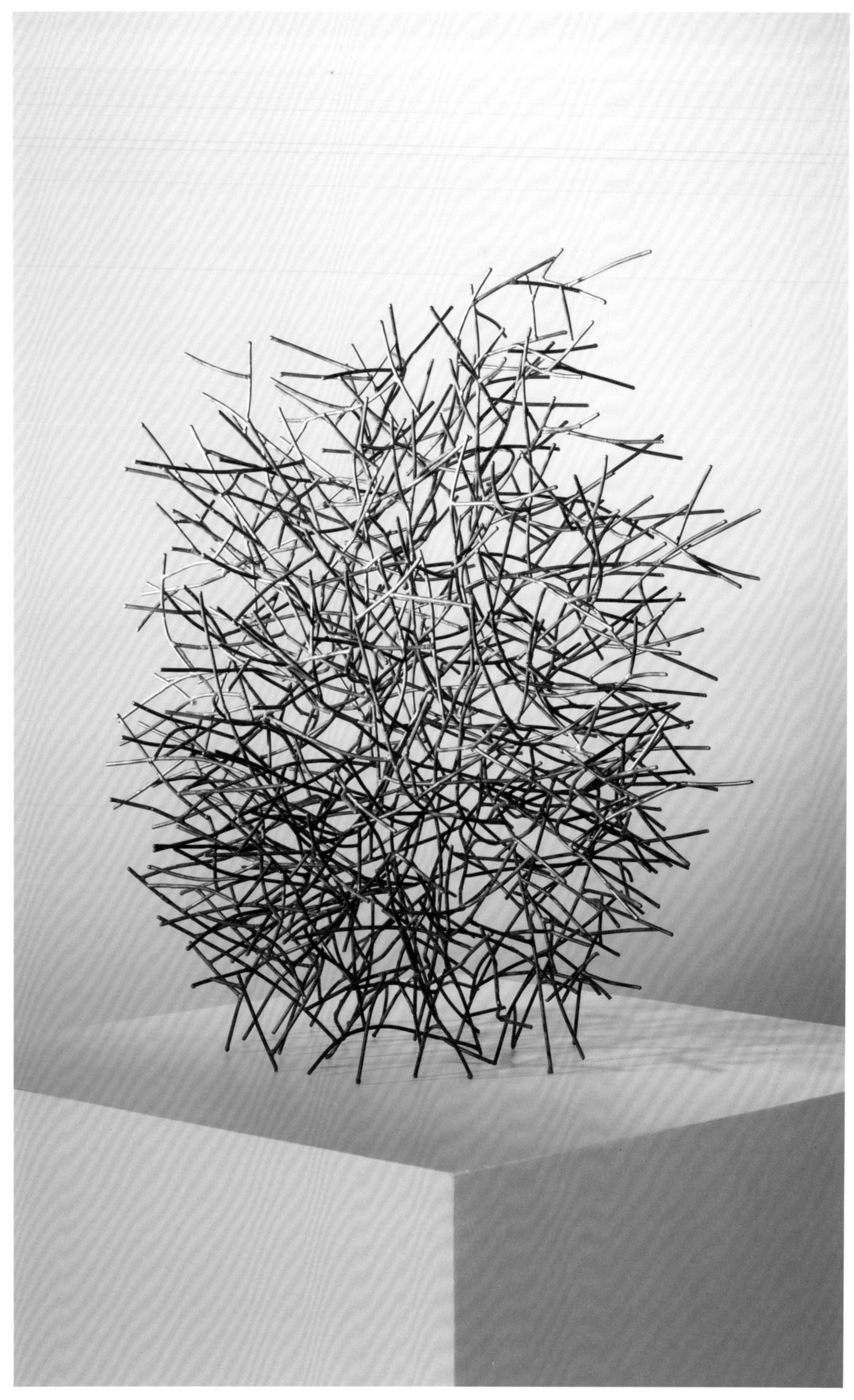

(B. 1937)

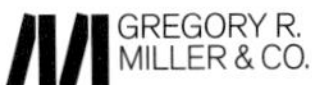
GREGORY R.
MILLER & CO.

Gregory R. Miller & Co.
62 Cooper Square
New York, NY 10003
grmandco.com

TINA KIM GALLERY

Tina Kim Gallery
525 West 21st Street
New York, NY 10011
tinakimgallery.com

Distributed worldwide by

ARTBOOK | D.A.P.
75 Broad Street, Suite 630
New York, NY 10013
artbook.com

978-1-941366-43-1

Edited by Natalie Danford
Editorial and research assistance provided by Tina Kim Gallery (Theodore Lau, SoYoung Kim, and Ami Yang)
Designed by Brette Richmond
Printed and bound in Italy by Conti Tipocolor

Library of Congress Control Number: 2022930823

Image Credits

Installation Views

Courtesy of Tina Kim Gallery and photographed by Dario Lasagni: 34–35, 36–37, 38–39, 40–41, 42–43, 44–45.

Leo Amino

Courtesy The Estate of Leo Amino and Western Regional Archives: 53, 54, 55, 61.
Courtesy The Estate of Leo Amino and David Zwirner Gallery: 50.
Courtesy The Estate of Leo Amino and photographed by Alex Yudzon: 76–77, 78, 81, 92, 93.
Courtesy The Estate of Leo Amino and Tina Kim Gallery and photographed by Dario Lasagni: 79, 82–83, 84–85, 91.
Courtesy The Estate of Leo Amino and David Zwirner Gallery and photographed by Kerry McFate: 66, 67, 68–69, 71, 72, 73, 74–75, 81, 86, 87, 89, 95.

Minoru Niizuma

Courtesy The Estate of Minoru Niizuma: 98, 101, 102, 103, 104, 105, 114, 115, 121, 126–27, 130–31, 135, 137.
Courtesy The Estate of Minoru Niizuma and Tina Kim Gallery and photographed by Dario Lasagni: 117, 118, 119, 123, 125, 129, 133, 138, 139, 140.
Courtesy The Estate of Minoru Niizuma and Tina Kim Gallery and photographed by Hyunjung Rhee: 136, 141, 143.

John Pai

Courtesy The Estate of John Pai: 149, 152, 163, 164–65, 168–69, 173, 174–75, 176, 177, 181.
Courtesy The Estate of John Pai and photographed by Geoffrey Quelle: 162, 166, 167, 171, 178, 179, 183, 185, 186, 187, 188–89, 191.
Courtesy of Pratt Institute Archives, Brooklyn, NY: 146, 150, 151, 153, 157.